Josh,
Merry Christmas
2003

Love,
Robyne & Brandan

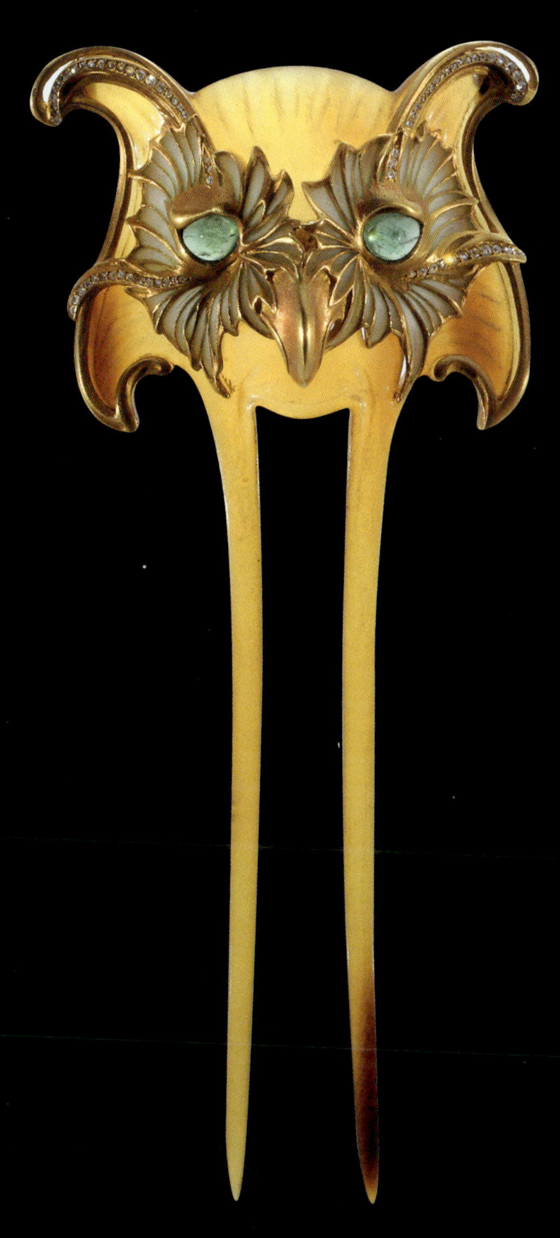

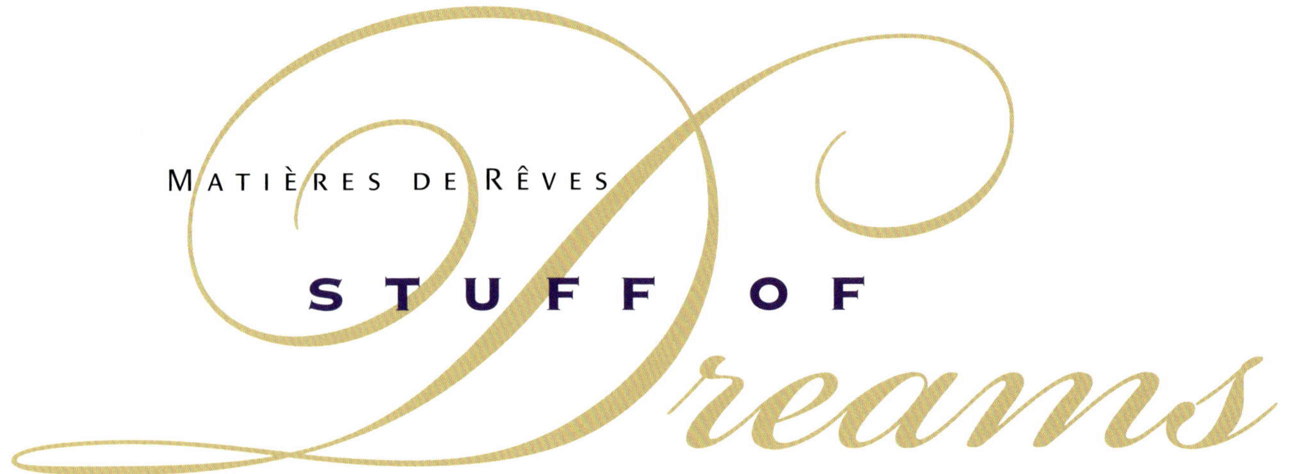

FROM THE PARIS MUSÉE DES ARTS DÉCORATIFS

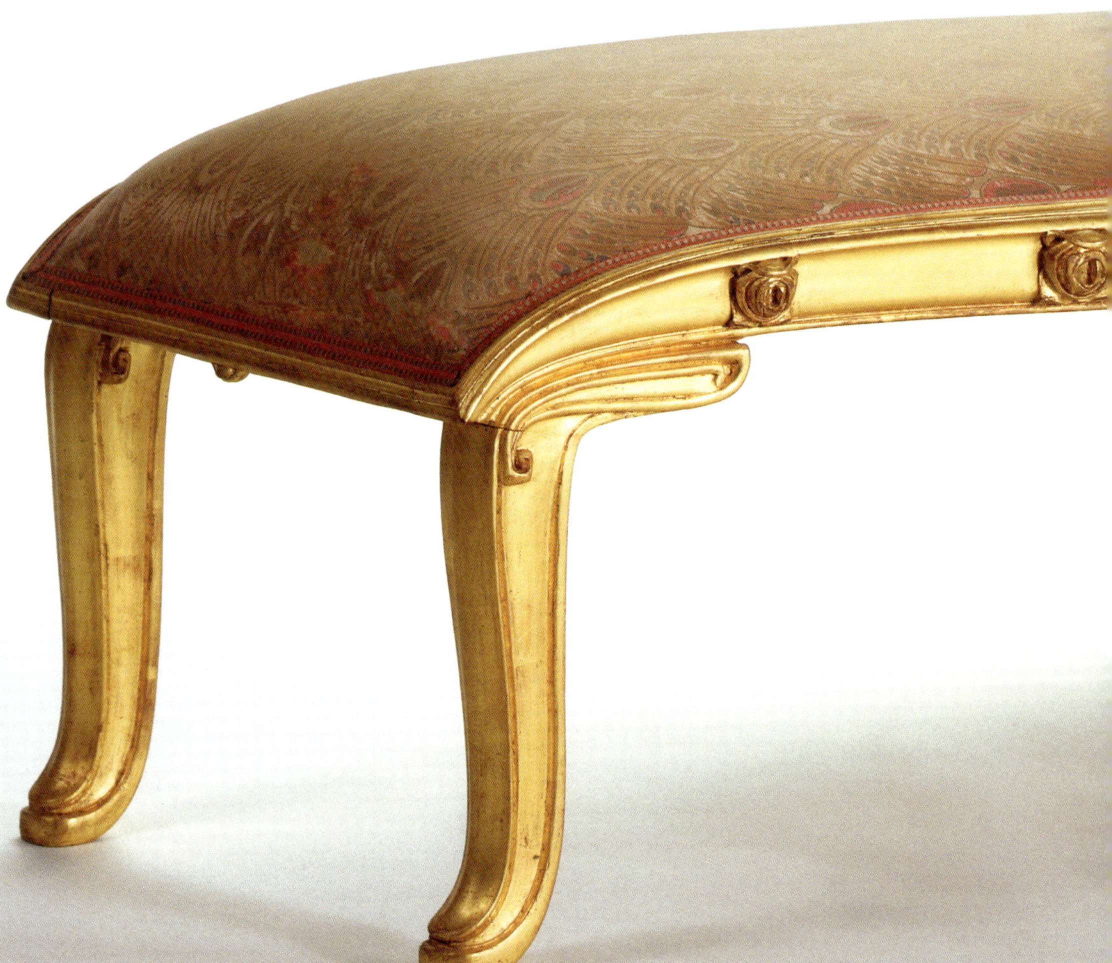

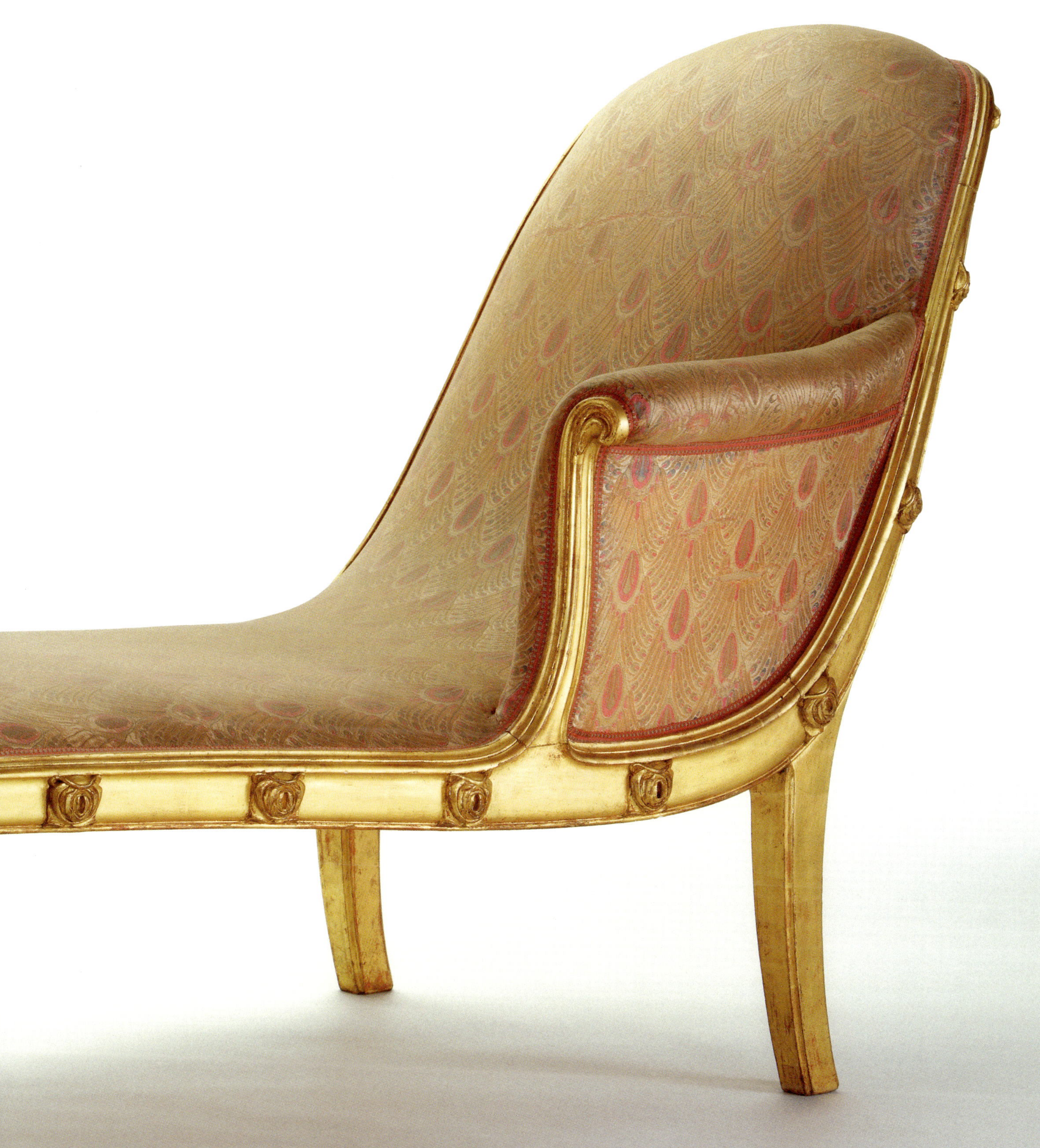

Penelope Hunter-Stiebel   Odile Nouvel-Kammerer

Portland Art Museum

Matières de Rêves: Stuff of Dreams from the Paris Musée des Arts Décoratifs

An exhibition organized by the Portland Art Museum, Oregon, and Musée des Arts Décoratifs, Paris. The exhibition is made possible by The Florence Gould Foundation and Dr. and Mrs. Robert B. Pamplin, Jr.

Itinerary

Portland Art Museum, Oregon
February 2–April 28, 2002

Wadsworth Atheneum Museum of Art, Hartford, Connecticut
June 1–August 11, 2002

Birmingham Museum of Art, Alabama
September 22, 2002–January 5, 2003

Published by the Portland Art Museum, Oregon

Library of Congress Control Number: 2001 135885
ISBN: 1-883124-14-X

Page 1: Paul Vever and Henri Vever, *Owl Comb,* 1900 (p. 109)
Pages 2–3: Paul Follot, *Chaise Longue,* circa 1912 (pp. 134–135)
Page 5: Eugène Feuillâtre, *Artichoke Vase,* circa 1903 (pp. 116–117)

General Editor: Penelope Hunter-Stiebel
Translated by Simon Pleasance and Fronza Woods
Copyedited by Marie Weiler, Sherri Schultz, and Laura Iwasaki
Designed by Ed Marquand and Jeff Wincapaw
Color separations by iocolor, Seattle
Produced by Marquand Books, Inc., Seattle
www.marquand.com
Printed and bound by CS Graphics Pte., Ltd., Singapore

Musée des Arts Décoratifs

General Director: Sophie Durrleman

Authors of Catalogue Entries

H.A. Hélène Andrieux
V.A. Véronique Ayrolles
M.B. Monique Blanc
F.B. Frédéric Bodet
D.F. Dominique Forest
V.L.H. Véronique de La Hougue
S.M. Sophie Motsch
O.N. Odile Nouvel-Kammerer
J-L.O. Jean-Luc Olivié
E.P. Evelyne Possémé
B.R. Bertrand Rondot
C.R. Constance Rubini

Contents

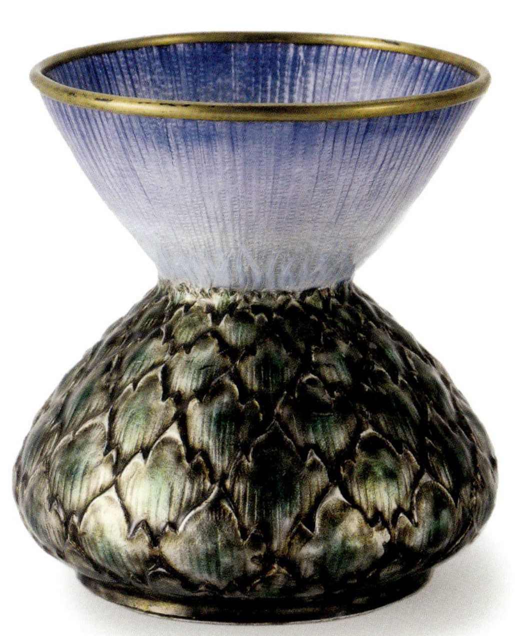

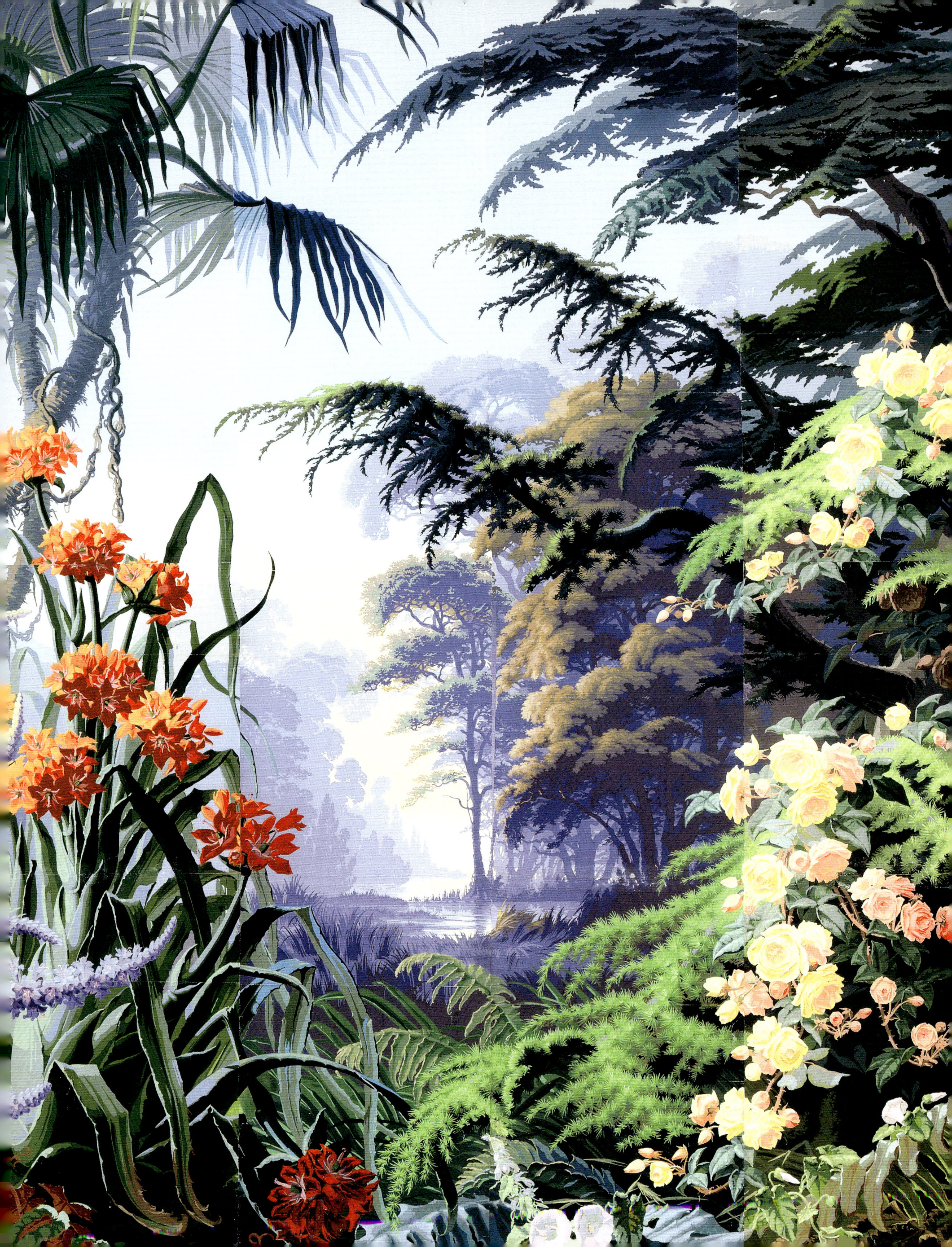

Foreword

JOHN E. BUCHANAN, JR.
EXECUTIVE DIRECTOR,
PORTLAND ART MUSEUM

Stuff of Dreams continues the Portland Art Museum's goal of presenting the highest-quality works of art from the greatest private and public collections around the world. It was during Portland's preparation for *Stroganoff: The Palace and Collections of a Russian Noble Family,* an earlier international exchange project, presented in Portland in winter 2000, that we made the initial contact with the Paris Musée des Arts Décoratifs. We are now able to "capture the moment" by organizing an exhibition of its treasures while the Musée is closed for renovation.

I am indebted to Musée officials Hélène David-Weill and Béatrice Salmon, who, rather than see their remarkable collections lie hidden, encouraged me to co-organize with them an exhibition for American audiences that would showcase the Musée's most important works of art. Many of the objects that make up the exhibition have never been viewed outside Paris and most of them have never traveled outside France.

The Musée des Arts Décoratifs is an international powerhouse of decorative arts and design. Because of their utilitarian nature, the decorative arts are among the most accessible of the arts—each of us has had an experience with some form of an object represented in this exhibition. And, for many of us, France is synonymous with the decorative arts.

The exhibition's co-curators, Penelope Hunter-Stiebel of the Portland Art Museum and Odile Nouvel-Kammerer of the Musée des Art Décoratifs, have selected over 100 artworks for display. Each object is exceptional in its quality, surpassing standards of tradition, craftsmanship, and utility in terms of beauty and artistry. Many of the pieces carry unique and fascinating stories about their origins, their makers, or those who commissioned, collected, used, or loved them. It is this opportunity to add a human dimension that brings life to art.

We expect this exhibition to have a lasting impact on the Portland Art Museum and its community as well as on the other venues hosting the exhibition. I extend my appreciation to my colleagues Kate Sellers, director of the Wadsworth Atheneum Museum of Art, and Gail Trechsel, director of the Birmingham Museum of Art, for their belief and investment in this project. I thank The Florence Gould Foundation and its president, John R. Young, for leadership support in making this dream a reality.

In addition, I extend my gratitude to the exhibition's curators and my other professional colleagues who have contributed to the success of this project, including Portland Art Museum registrar Karen Christenson, exhibition coordinator Lisa Morgan, and public relations and communications director Beth Sorensen. We are indebted once again to Lucy M. Buchanan, whose development efforts have enabled the project to move forward; to talented exhibition designer Clifford La Fontaine; and to the staff of Marquand Books, for producing this accompanying publication.

Joseph Fuchs, *Eden Scenic Wallpaper,* 1861 (detail; pp. 82–85)

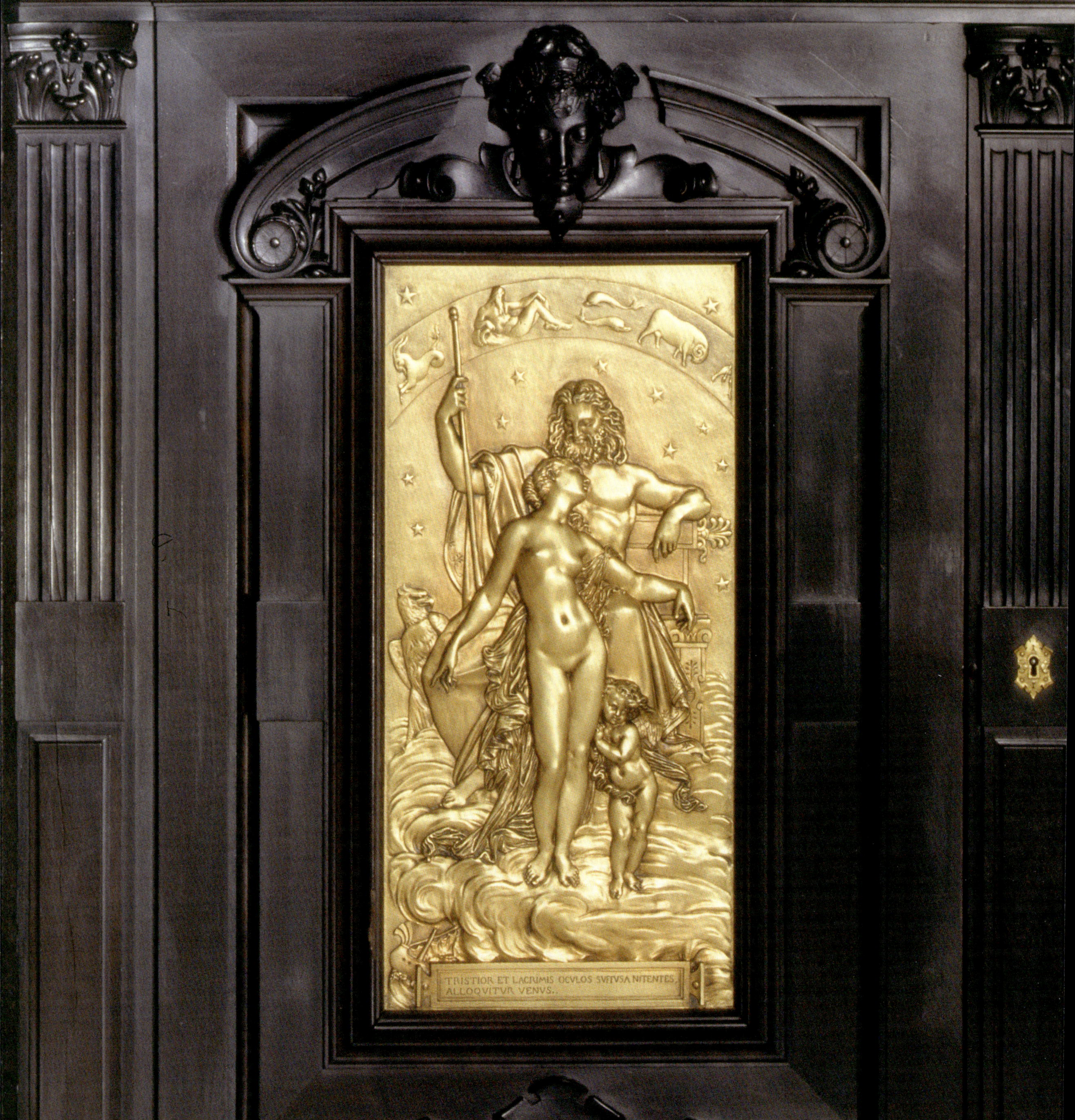
TRISTIOR ET LACRIMIS OCVLOS SVFFVSA NITENTES
ALLOQVITVR VENVS.

Foreword

HÉLÈNE DAVID-WEILL
PRESIDENT, UNION CENTRALE
DES ARTS DÉCORATIFS

The Union Centrale des Arts Décoratifs (UCAD), a private institution, came into being as the brainchild of late-19th-century collectors and manufacturers. The purpose of this unique institution is to promote a link between beauty and usefulness. Today it holds fast to its original mandate of providing national references in an area where industrial and economic challenges are taking on an international dimension.

Several tools have been introduced to meet the expectations of a diverse public: a library, a museum of decorative arts, and educational programs. This triad is still valid today and sums up the uniqueness of our institution within the cultural landscape of France.

Our collections stem mainly from the generosity of private donors and enjoy a national status. The Musée des Arts Décoratifs (Museum of Decorative Arts) emerged a century after the national museums but is still a mirror of upper-middle-class taste, with its very broad interests. The museum is home to several impressive collections illustrating a comprehensive range of traditional techniques: cabinetmaking, joinery, metalwork, ceramics, and glass.

Among those backing this institution there is a desire to develop an interest in the art of our time. Because of its very open and many-faceted structure, the UCAD has regularly adapted itself to contemporary issues and will never falter in its desire to be part and parcel of modernity. The year 1969 saw the foundation of the Centre de Création Industrielle (Center for Industrial Creation), which became part of the Centre Georges Pompidou when it opened in 1977. In 1985 the Musée de la Mode et du Textile (Museum of Fashion and Textiles), which gives fashion designers a full-fledged status of their own, was created. After the founding of the Musée de l'Affiche (Poster Museum), 1999 saw the inauguration of the new Musée de la Publicité (Museum of Advertising), a unique concept encompassing all the variations of this creative medium.

The Musée des Arts Décoratifs is in the midst of change, while remaining true to its wish to espouse the requirements of its day and age. It was in this spirit that the decision was taken concerning a major renovation project, planned for completion in 2004.

Rather than confining our masterpieces to the silence of the storeroom, we are pleased to be able to share them with the American public, which has shown much interest in French taste, as can be seen from the major financial support offered by many patrons for our new Musée des Arts Décoratifs.

Pierre Manguin, *Cabinet,* circa 1856
(detail; pp. 80–81)

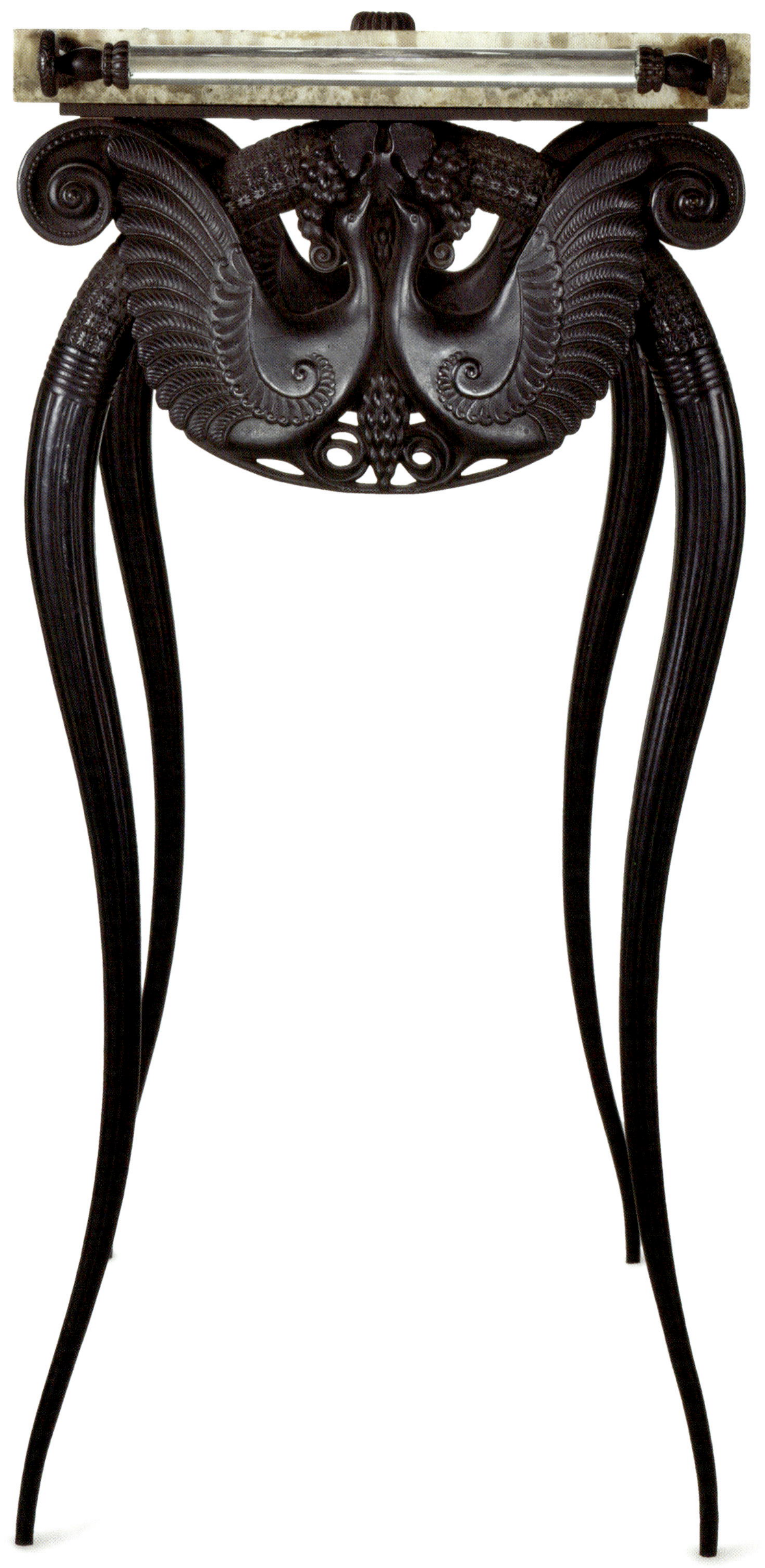

The New Musée des Arts Décoratifs

Béatrice Salmon
Director of the Museums,
Union Centrale des Arts Décoratifs

When the new building for the Musée des Arts Décoratifs opens its doors to the public in 2004, almost one hundred years will have elapsed since the museum's original inauguration in 1905 in a portion of the Pavillon de Marsan, a wing of the former royal palace mainly occupied by the Louvre Museum.

The Musée's location in the heart of Paris, at the prestigious Louvre site, became a must after the many long years during which its collections had been in various locations. The choice of such a symbolic place has underscored the importance attached by the powers-that-be to a museum unlike any other.

The initial Place Royale (now the Place des Vosges) location, which already housed the "modern and retrospective" museum and the library, was not particularly well-suited to the aims of the founding fathers of the Union Centrale des Beaux-arts appliqués à l'Industrie (The Central Union of Fine Arts Applied to Industry), and in no time there was a severe shortage of space to house the major growth of the collections.

After the war of 1870, a move in 1875 to other premises at the Place des Vosges helped temporarily to provide areas better suited to the development of the Union Centrale's cultural project, which was thereafter combined with a teaching program. However, the creation in 1877 of a Société du Musée des Arts Décoratifs, which rivaled the Union Centrale, complicated matters considerably.

From 1879 on, the glass roofs of the Palais de l'Industrie housed both organizations, which eventually joined forces to form the Union Centrale des Arts Décoratifs (UCAD). The principal concern of UCAD chairman Antonin Proust, a brilliant Minister for the Arts in the Gambetta government, was to find a site for the Musée des Arts Décoratifs, once again too cramped in the Palais de l'Industrie. At the same time, however, he had to make sure this undertaking would be adequately funded. Proposals abounded, involving rentals, purchases, and constructions ranging from the Palais du Quai d'Orsay to the Folies Bergères theater.

The Pavillon de Marsan, at the end of the North Wing of the Louvre, was suggested, but was turned down by the Council in 1887. Yet it was this solution that would eventually be adopted. In 1896 an agreement was signed between the government and the UCAD making this building available for a fifteen-year period to commence with the inauguration of the museum. For the UCAD, the move from the Palais de l'Industrie to the Louvre was much more than a mere relocation to a larger venue. It was a transition charged with significance. In 1882 the Union Centrale des Beaux-arts appliqués à l'Industrie changed its name to the Union Centrale des Arts Décoratifs, thus giving preference to the "decorative" over the "industrial." The change of premises followed suit, and in the eyes of contemporary

Armand-Albert Rateau, dressing table from the bathroom of Jeanne Lanvin, circa 1920–1922 (pp. 136–139)

observers, the Union Centrale's installation in the Louvre stressed a desire to lend the youthful institution a genuinely cultural dimension.

Needless to say, the Pavillon de Marsan rooms were never designed to house a museum. The pavilion had burned down in the fire that ravaged the Palais des Tuileries in 1870, and it was rebuilt in 1874 to house the national audit administration. When it was allocated to the UCAD, the interior areas were in the process of being renovated. Once again many difficulties cropped up, and the wish entertained by the new president, Georges Berger, to have the opening of the museum coincide with the inauguration of the 1900 Paris World's Fair came to naught. But nothing seemed to get in the way of the intentions of the project's main backers. The collections continued to grow, thanks in particular to the unfailing commitment of Jules Maciet, and major exhibitions were nevertheless put on in the huge unfinished premises of the Marsan wing.

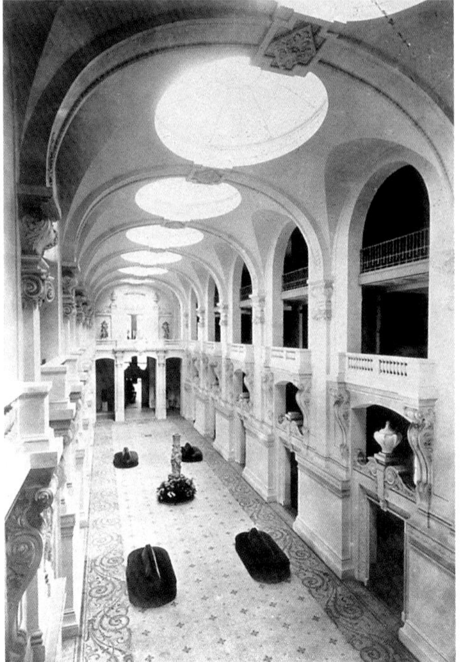

View of the central hall, Musée des Arts Décoratifs, Paris

Finally, on 29 May 1905, French President Emile Loubet opened the long-awaited Musée des Arts Décoratifs. Unfortunately, it was not until the end of the 20th century that it was possible to envisage a complete overhaul of the museum. Opportunity knocked when the Grand Louvre project, announced in 1981 by French President François Mitterrand, got under way. Various solutions were entertained for increasing the display areas for the ever-burgeoning collections in storage. There were even thoughts of moving the museum outside Paris, but it was soon evident that these collections dedicated to *l'art de vivre français* (French art of living) had a legitimate place in the Palace of the Louvre. The considerably larger display areas made possible by earmarking a part of the Rohan wing, allocated since 1997 to the Musée de la Mode et du Textile (Museum of Fashion and Textiles) and in 1999 to the Musée de la Publicité (Museum of Advertising), made it possible to completely reorganize the collections, especially when combined with the construction of large storerooms in the basement of the Carrousel gardens.

Toward the end of 1999, four teams of architects were appointed to undertake this enormous project covering some 65,000 square feet. Oscar Tusquets was in charge of the historical collections, Sylvain Dubuisson the contemporary section, Bernard Desmoulin the study galleries, and Daniel Kahane the temporary exhibition area and circuits, or tours of the museum.

Faced with the scale of the collections dating from the Middle Ages to the contemporary period, along with their type, size, and quality, the curatorial and architectural teams had to make choices, encouraging a twofold way of looking at the collections, while still respecting the initial goals of the UCAD's founders. The twofold perspective includes a chronological circuit and the study galleries.

The chronological circuit leads visitors from the Middle Ages to the contemporary world, traversing several levels in the building. The itinerary is not without surprises, which help to keep the material from becoming systematically and tediously linear. There is a series of thematic areas that highlight either a prominent figure; an ornamental motif, technique, or typology; or an iconographic issue. The challenge here involves helping visitors to approach the decorative arts on the basis of a far richer perspective than merely formal and stylistic factors. Each object is displayed like a finished product meeting many different criteria: user requirements, economic restrictions, and technical know-how. It is also an element of social refinement, in dialogue with the arts of the day. This explains why the circuit is punctuated by period rooms. These re-creations, be they comprehensive or partial, also help to introduce the personality of the person to whom objects and sets of objects once belonged, thus situating them in the context of their appearance and dissemination.

Study galleries, complementary or alternative to the circuit described above, are organized by material regardless of chronology. Here we return to the method of classification originally used by the museum and the great 19th-century expositions and world's fairs.

First passing through a gallery devoted to the history of the UCAD, the visitor to the study gallery might follow a lively presentation of the various works, based on comparisons between series of works, to convey an understanding of the problems peculiar to a particular material or technique. The modular arrangement designed for these rooms and the desire to present the collections on a rotating basis allow for a variety of scenarios.

Additionally, specific collections—e.g., the Dubuffet donation, the jewelry collection, or the toy collection—benefit from special presentation. Lastly, the documentation center, which specializes in the decorative arts, the drawings department, and the wallpaper department have all been designed for the needs of researchers.

The establishment of the new Musée des Arts Décoratifs is a major undertaking. Its confirmed location in the Louvre and the scale of government investment, compounded by the generosity of private patrons—be they French or foreign—all won over by our project, go to strengthen my persuasion that we are involved in an enterprise that is at once necessary, important, and rare.

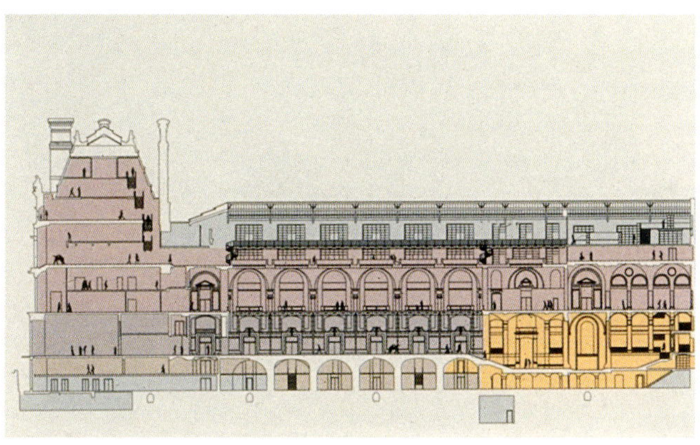

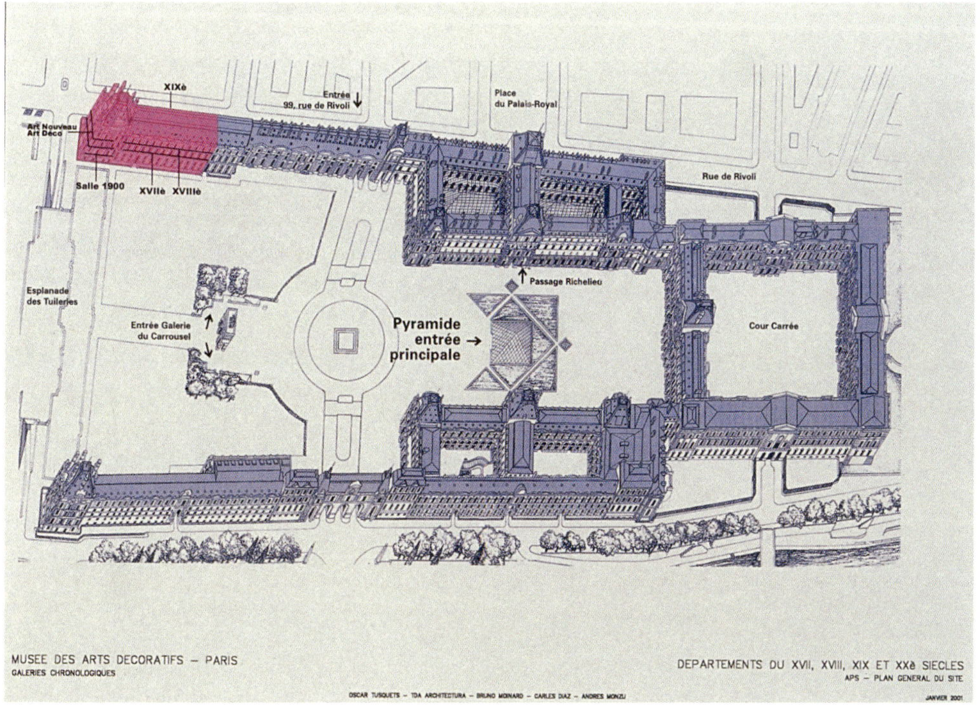

Top: Elevation of the Pavillon de Marsan, which houses the Musée des Arts Décoratifs

Bottom: Plan of the Palace of the Louvre. The Pavillon de Marsan is shown in pink, with the locations of the various galleries of the Musée des Arts Décoratifs indicated

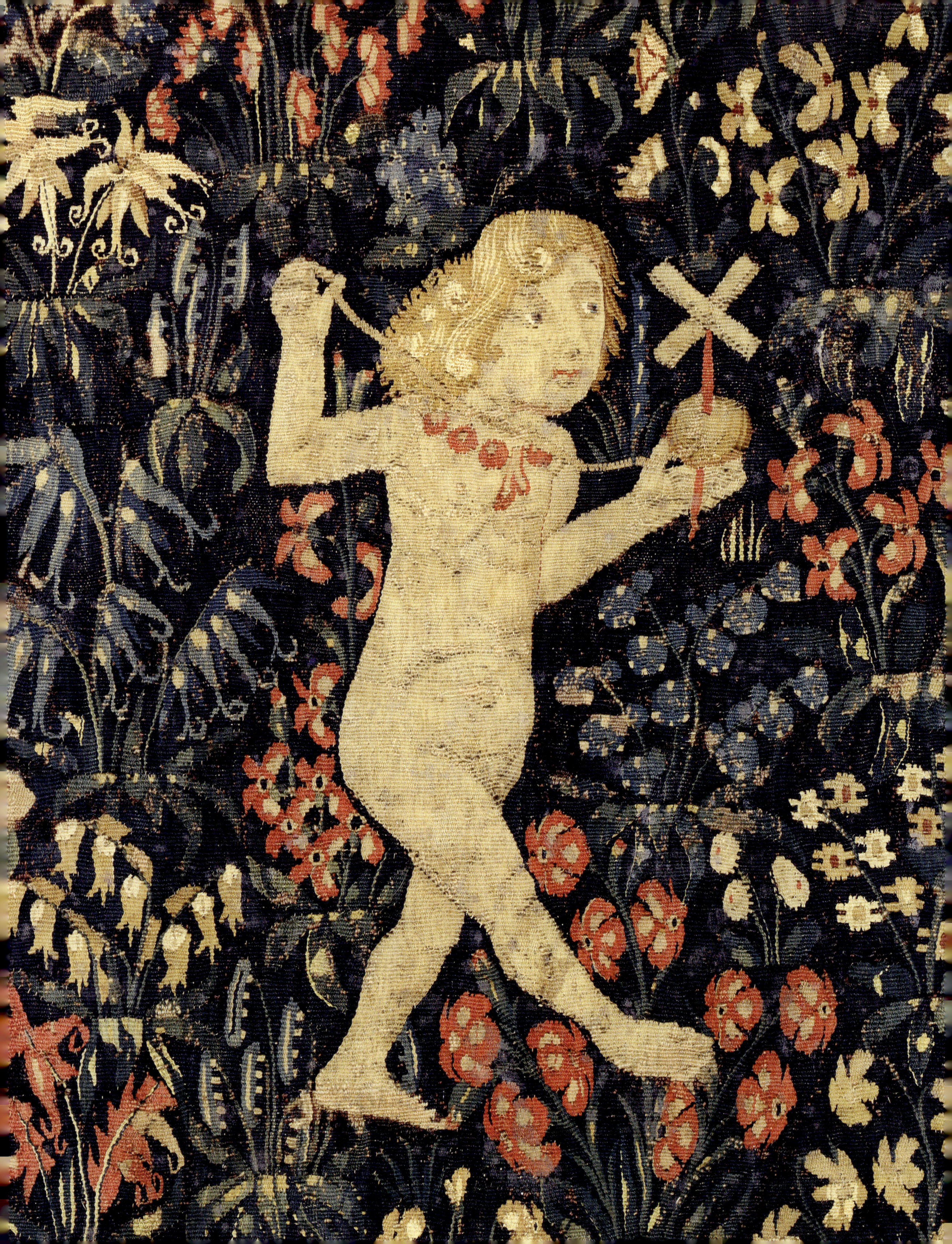

The Collections of the Musée des Arts Décoratifs

Odile Nouvel-Kammerer
Curator of the 19th-Century Department, Musée des Arts Décoratifs

For the first time, the Musée des Arts Décoratifs is showing the American public a selection of its masterpieces. Each object conveys the magical stuff of dreams, whisking us out of the present, away from contemporary cares and the humdrum, day-to-day lives we all lead. This major exhibition called for lengthy and painstaking preparation, and the press conference—that crucial stepping-stone for launching any kind of exhibition—had been organized in an extraordinarily effective way by John and Lucy Buchanan.

The conference was scheduled for 11 September 2001, in New York. Needless to say, it was canceled because of the tragic events of that day. In light of the horrors of the attack on Manhattan, our exhibition suddenly seemed fearsomely trivial. Many issues were raised by the act of proceeding so abruptly from an exhibition based on the idea of the "stuff of dreams" to the harsh reality of so much death and destruction. What significance does a museum of decorative arts have in this day and age, along with the objects it houses and the luxurious imagery with which it is associated? What values are its curators championing?

On further reflection, it seems apt to remind readers that a museum of decorative arts does have a decisive role. More than any other museum, this one is a supreme example of a place that houses the collective heritage. As such, its task is to make this heritage available to all of humankind, past and present. In such a museum, everything to do with the furnishing of the home is spared destruction, precisely because the object is here regarded as the special witness of people's tangible, material lives. Visitors are invited to a practical reading of many-faceted everyday life, be it luxurious or lowly, and those thousands of "overlooked" gestures that make up the warp and woof of life.

A museum of decorative arts is not a mere accumulation of collections, oriented toward a past that has once and for all vanished. It is a place for reflection, straddling time, and finding a place for contemporary works—those we can see being created today—against a backdrop that is both historical and ethnological, giving them their full due as something novel.

The history of the Union Centrale des Arts Décoratifs is part and parcel of this context, and, from the outset, has conveyed a far-reaching yet simple conviction: objects are worlds unto themselves, with the power to reveal human creativity and talent. The artist, craftsman, or manufacturer who has designed and produced an object, the purchaser who has been won over and actually used that object in his or her own home and then either bequeathed or sold it, the collector adding it to his trove, the donor offering it to the museum for ever and a day—this whole human sequence can be perceived in its finest moment at the Musée des Arts Décoratifs, because the final link in the chain—the donors—has been especially conspicuous.

Millefleurs Tapestry, Flemish, early 16th century (detail; pp. 28–29)

The collections of the Musée des Arts Décoratifs boast more than 250,000 items and objects, ranging in date from the Middle Ages to the present. From period rooms to series of snuff boxes, from toilette accessories to a collection of walking sticks, from thimbles to huge Norman wardrobes or to wallpapers—this accumulation of eclectic objects speaks to us of life's most diverse situations, from the most private to the most urbane, and from the most vital to the most trivial. How has this crucible come about, in which the dreams of thousands of generations intermingle, forming the very fabric of our culture?

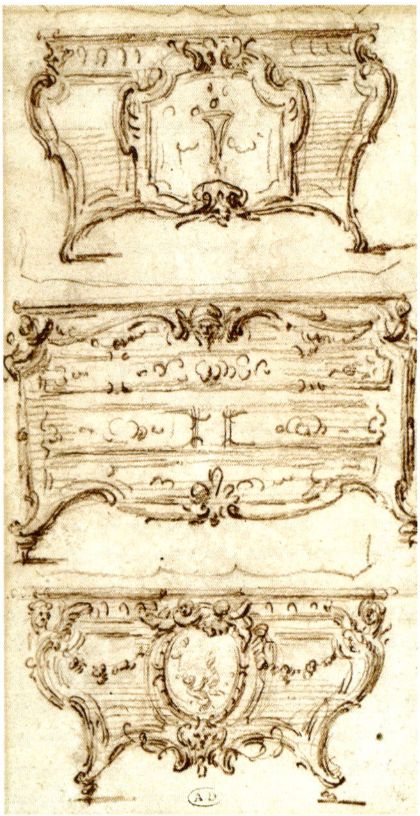

Nicolas Pineau, *Designs for Furniture,* French, 18th century. Musée des Arts Décoratifs, Paris

The Reproductions Policy

The plan to set up a new type of museum in France came to the fore in the mid-19th century, in the wake of the Expositions des Produits de l'Industrie (Industrial Products Exhibitions). These exhibitions were organized at the prompting of Napoleon, their aim being to show Paris the very best of French production, in every area of economic activity, be it farming, trade, or industry. The nine Industrial Products Exhibitions that were held between 1796 and 1849 also saw people taking a public stance, and the sector of household arts and deluxe production found itself at the hub of a great deal of discussion and salon chatter. Between about 1830 and 1835, enlightened minds became more and more alarmist. They noted that, with the pressure of mass production and competition from the English, France's famous "good taste" was vanishing beneath a heap of objects derived from an eclectic past and disconcerting historical bric-a-brac. On reflection, people also realized that after the suppression of the guilds during the French Revolution, there were no longer any schools to fashion the tastes of draftsmen, craftsmen, and manufacturers. The situation was so serious that in 1846 a group of artists headed by the extremely gifted sculptor Jean Feuchère decided to draw up a plan for an industrial-design school where classes would be associated with a *galerie d'étude* (study gallery). Objects deemed to be exemplary would be put on view to help train young craftsmen. Here we have the premise of Paris's future Musée des Arts Décoratifs, and the idea of having a selection of objects, chosen on the basis of both aesthetic and technical criteria, was very much in line with the juries presiding over the Industrial Products Exhibitions.

In 1856 the sculptor Jules Klagmann submitted a second project to Emperor Napoleon III, requesting the creation of schools and an industrial arts museum in every major French city, so as to establish "that close link between *the workshop, the school and the museum.*" The "study gallery" concept had evolved in the direction of the loftier "museum" concept. The Union Centrale des Beaux-arts appliqués à l'Industrie (The Central Union of Fine Arts Applied to Industry) was founded in 1864 with the aim of "maintaining in France the culture of the arts focusing on the execution of the Beautiful within the Useful." It remained true to the goals listed by Feuchère and created a library and a "retrospective museum" connected with the organization of courses and lectures.

This earliest museum, which sadly left no trace of any inventories, formed its collections essentially through gifts made by artists, manufacturers, and collectors, all eager to turn "their" museum into an exemplary venue.

The Union Centrale des Arts Décoratifs was created in 1882. The replacement of the idea of "fine arts applied to industry" by the "decorative" concept went hand in hand with the introduction of two new directions for the museum. On one hand, at the suggestion of the jeweler Lucien Falize, exhibitions were organized around a then very modern concept: the theme of "natural products," such as metal, fabric, and paper; hides; wood and stone; clay and glass; plants; and so on. These exhibitions attracted many gifts. The first museum inventory was drawn up and the museum filing system was organized around a classification method arranged by material.

The second innovation, which is more surprising for us, was the launch of a vast policy involving the reproduction of works. The museum saw itself as an encyclopedic place, capable of showing its public the best of every technique and technology, from every period. Faced with the problems attached to such an ambitious project, the UCAD chairman, Antonin Proust, decided to go along with reproduction techniques using casting and electroplating. "The Union Centrale reckons that it must, above all, create a huge reproduction factory not limited to producing models for its museum, but enabling it, further, to make these models available to every workshop and every school." A choice of models was developed, a workshop for plaster casts was set up, and a contract was signed with Christofle (a factory of gold- and silverworks that specialized in electroplating), where one of the directors, Henri Bouilhet, was incidentally vice-chairman of the UCAD. Casts and molds were dispatched to France's art schools, and casts were also exchanged with other great museums of decorative arts in Berlin, Budapest, Vienna, and elsewhere.

From Reproduction to Masterpiece: Creating a Unique Collection

Faced with the growth of its educational activities and its collections, the Union Centrale was granted leave by the government to move to the Pavillon de Marsan in the Louvre, where it is currently located. The Musée des Arts Décoratifs and the Library opened their doors on 29 May 1905, in the presence of Emile Loubet, president of the Republic.

People visiting at that time found that a major change had occurred within the museum. There were no longer any reproductions—only original works. In 1891 the new UCAD president, Georges Berger, had done away with the reproductions policy involving casting and electroplating, fearful of developing a spirit of copying. He accordingly gave up the idea of an encyclopedic collection of objects in favor of a museum filled with works of art.

The collections grew conspicuously richer. The Mobilier National, the Louvre, and Versailles all agreed to loan important pieces to the Pavillon de Marsan. One of the UCAD's very rare commissions, the famous *1900 Room*, created by Georges Hoentschel for the UCAD pavilion at the 1900 Paris World's Fair, was reassembled as testimony to contemporary taste. For its part, the Union Centrale's purchasing committee introduced many contemporary objects—bought from artists at salons and world's fairs—on a regular basis. It was in this way that the outstanding collection of Emile Gallé glass was gradually put together, likewise the Delaherche ceramics and the Gaillard pieces of gold- and silverwork.

But it was private donors who played a crucial role in forming collections that made sense. Two powerful figures triggered the long series of generous gifts that enabled the Musée des Arts Décoratifs to amass its treasure trove. Emile Peyre made the UCAD his sole legatee when, on his death in 1904, he bequeathed a collection of more than 1,900 objects worth close to one million francs. This tireless collector of medieval and Renaissance art was described by a contemporary as "a slightly wild one-off character, receiving his friends in the incredible hodge-podge of Rue Malakoff, wearing a chef's hat, and trotting through his rooms," taking note of all his acquisitions in dogged detail in little notebooks, and rewriting them precisely on the plans of his private mansion.

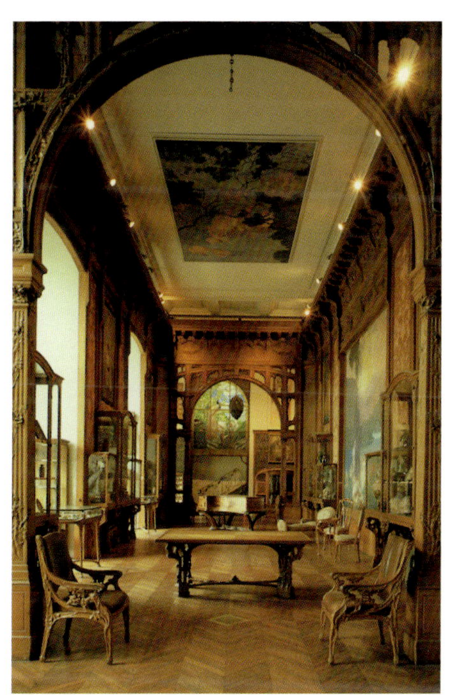

Georges Hoentschel, *1900 Room,* created for the UCAD pavilion at the 1900 Paris World's Fair. Musée des Arts Décoratifs, Paris

Unlike his friend Peyre, Jules Maciet showed a highly eclectic taste. On many occasions, and at his death in 1911, he donated more than 2,000 works, including many French items from the 17th and 18th centuries, 15th- and 16th-century Flemish tapestries—all masterpieces —original carpets and rugs, Japanese porcelain, Persian miniatures, earthenware, and much more. He was also a great collector of pictures (prints, photographs, reproductions from books and magazines), which he would cut out, day after day, until they methodically filled the 3,500 large volumes lining the walls of his library, thus forming an outstanding source of iconographic reference.

In the wake of Peyre and Maciet, many collectors, artists, and craftsmen, or just modest men and women in love with a beautiful object, have all been movingly generous to the museum.

Collectors, in droves, donated. Between 1898 and 1931 Raymond Koechlin offered in succession 150 gifts, including many items from the Middle East and the Far East. Miss Louise Grandjean, with her eclectic taste, contributed, by gift and bequest, more than 1,000 works in 1910. The Marquess of Arconati-Visconti, also a benefactor of the Louvre Museum, gave jewels and Art Nouveau works. In 1922 Samuel Bing bequeathed the impressive collection of Art Nouveau objects, drawings, and wallpaper that he had promoted and offered for sale, as well as items from the Far East that he had collected. Félix Doistau donated his amazing collection of walking sticks and swords, along with many ceramic pieces. Some 160 carved ivory skulls, collected by Baroness Henri de Rothschild, were bequeathed in 1925. In 1930 Mrs. Géo Rouard entrusted the museum with the bedchamber that she and her husband had commissioned in 1900 from Louis Majorelle. In 1934 the legacy of Alfred Heidelbach greatly enhanced the porcelain collection with almost 600 18th- and 19th-century French and foreign pieces. In that same year Mr. and Mrs. Barthou bequeathed their important collection of 43 works in glass by Maurice Marinot, which today form an important set. In 1937 Thierry Délicourt added more than 1,000 18th-century works. In the 19th century, the heirs of Léon Nozal donated the bedroom he had commissioned from Hector Guimard.

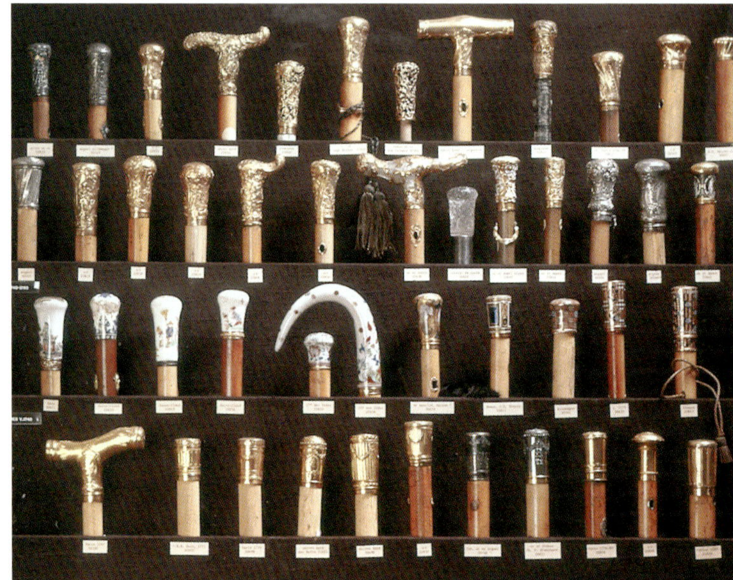

Walking Sticks, French, 18th century.
Musée des Arts Décoratifs

After the war, several important suites of furniture found their way to the museum. In 1958 Jean Edouard Dubrujeaud donated the sophisticated furniture that Jacques Doucet had commissioned from Pierre Legrain and Louis Mergier for his Neuilly studio. In 1965 Prince Louis de Polignac, who had married the couturier's daughter, donated Jeanne Lanvin's extremely famous apartment, designed by Armand-Albert Rateau. The dining room of the old Lavenne Hotel in Brussels, made by Emile Gallé, was donated in 1968 by the heirs of Léo Hannon, the patron who commissioned it. The heirs of Pierre Charreau decided to donate his study to the museum in 1999. And most recently, the patronage of Michel and Hélène David-Weill, with the participation of the Heritage Fund, has made it possible to acquire André Groult's extraordinary chiffonnier. The extraordinarily large number of these major collectors who have entrusted the museum with the fruits of their enthusiasm means, sadly enough, that I cannot mention all of them personally. Today, however, we can still very much feel the effects of their generosity.

Among all these lovers of objects, two figures seem especially touching in their generous loyalty. David David-Weill, who was vice-chairman of the UCAD, chairman of the Artistic Council of the Réunion des Musées nationaux, and a very influential member of many Paris museums, made more than 60 donations, all of them major ones and chosen with sure and exceptional taste. They include several unique and world-renowned pieces, such as the Meissonnier-Duvivier candelabra, an absolute masterpiece of French Rococo; the blue lacquer desk of Madame de Pompadour; and a superb collection of Chinese cloisonné enamel pieces. His son Pierre David-Weill followed his example, and today his grandson, Michel David-Weill is still demonstrating the same unflagging generosity.

On his death in 1935, Comte Moïse de Camondo, a close friend of David David-Weill, who also played a very active role in the UCAD, bequeathed his rue de Monceau mansion and the entirety of his 18th-century collections in memory of his son Nissim, who died in the First World War. The coherence of this extraordinary collection has enabled it to be turned into a house museum that is unique in Paris.

Artists, too, have been major donors. In 1889 Jean-Baptiste Carpeaux's widow donated some ten terra-cotta statuettes. In 1910 Ernest Chaplet bequeathed more than 60 ceramic pieces, all much appreciated today. The famous jeweler Henri Vever in 1924 gave more than 600 pieces of jewelry, most of them his own production, to which he added various older pieces, thus forming a reference collection for the 19th century. In 1958 the widow of Robert Mallet-Stevens offered the entire personal office of this famous architect, and in 1967 Jean Dubuffet made a donation of almost 300 of his works, out of his friendship for François Mathey, then the museum's chief curator. The exhibition *Assises du siège contemporain* (Contemporary Seating), organized in 1968, led to many gifts from manufacturers of contemporary furniture, making it possible to set up an important design collection. In 1969 the architect Emilio Terry bequeathed his wildly imaginative drawings, and in 1980 the decorator Jean Royère donated more than 500 drawings and almost 800 works on tracing paper. The important collection from the studio of decorator André Arbus was given by his daughter Madeleine Thorel Arbus in 1997. Lastly, the artist Niki de Saint-Phalle has just donated an amazing set of her furniture and objects, some of them unique works.

There has always been a host of less well-known donors—collectors all, and all sensitive to the beauty of objects. More than that of any other group, their generosity helps to turn our collections into a museum of "series," in other words, a significant gathering of objects, whose use, technique, and decoration are similar, thus permitting endless comparisons, the better to grasp the many-faceted nature of creative work.

Our collections are a special record of expertise, of the passionate experience of beauty and collecting, of the ability to give generously, and, last of all, the absolute need to hand things on. Surpassing the status of a functional object that may be neglected through everyday use, the beautiful objects here exhibited were made precisely to *not* be forgotten. Their virtue lies in offering a dash of pleasure day after day down through the ages. This is why they deserve to be lovingly safeguarded and bequeathed to others in museums like that of the Musée des Arts Décoratifs.

Salon Barriol, late 18th-century period room. Musée des Arts Décoratifs

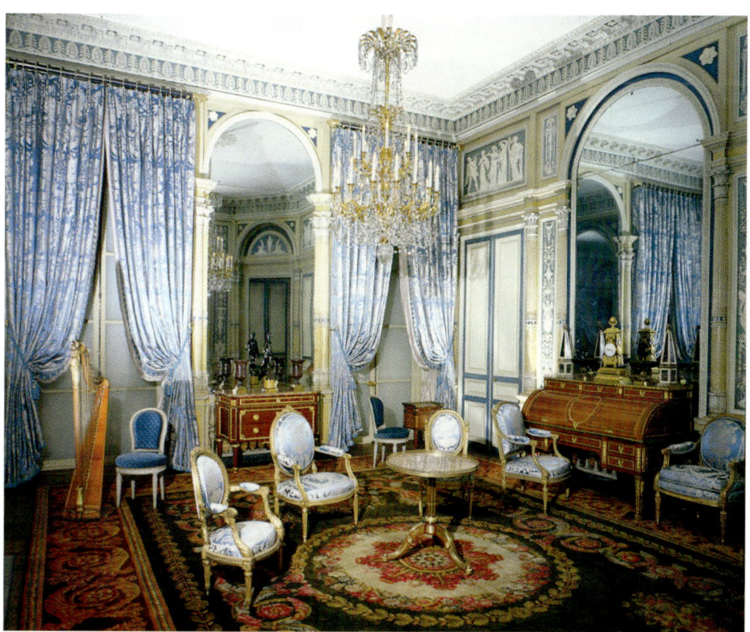

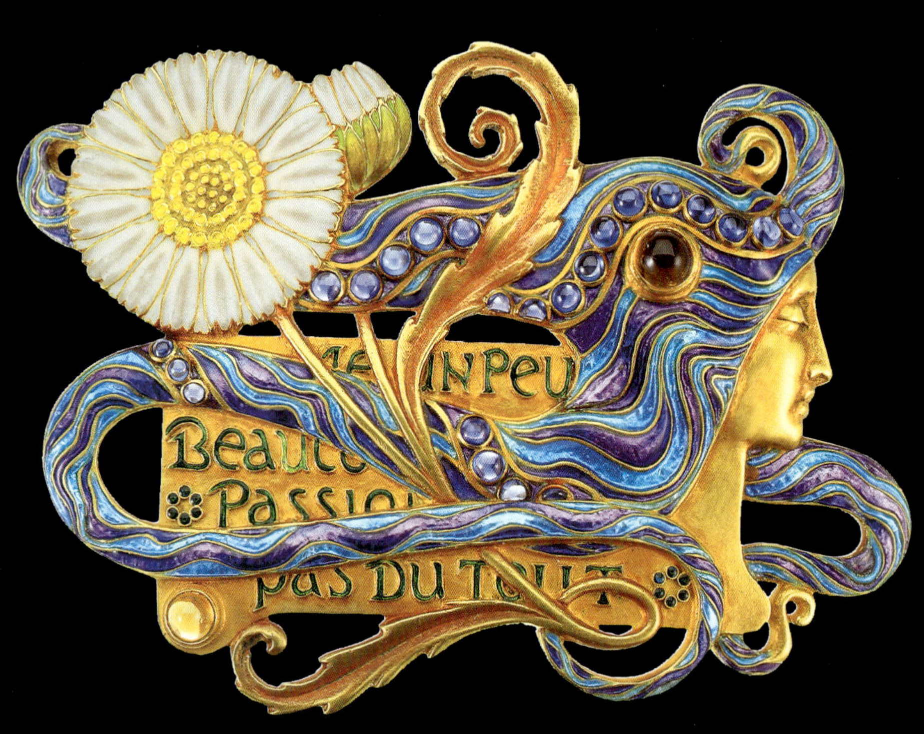
UN PEU

Stuff of Dreams

Penelope Hunter-Stiebel
Consulting Curator
of European Art,
Portland Art Museum

The stuff of dreams—that is what they are, these extraordinary objects that surpass all standards of technical excellence, demands of utility, and traditional precedents to make the leap from artifact to work of art.

They have come down to us over the ages with the surprise of their unexpected forms and the irresistible power of their sensual appeal. From their humble roots as useful objects, they have pushed into a territory of exotic individuality. They are made to realize the dreams of people: not just the people who have made them, but also the people for whom they were made.

These objects translate intangible flights of fantasy into aspects of reality that become an integral part of the life span of their owners. They are made to be used, touched, and handled as well as admired. In the intimacy of physical contact, they differ from what has been termed the "fine arts."

Yet they can be as fine as any art form, and that should, but cannot, go without saying. It is only since the 19th century that outstanding aesthetic achievements in ceramics, glass, metalwork, textiles, or furniture have been set apart from painting and sculpture. Classed as a lesser category of artistic expression, they have been designated "applied arts" or "decorative arts," as distinct from "fine arts."

History offers no support for this distinction. For the classical civilizations of Greece and China, there was no higher form of art than ceramics. The goldsmithswork of tribal hordes argues for a well-developed sensitivity to beauty in what history books have called "the Dark Ages." Nothing was more highly valued in the Europe of the Middle Ages than tapestries, and the messages of religion shone most clearly through the images of stained-glass windows. Weavers of the court of the 16th-century sultans are familiar to our own children through tales of the magic powers of the Persian carpet. Renaissance rulers competed for the talents of Benvenuto Cellini, and his gold-and-enamel saltcellar was as highly prized as any painting or sculpture of the time. In the Baroque age an intricately veneered cabinet became the ne plus ultra showpiece of any prince, eclipsing the treasures contained in its drawers. In 18th-century France, painters jockeyed to provide subjects to be woven at the tapestry workshops of Gobelins and Beauvais, and sculptors were honored to supply models to the royal porcelain manufactory of Sèvres.

To pass muster in a competitive environment, these works had to demonstrate exceptional technical skill without sacrificing function. To be recognized as art, they had to be invested with the imagination, the dreams, of their creator. To be passed on as treasures and preserved from generation to generation, century to century, they had to inspire the desire of possession. They had to correspond to their owners' (in actuality, their temporary custodians') sensibilities, aspirations, and dreams.

Eugène Grasset, Paul Vever, and Henri Vever, *Marguerite Brooch,* 1900 (p. 108)

So it was the idea of the dream that the two curators, Odile Nouvel-Kammerer and I, decided upon as the ultimate criterion in selecting works for an exhibition that would represent the unique character of the Paris museum dedicated to the decorative arts. In an extraordinary adventure, I followed my colleague up shaky ladders in dark attics and through the fluorescent brilliance of subterranean corridors as we visited every storeroom, leaving no corner uninvestigated, no shelf unexamined, no drawer unopened, in our self-appointed task as dream-catchers.

As a student I became a regular visitor to the Musée des Arts Décoratifs, using its extensive collections to gain expertise in the field of French decorative arts. I continued to learn, not just from the objects themselves, but also from the scholarship of the museum's curators. The pioneering work in the 1960s and '70s of curator (and later director) Yvonne Brunhammer was my guiding star in developing the Twentieth Century Decorative Arts collection at the Metropolitan Museum of Art.

But it has not been for education alone that I have spent hours in the galleries of this unique Parisian institution. They have captivated me with their presentation of art in the most accessible of forms.

These works of art are talismans that require little or no decoding. Whether from a near or distant past, they speak in the universal language of utility. These are not works made simply to satisfy a creative impulse. Each one was conceived with the idea that it would become a part of someone's private world. Often the object's provenance, the person for whom it was made (from Queen Marie Antoinette to the most notorious courtesan of Paris), or the person who would later acquire it, adds another level of fascination. No matter how extravagant and foreign to contemporary circumstance a work may appear, it is accessible, because it deals with the needs of daily life in any age. Those are needs as basic as providing light or accommodating sleep. Yet the difference between the light fixture or bed that is familiar to us and Meissonnier's free-form silver candelabra or the boat bed by Baudry is the difference between prose and poetry.

To introduce you to the delights of decorative arts as represented in the Musée des Arts Décoratifs, we have arranged a night of dreams. Starting in the Middle Ages with the most fantastical of water jugs—half-man, half-beast—you will pass through extraordinary episodes of fantasy, from the molten world of French 18th-century Rococo to the delirium of Art Nouveau to modernistic visions of mythical simplicity. When you come to the last of these works, which connect so eloquently to their predecessors in materials and techniques, you will know that even in our post-industrial age, dreams have not ended.

Catalogue

Aquamanile

Southern German, early 13th century
Bronze. H. 9½ in. (24 cm)
Jacques Martin Le Roy bequest, 1929

The strange vessel known as an "aquamanile" (from the Latin *aqua,* water, and *manus,* hand) originated in the church sacristy, where the priest used it to wash his hands before and after celebrating Mass. Artists have given this liturgical object various surreal forms drawn from the repertoire popularized by the Catholic Church. Most aquamaniles are rich in fantasy, with imaginary beings having animal forms, preferably lions or horses, at times combined with human faces.

In this example, a fantastic bird with a human torso and face holds in its slender arms a kind of spout that serves as an air inlet. A second animal's head between the two legs functions as a spout for pouring. The bird's wings and tail are curved to form the aquamanile's handle, and they hold the hinged lid of the opening into which the water was poured.

Works such as this come mainly from northern countries, and more specifically from Germany, the Meuse region, and the Netherlands. Production of aquamaniles reached its height in the 12th and 13th centuries, when they were used not only in sacristies but also in private homes. The form died out altogether during the Renaissance. —M.B.

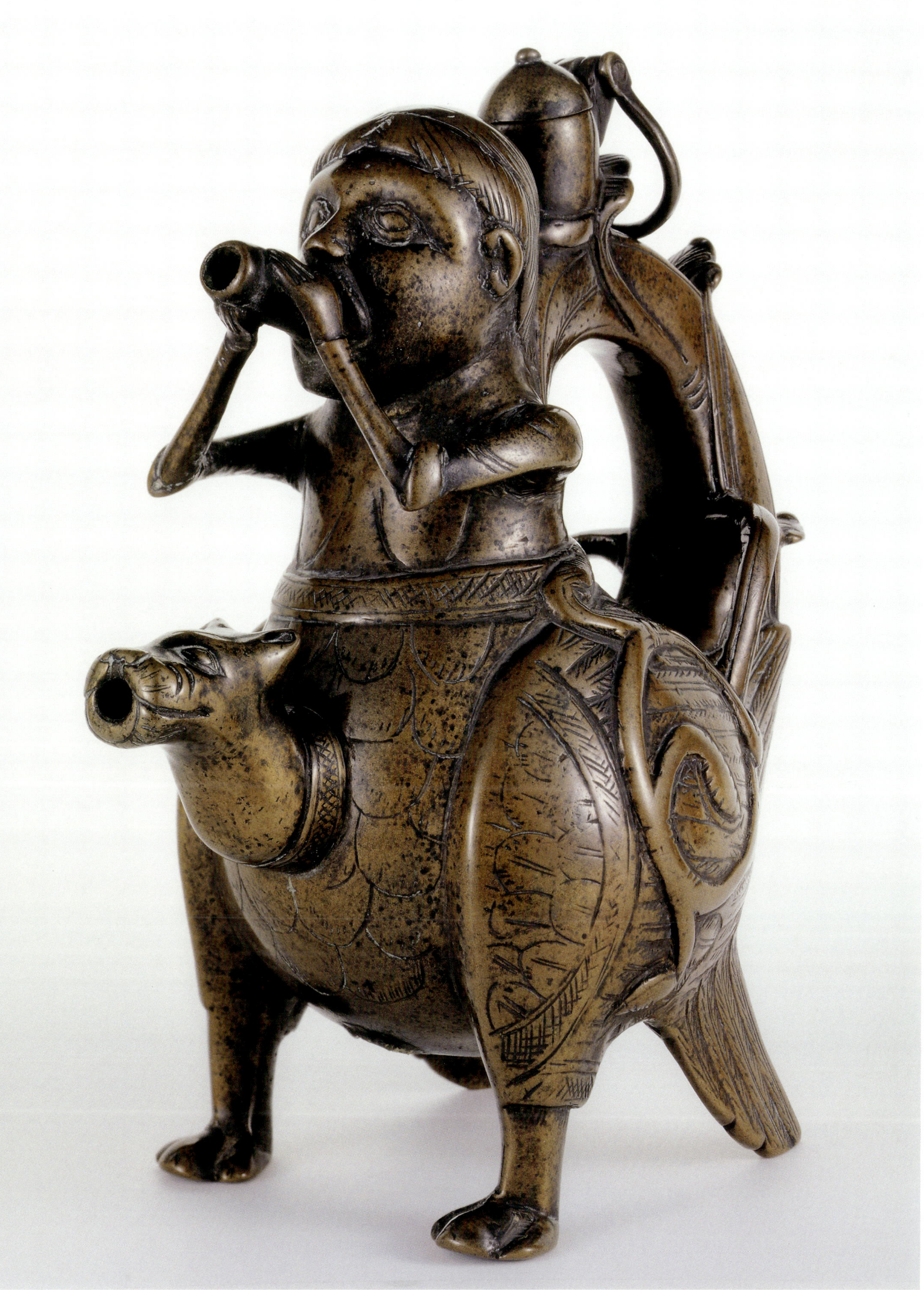

CHEST

FRENCH, LATE 13TH CENTURY
OAK, WROUGHT IRON. H. 35 IN. (89 CM),
W. 65 IN. (165 CM), D. 31⅛ IN. (79 CM)
EMILE PEYRE BEQUEST, 1905

In the Middle Ages, chests were used for storing textile hangings, tapestries, clothing, and miscellaneous everyday objects. They had to be sturdy because they served as luggage when lords and ladies traveled, which they did frequently.

Chests were constructed of thick panels held in place by an armature of iron straps nailed to the wood to ensure solidity and rigidity. The repeated decorative devices of the ironwork enlivened the simple facades of these rustic pieces with rhythmic patterns.

Few chests survive from the Middle Ages, and the origin of this superb example is unknown. But its iron armature of spiraling stems, ending in small flowers and growing both vertically at the center front and horizontally in five rows wrapping around from the sides, distinguishes it as an object of extremely high quality. —M.B.

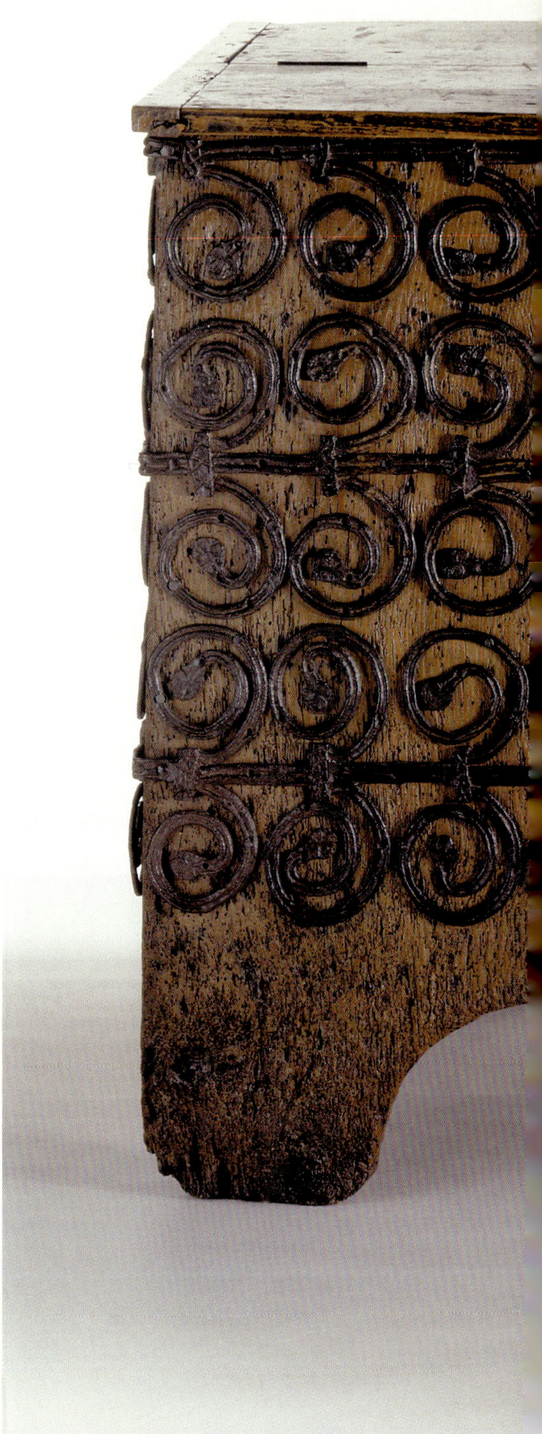

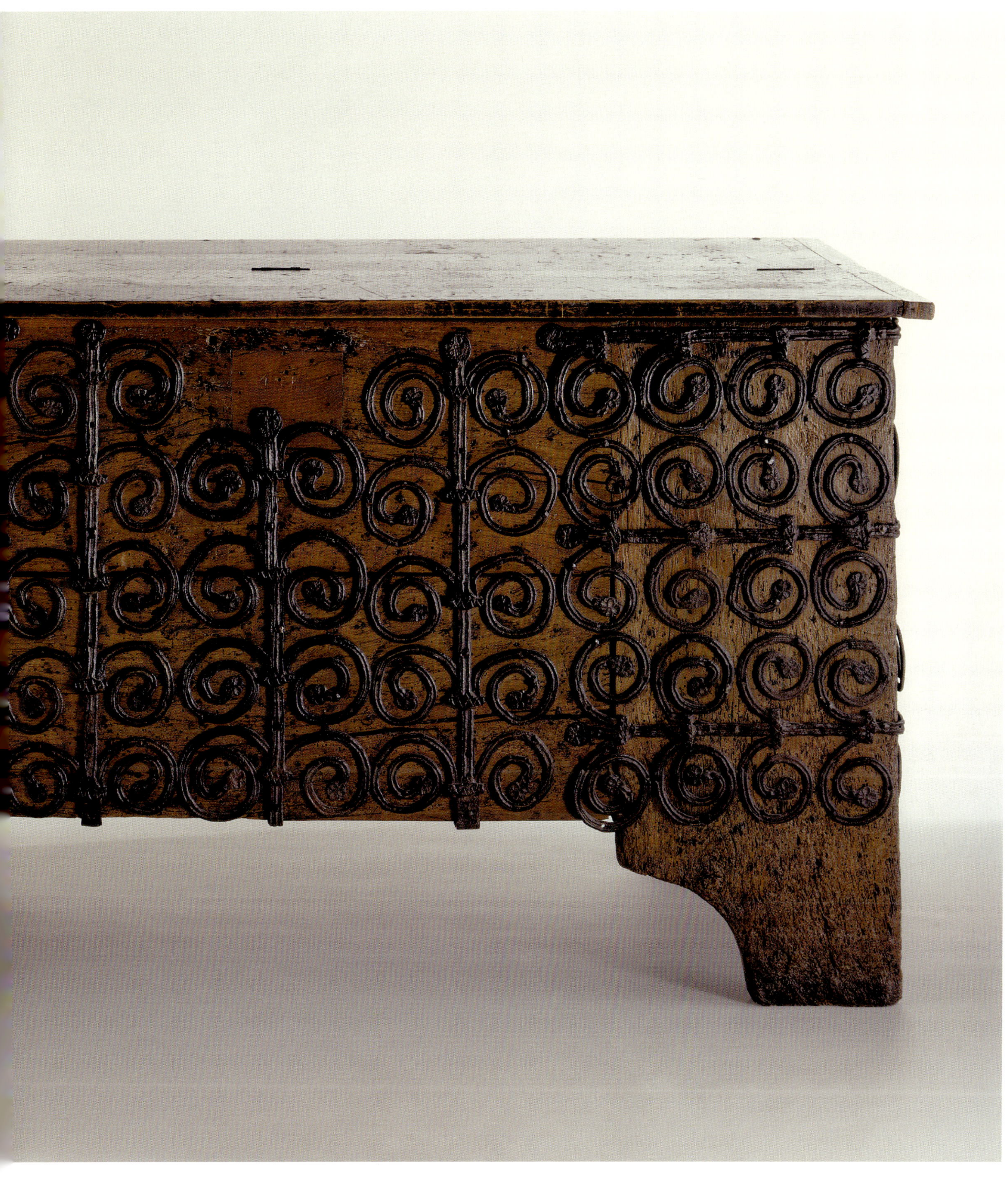

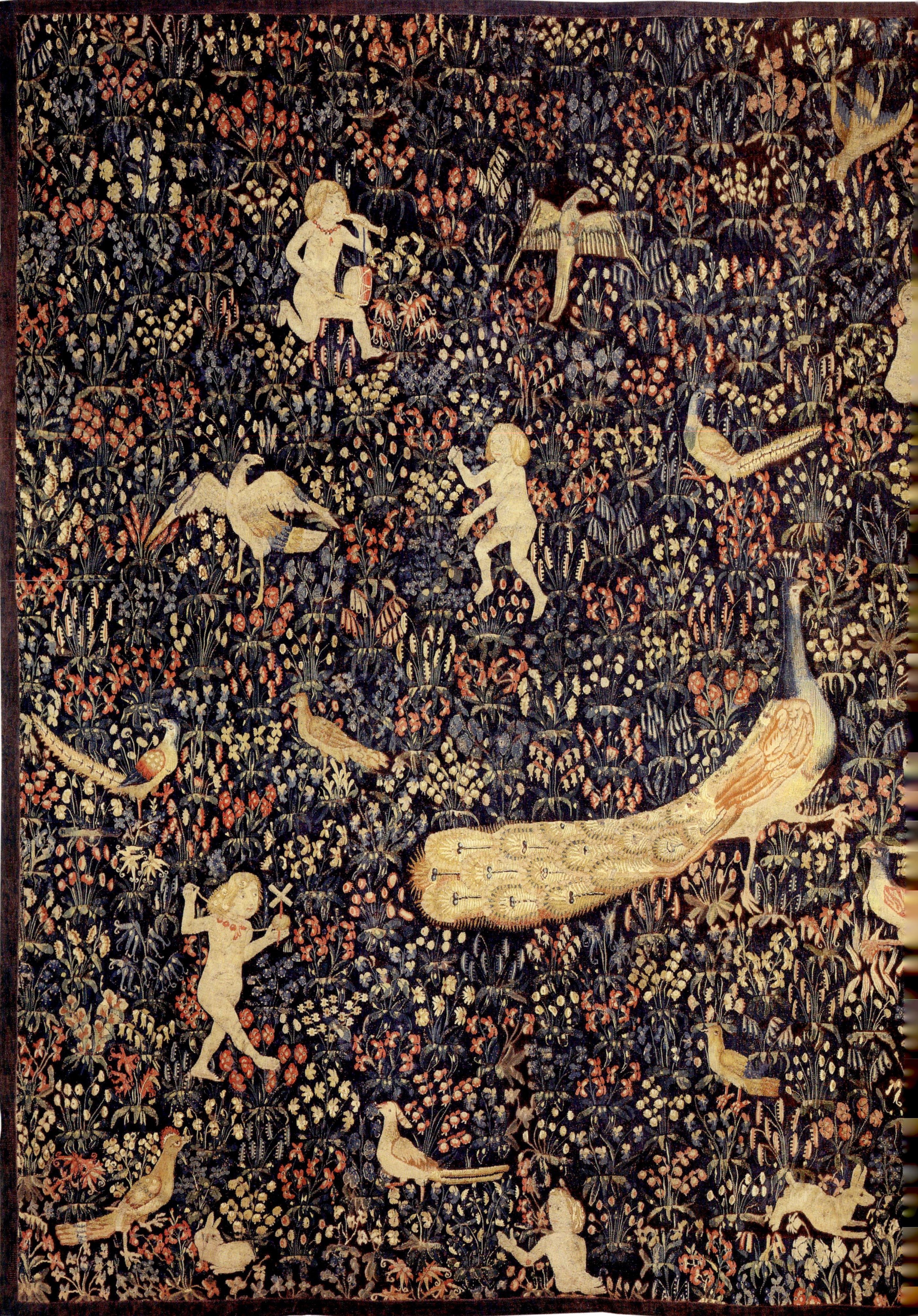

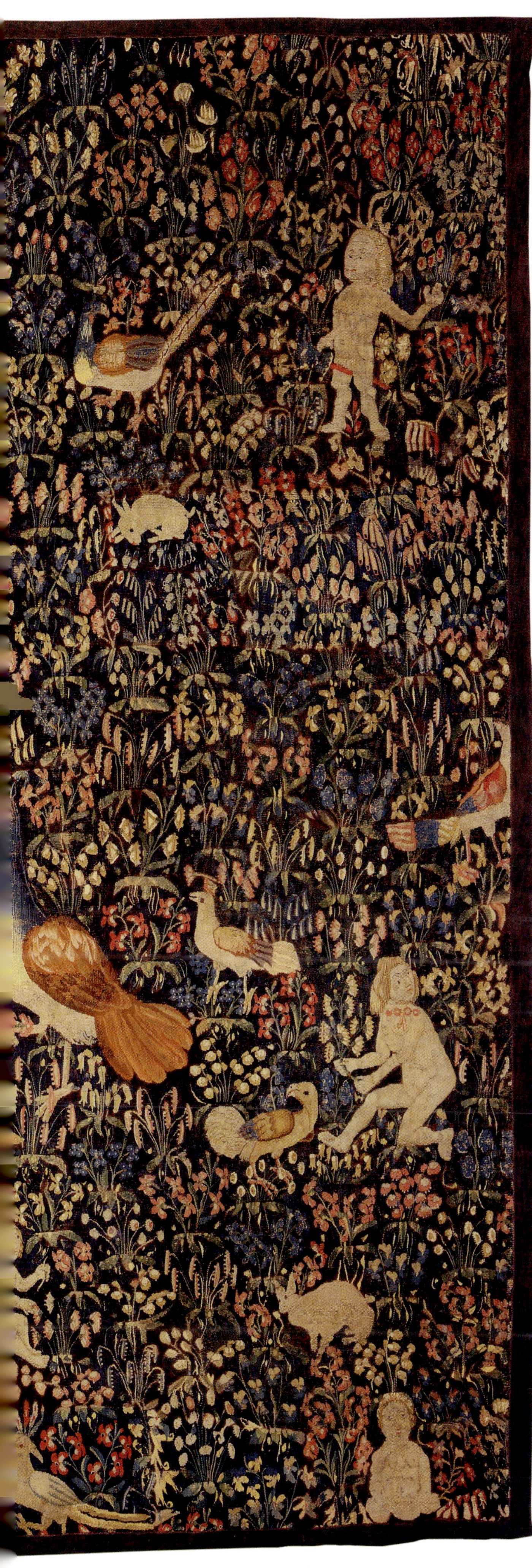

MILLEFLEURS TAPESTRY

FLEMISH, EARLY 16TH CENTURY
WOOL, SILK. H. 110¼ IN. (280 CM),
W. 132¾ IN. (337 CM)
GIFT OF JULES MACIET, 1903

This type of tapestry, poetically called "millefleurs" (literally, a thousand flowers), is strewn with a host of little motifs scattered through a paradise of Nature, often featuring clumps of irises, aquilegia, thistles, hyacinths, wallflowers, strawberries, and daisies. In addition, the tapestries may be decorated with coats of arms, little animals, or illustrations of courtly scenes and episodes from the life of the nobility. In this tapestry, naked toddlers frolic amid flowers, birds, rabbits, and peacocks. One child is beating a drum and blowing a horn, while others are picking flowers and laying them in a wicker basket. Still another child rides a hobbyhorse, while his friend spins a top with a whirligig.

Such tapestries were costly luxury items available only to an elite. They were valued for the comfort and warmth they offered in winter as well as for their beauty and harmony of color. Dating from an era when windows gave onto Italianate enclosed gardens, the tapestries conjure up an imaginary vista of a paradise encompassing innocent happiness.

The origin of these prized millefleurs is not easy to pin down. A large number of them were found in central France, so it was long thought that they were made in itinerant weaving workshops on the banks of the Loire. Current thinking, however, posits that the main production centers of millefleurs were in Brussels, Tournai, and Bruges. —M.B.

Two rosary beads

Northern German, 16th century
Lime wood. Left: H. 1¾ in. (4.5 cm), Diam. 1½ in. (3.8 cm);
right: H. 2⅛ in. (5.5 cm), Diam. 1¾ in. (4.5 cm)
Louise Grandjean Bequest, 1910

In the practice of the Catholic religion, a rosary is used to assist in the recitation of a lengthy series of prayers. Small beads are arranged in groups of fifteen, each to be fingered with the repetition of a prayer known as the "Hail Mary." A larger bead separates the sets and prompts the recitation of the Lord's Prayer.

These two Lord's Prayer beads are exceptional examples that are hinged so their owner could open them to meditate on the miniature scenes of Christ's Passion inside, then close them after reciting the prayer.

In the upper part of the first bead, we see Golgotha and the Virgin Swooning; in the lower part, Christ Bearing the Cross. Two circular inscriptions, in Latin, are featured on both parts: "Levemus corda nostra cummanibus ad.D" and "Dolore sicut. dolore me. attendite.et.videte.si. est.dolore. . . ."

In the second rosary bead, we are shown Christ on the cross flanked by two angels bearing the attributes of the Passion; in the lower part, the Virgin Swooning.

Both beads were made in the same way: two half-spheres of lime wood were hollowed and finely perforated, using gouges and small scalpels, to produce a décor resembling the tracery of Gothic windows. The religious scenes inside the beads were fashioned out of separate pieces of lime wood. Several episodes of Christ's Passion are carved in high relief with tiny figures in remarkably readable perspective recession. They were then inserted in each hollowed half-sphere, the space between the carved scene and the wall of the sphere creating a subtle sense of depth.

The work is typically German in style and relates to the finely detailed scenes of carved wooden altarpieces in churches in northern Germany.

—M.B.

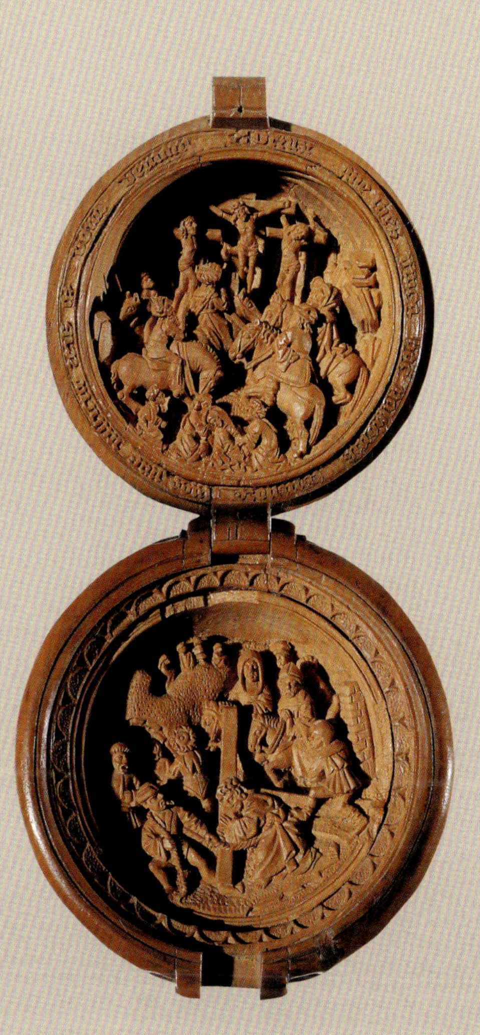

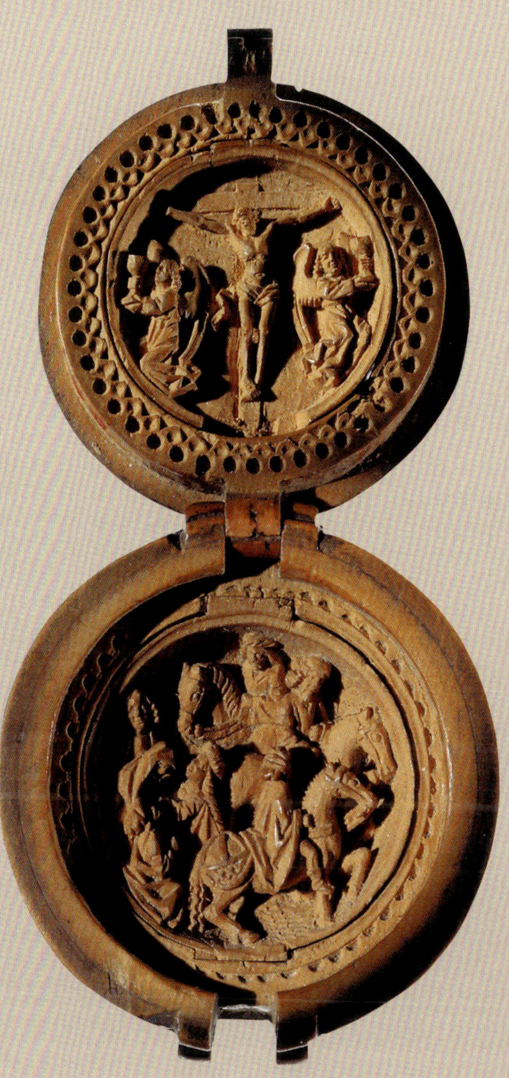

Dresser

French, Ile-de-France or Burgundy, circa 1580
In the style of Jacques Androuet Du Cerceau
Walnut. H. 58¼ in. (148 cm), W. 42½ in. (108 cm), D. 19⅝ in. (50 cm)
Emile Peyre bequest, 1905

The dresser originated in the late 16th century. It was usually designed as a cabinet with one or two doors above a medial drawer, the whole raised on slender columns that rest on a footed plinth base. Carved ornaments and figures generally embellished the entire dresser, with molding framing the doors. During the 17th century, the form, minus columns, evolved into the full-length armoire.

The Musée des Arts Décoratifs dresser follows a design by the great architect Jacques Androuet Du Cerceau that was engraved and published in 1550. At the request of Queen Catherine de Médici, Du Cerceau made a collection of seventy-two designs for furniture. Most were heavily charged with carved decoration. This example, however, is conceived as a piece of classical architecture characterized by purity of line and restraint of form. Spare and abstaining from all ornament, this exceptional dresser achieves a powerful presence. —M.B.

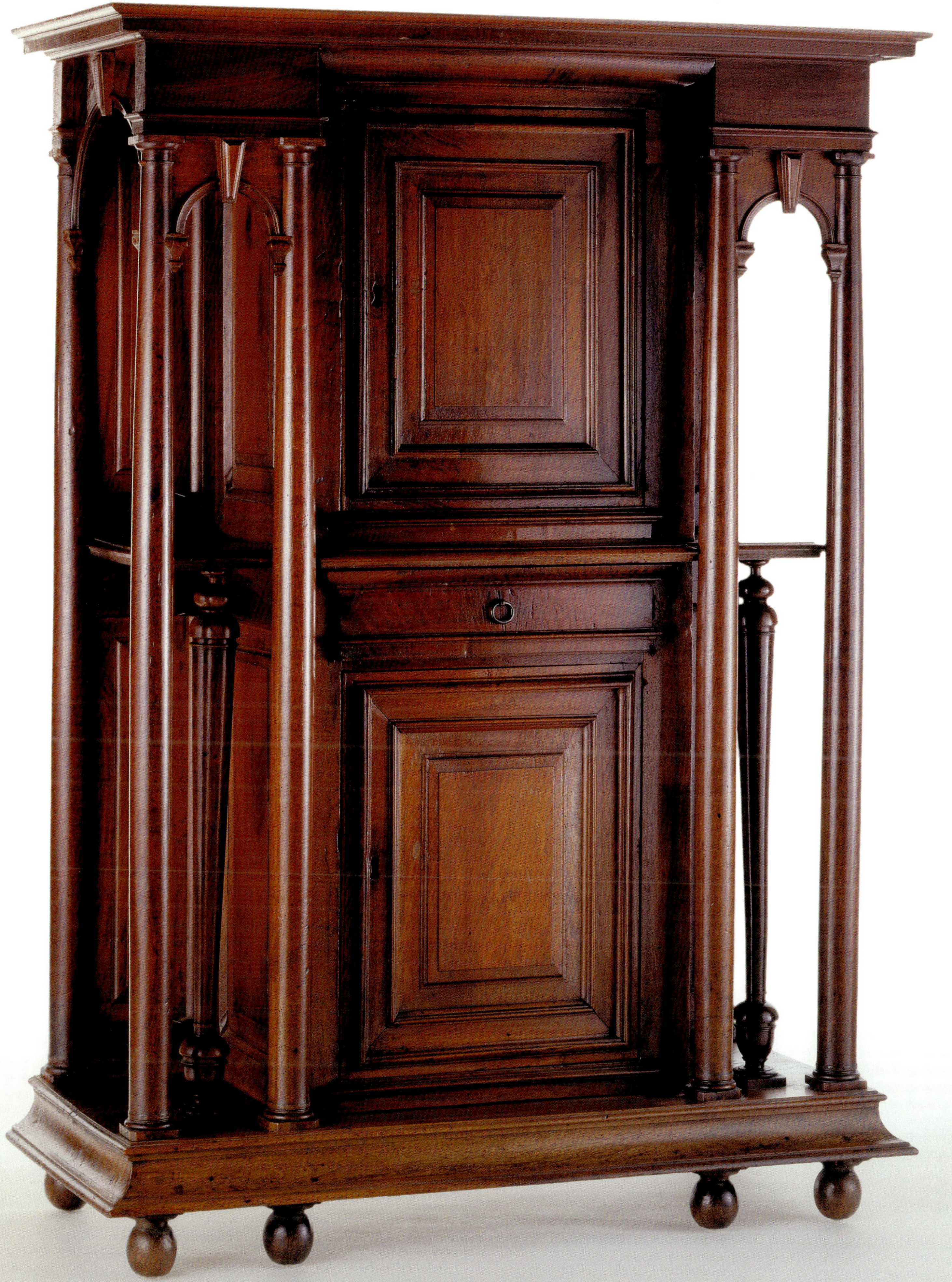

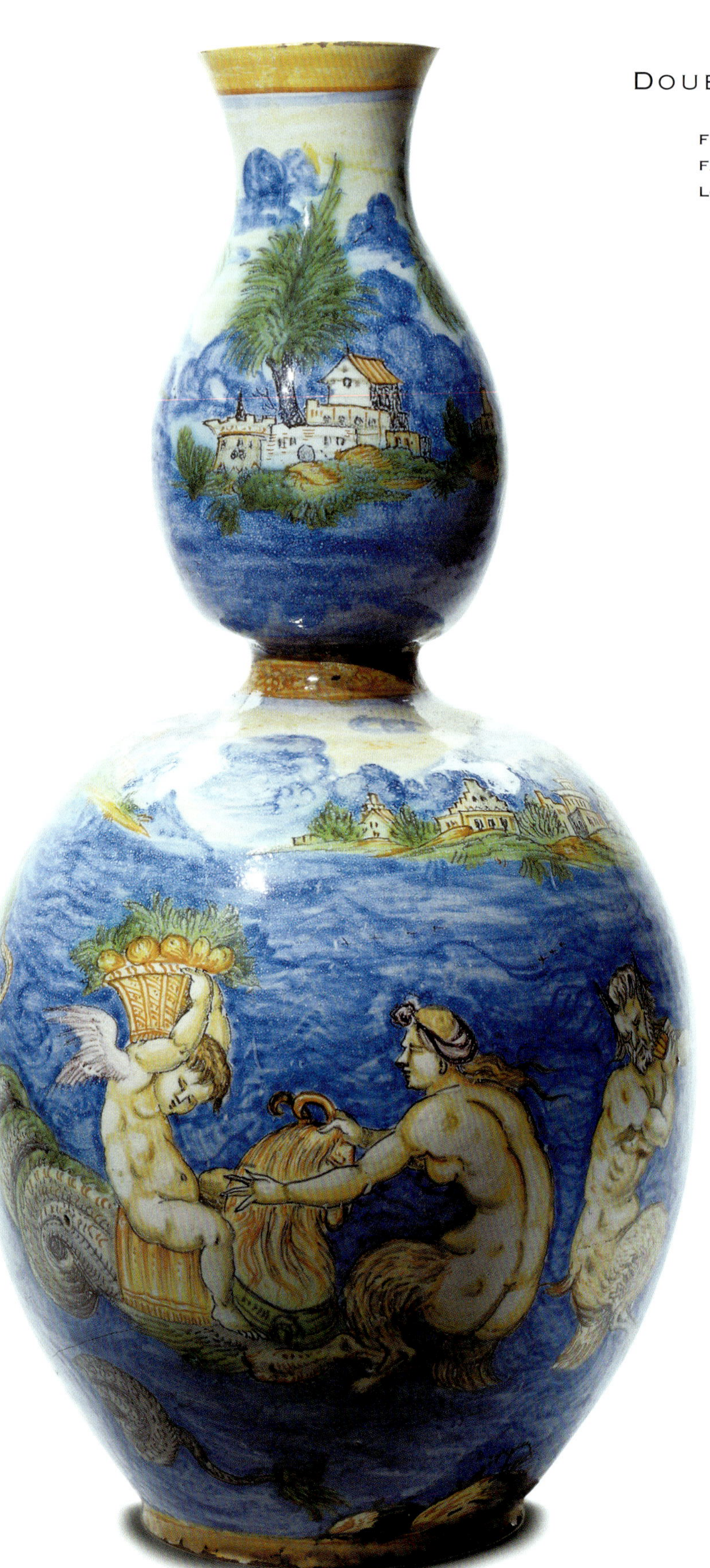

Double gourd vase

French, Nevers, early 17th century
Faience. H. 18⅛ in. (46 cm)
Louise Grandjean Bequest, 1910

The double swelling of the silhouette of this vase recalls the shape of the calabash gourd. This type of vase would have been lined up with others of various shapes—roll (cylindrical), horn (beaker), urn—for collective display on top of a cabinet. These forms were borrowed from Chinese porcelain at a time when its features were copied, even though the secrets of its manufacture had not yet been mastered by European imitators.

The decoration is of Italian inspiration. In two registers conforming to the contours of the vase, the painter has depicted two connected landscapes enlivened by architectural features. The main scene, in the lower part, is probably a depiction of the Flood: various mythological figures (e.g., naiads, tritons, fauns) are caught in the watery surge, from which narrow tongues of land emerge. The scene is based on a print by Bernard Salomon illustrating the *Quadrins Historiques de la Bible,* first published in Lyons in 1553, which served as a source for ceramic decoration in Italy and France in the latter half of the 16th century.

The first workshop for producing faience (tin-glazed earthenware) in Nevers was set up in 1588 by two Italians: Augustin Conrade, who came from Italy, and Julio Gambin, who had been living in Lyons. In the 16th century, Lyons was a major financial and banking center with ties to Italy and was home to many Italian craftsmen as well as bankers. In addition, Nevers, situated in the very middle of France, had become an Italian principality when its heiress married Prince Luigi di Gonzaga in 1565. It was quite natural, then, that the new duke would summon his fellow countrymen to Nevers, drawing Italian masters of ceramic and glass who would in due course bring renown to the city. —B.R.

Reliquary cross

French, 1645
Inscribed: *Ce pnt Reliquere apartien A Mre Claude Laborieux Archipbre de St Pierre de Venne 1645*
Silver. H. 4¼ in. (10.8 cm)
Jean-Jacques Reubell bequest, 1933

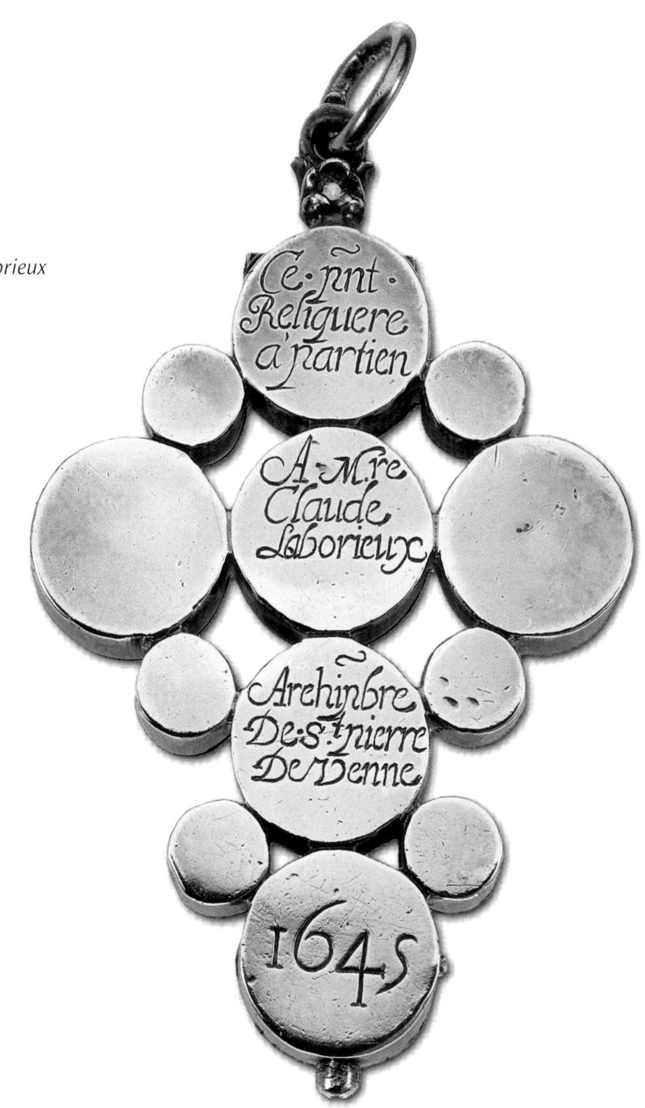

The cult of relics—fragments of the mortal remains of holy people and of objects that had belonged to them—emerged in the early days of Christianity and gathered momentum in the Middle Ages, particularly in the wake of the Crusades, which flooded the West with relics from the Holy Land.

Originally, relics were housed in sumptuous reliquaries made for their public display in sanctuaries that became pilgrimage destinations, but they soon migrated into the private sphere, where they played a part akin to that of the talisman, with its protective powers. Then came the appearance of portable reliquaries to be worn like necklaces. This type of small, private devotional reliquary is known as an "enkolpion." It may be in the form of a cross, medallion, or pendant.

The wearing of crosses containing numerous relics gained popularity in deeply religious Spain in the late 16th century and then spread to the other Catholic countries of southern Europe.

Here, the goldsmith skillfully created a cross by using an unusual geometric design composed of six large circles interlocked with six smaller ones. The back is hinged to form a cover that opens, with a catch at the bottom of the lowest compartment.

Contrary to usual practice, the silver has no hallmarks, which makes it difficult to identify its place of manufacture. Only an inscription with the date 1645, carefully engraved across the front, tells us that this reliquary belonged to a man of the cloth, one Claude Laborieux, archpriest of St. Pierre, one of many parish churches in France consecrated to the first apostle. —B.R.

Skeleton on a tomb

Southern German, 1547
Ivory. H. 3¾ in. (9.6 cm), W. 3½ in. (8.8 cm),
D. 1⅛ in. (3 cm)
Baronne Henri de Rothschild bequest, 1926

Death, personified as a skeleton swathed in a shroud, is sitting on the edge of his tomb. The skeleton's elbow is propped on an hourglass, and his right hand is resting on a half-opened scroll with the inscription: ". . . tu es tu deviendras comme je suis" (. . . you are you will become as I am). Two attributes are usually associated with the skeleton as a reference to the inevitability of death: the hourglass and the scythe, both of which symbolize the relentless passage of time. This association of time and death was ever-present in people's minds following the Black Death of 1348 and the onset of the terrible Hundred Years' War. From that period on, representations of death, macabre dances, and ossuaries became widespread in prints, sculptures, and paintings, as they illustrated the idea of the equality of one and all before death *(mors aequat omnia).*

The sculptor of this ivory piece has not omitted a single anatomical detail, and the raw realism of the skeleton, contrasting with its almost offhand posture on the edge of the tomb, serves to increase the dread aroused by all representations of Death. Works of this type were probably objects of private devotion, assisting meditation.

This skeleton is one of 160 small sculptural objects bequeathed to the museum by the wife of Baron Henri de Rothschild. Ranging from rosary beads in the form of skulls to macabre ivory cane handles to jeweled tie tacks, each object is a representation of Death, the subject of the collection assembled by the baroness. —M.B.

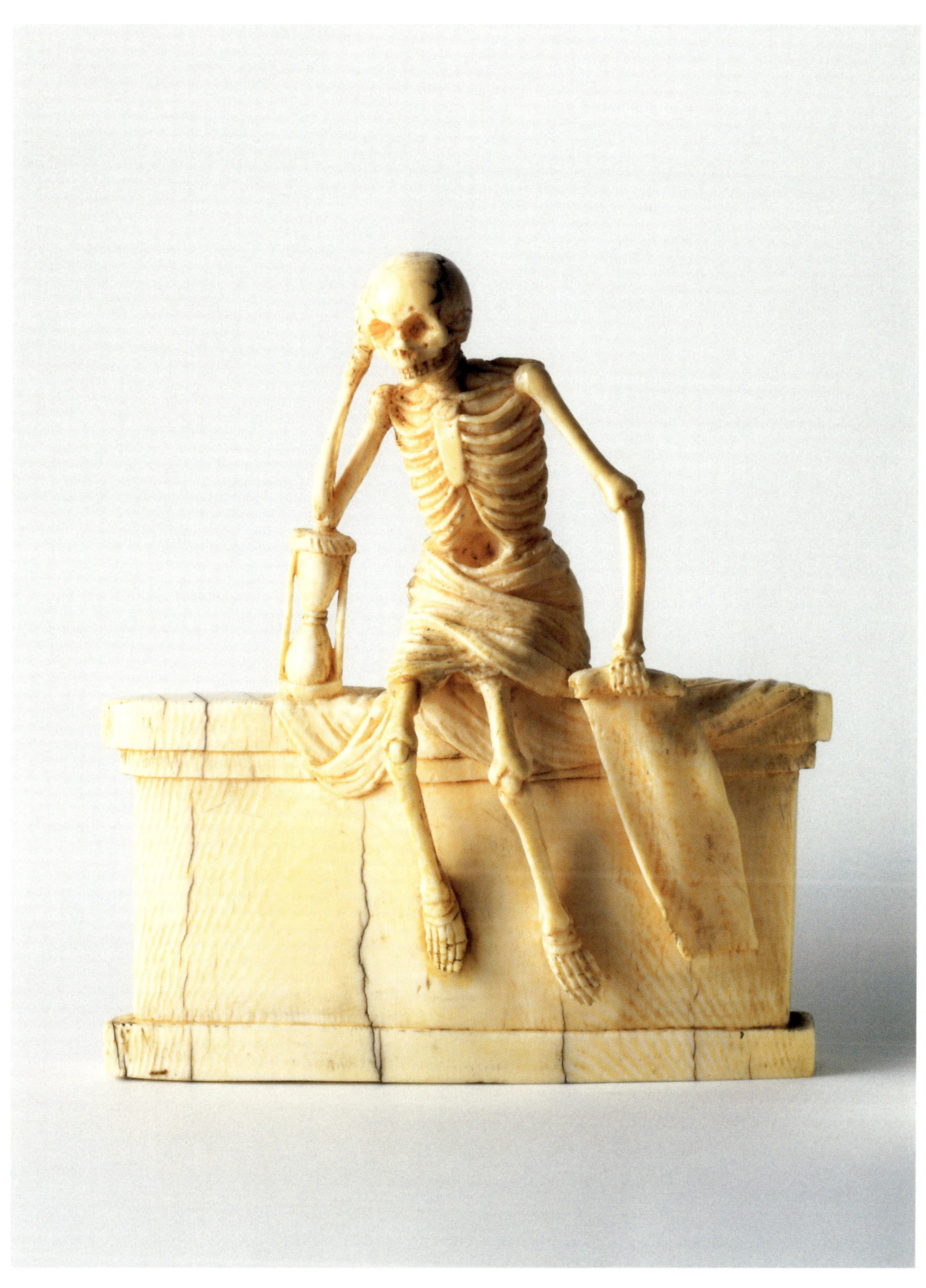

Armchair (Fauteuil à la Reine)

French, circa 1720
Gilt beech wood. H. 44 in. (111.5 cm),
W. 32¼ in. (82 cm), D. 34 in. (86.5 cm)
Gift of Rodolphe Kahn, 1888

Reeds coiled around long, jagged leaves and shell cartouches carved on curving legs are part of the decoration announcing this chair's place in the new art of living that developed in France at the end of the reign of Louis XIV. Between 1700 and around 1735, the French Regency style was marked by an easing of etiquette. The new aesthetic was based on the desire for softer, suppler lines, open, curved legs, and the increased importance of ornamental carving. Chair backs were no longer rigidly vertical but rather angled at a slight recline, and from 1715 on, the armrests were set back to accommodate the fashion for full skirts worn over panniers, or hoops.

Chairs designated as *chaises meublants* served as fixed elements integral to the architecture of a room. Lined up along the walls, the chair backs closely followed the outlines of the wall paneling. Hardly anyone ever sat on them, as their function was essentially decorative, in accord with the prevailing concepts of harmony and symmetry that carried over from the reign of Louis XIV into the Regency.

This example, a flat-backed armchair termed *fauteuil à la Reine,* is also *à chassis,* which means the upholstery of the back and the seat are mounted on removable frames, and the arm pads are designed to be laced on. This allowed for a regular changeover from summer to winter upholstery. The artistry of this chair is the product of a team endeavor by the wood-carver, the joiner, and finally the gilder. —S.M.

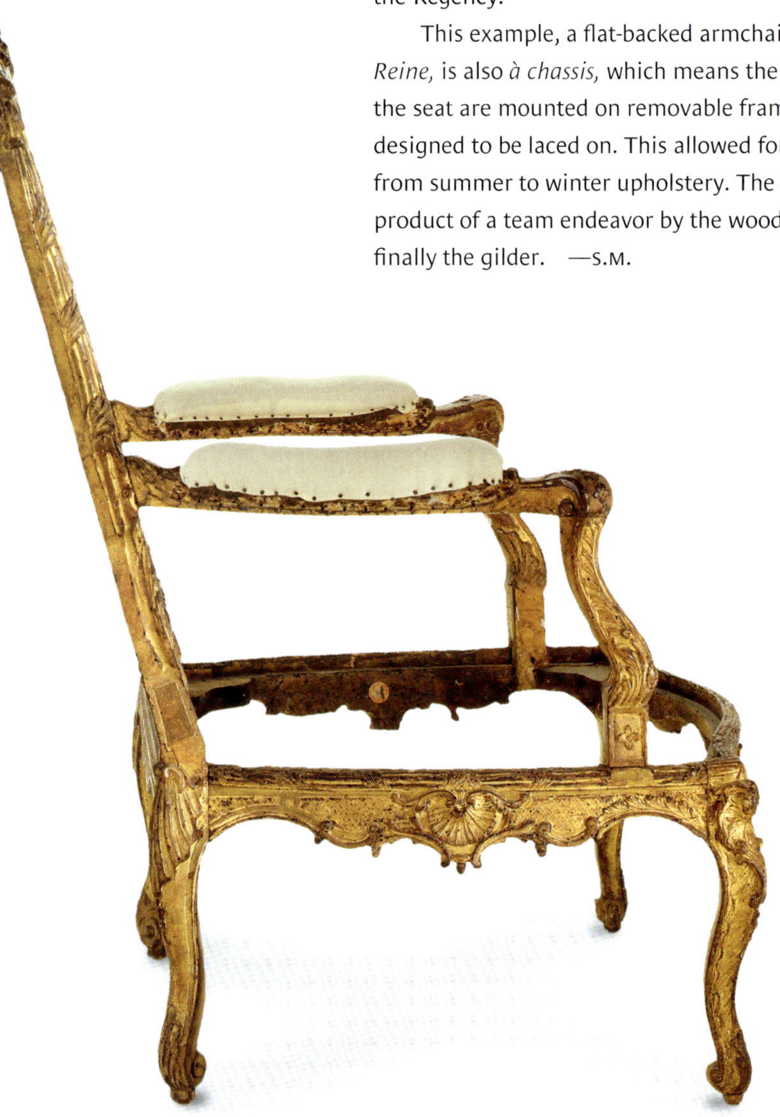

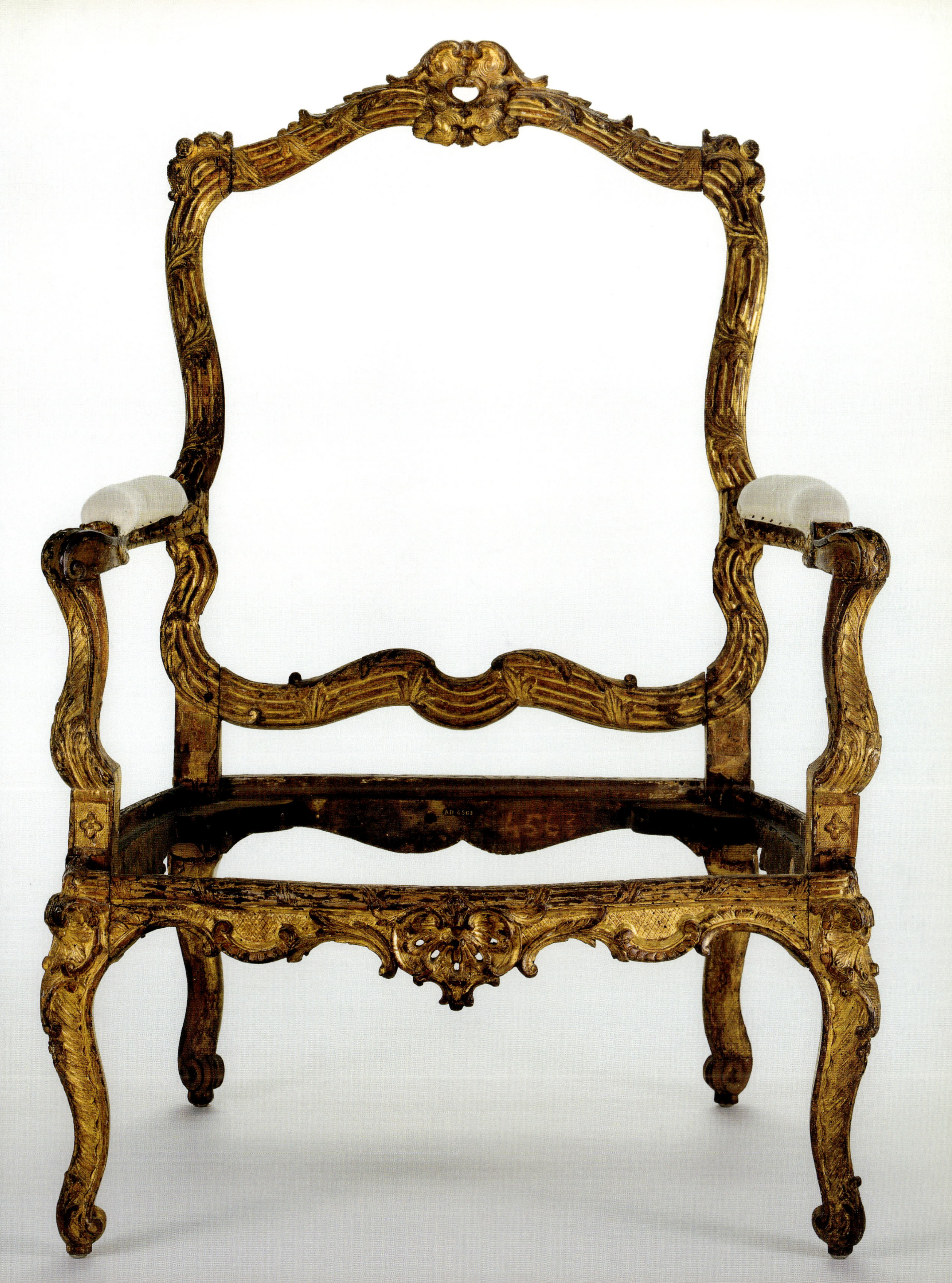
AD 4563

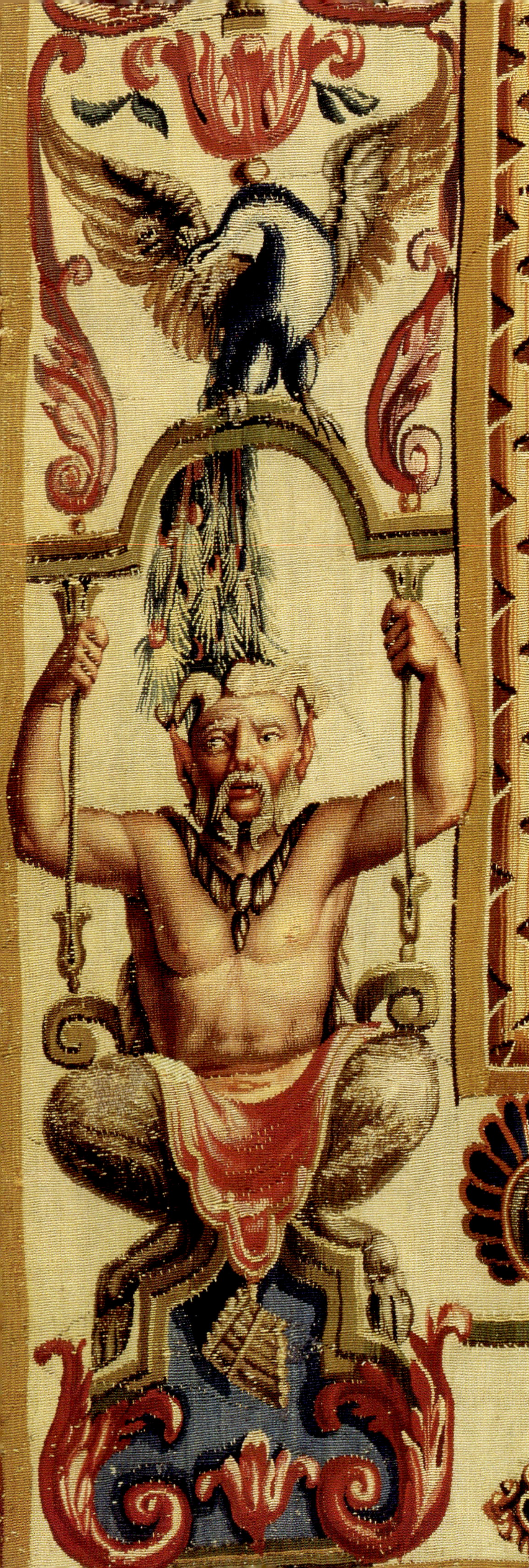

The Offering to Pan

French, Beauvais factory, early 18th century
Cartoon: Jean-Baptiste Monnoyer (1636–1699)
Border design: possibly Guy Vernansal (1648–1729)
Wool, silk. H. 120 in. (305 cm), W. 126 in. (320 cm)
Purchase, 1907

This tapestry was one in a series of six wall hangings called *Grotesques,* which included *The Musicians, The Trainers, The Dromedaries, The Elephant, The Offering to Bacchus*, and this, *The Offering to Pan.* In antiquity, the cults of Bacchus, god of wine, and Pan, god of pasture and livestock, were celebrated at merry and—with the aid of wine—uninhibited feasts.

On the tapestry, however, the ephemeral architecture, enhanced by garlands of flowers and trees in gilt pots as well as richly robed dancers and musicians, conjures up not so much classical antiquity as the sumptuous entertainments put on by Louis XIV at Versailles.

The composition of the tapestry—where humorous and imaginative details engage the eye—was part of a trend that emerged in the late 15th century, when the Domus Aurea, once Nero's imperial palace, was discovered in Rome. The originality and fantasy of its interior decoration—especially the carved and painted motifs of foliated scrolls decorated with fantastic beings, half-human, half-monster, engaged in mischievous tricks—made a great impression. This type of decoration would subsequently be called "grotesque," due to its discovery in the buried ruins of the palace, which had been mistaken for grottoes.

The Beauvais factory, in Picardy, was set up in 1664 at the instigation of Colbert, Louis XIV's minister and comptroller of finance, not long after the Gobelins factory in Paris was established. Whereas the Gobelins factory, a State enterprise, produced solely for the Crown, the Beauvais factory also had a private clientele.

With this set of wall hangings, the Beauvais factory introduced a breath of fresh air into the art of tapestry in France. It abandoned its previous mythological and historical subjects in favor of purely ornamental designs. The flower painter Jean-Baptiste Monnoyer was given responsibility for creating the cartoons. The success of the *Grotesques* was huge—around 150 pieces were woven—due in part to the attractive yellow background color known as "Spanish tobacco." —B.R.

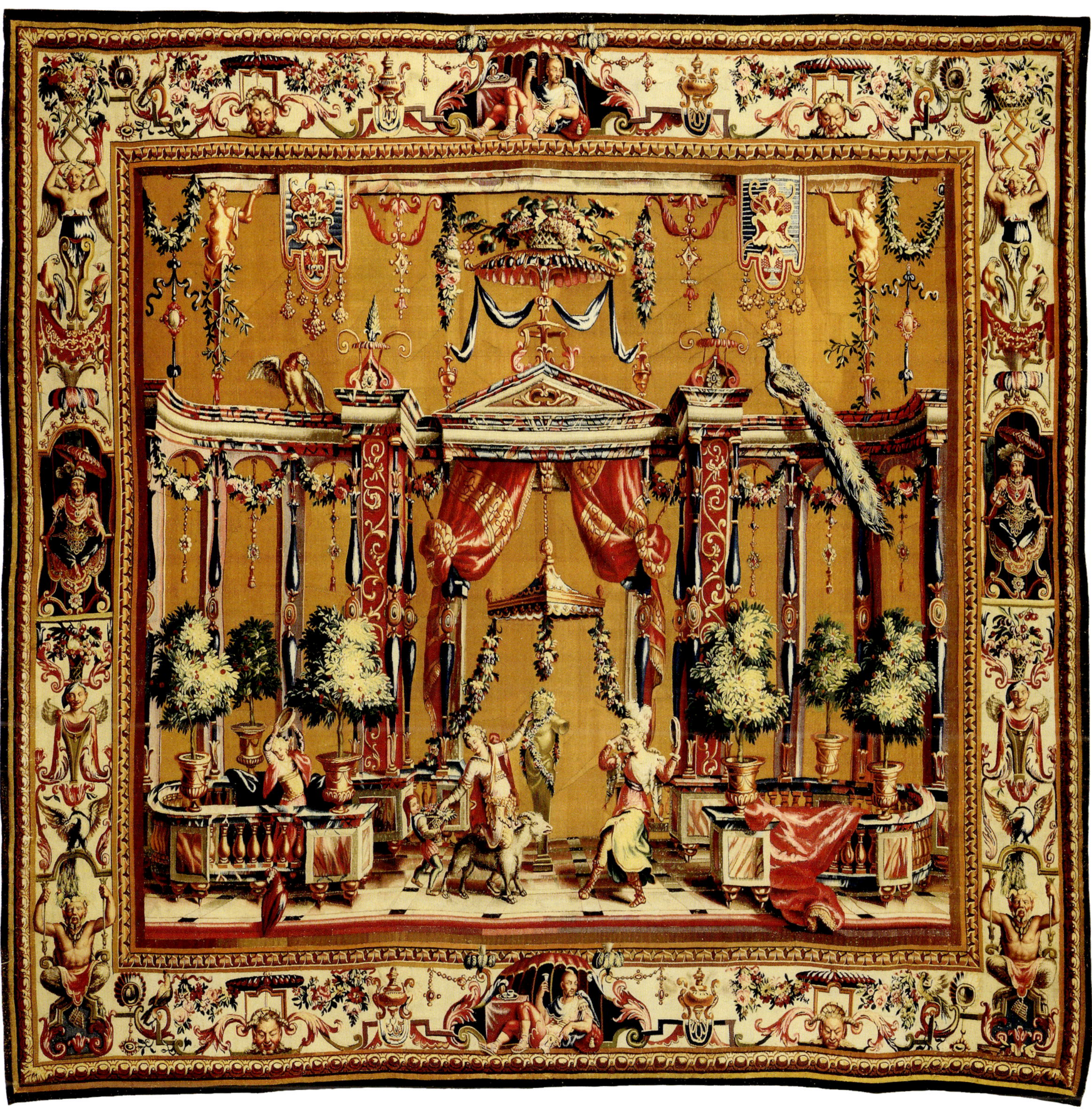

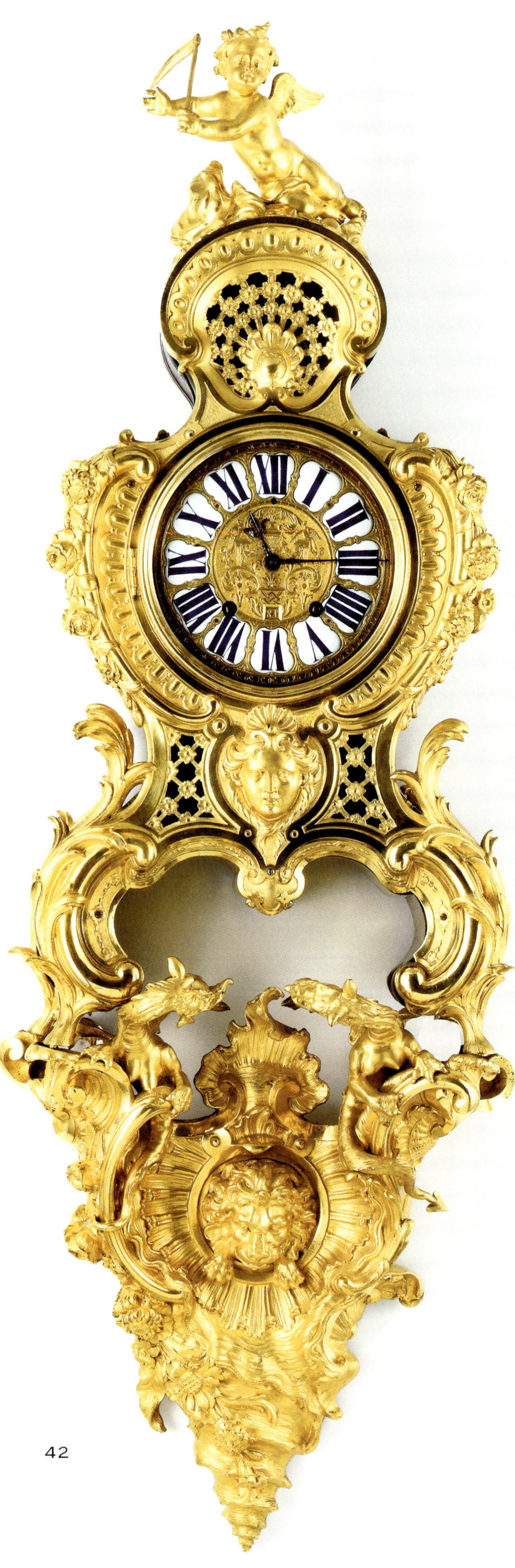

Bracket clock

French, circa 1733
Charles Cressent (1685–1768)
Gilt bronze, copper, oak, tortoiseshell, enamel, glass
H. 51⅛ in. (130 cm), W. 17¾ in. (45 cm), D. 7⅝ in. (19.5 cm)
Louise Grandjean bequest, 1910

This clock is a piece of sculpture in its own right. At the top, Cupid holds the scythe of Time, symbol of the relentless passing of the hours, while on the bracket two dragons frame a lion's head emerging from a rocaille, or Rococo, cartouche. Only the face of a woman placed below the dial brings a touch of serenity to the turbulent curves and countercurves of this object.

This sculptural piece was made by a cabinetmaker. The gilt bronze front is affixed to an oak frame, while the sides are clad with tortoiseshell and brass in a marquetry technique known as "Boullework." Only the bracket is made entirely of gilt bronze.

Behind the unique quality of this object lies the persona of Charles Cressent. As the son of a sculptor and the grandson of a cabinetmaker, Cressent had the advantage of dual training. He sculpted the models for the bronzes that would decorate his furniture, and he made them in his own workshop, ensuring exclusive use. Thus he foiled the strict separation between the different professional corporations and guilds observed in France before the Revolution. His colleagues had to buy bronzes designed to decorate their furniture (e.g., locks, corner brackets, feet, hooks) from the bronzeworkers who cast and chased them, and as a result bronze ornaments of the same model cropped up on pieces of furniture by different cabinetmakers. Because Cressent was not a registered bronzeworker, he did not have the right to cast, chase, and gild on his premises as he did, and the guild of casters and chasers, protective of its privileges, brought legal action against him on several occasions.

This spectacular model of wall clock remained popular throughout the 18th century, and Cressent came up with several versions. One variant, with the head of Boreas, god of wind, replacing the lion's head, was delivered in 1745 for the bedroom of the dauphine, daughter-in-law of Louis XV, at Versailles and was later transferred by Marie Antoinette to the queen's bedroom.

—B.R.

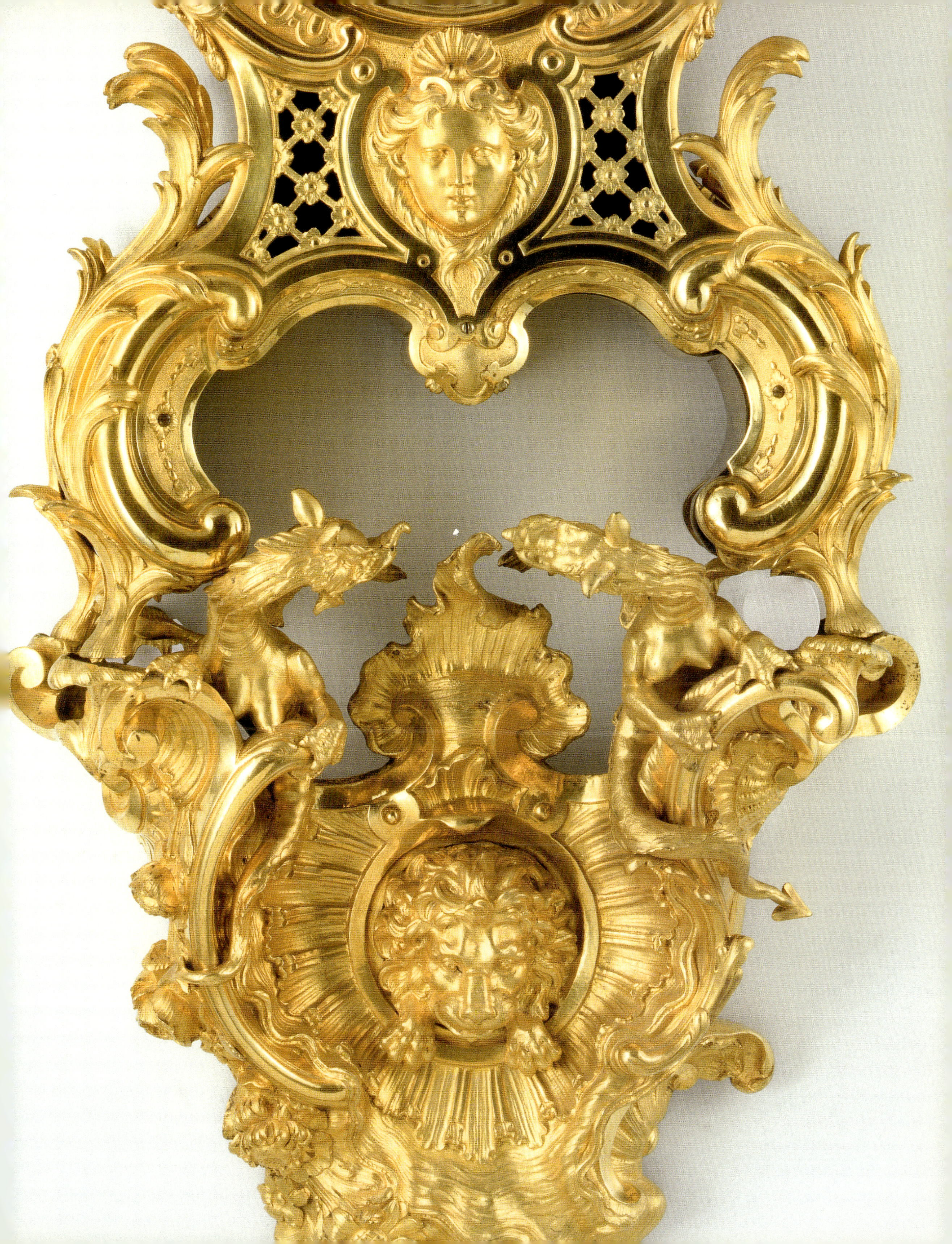

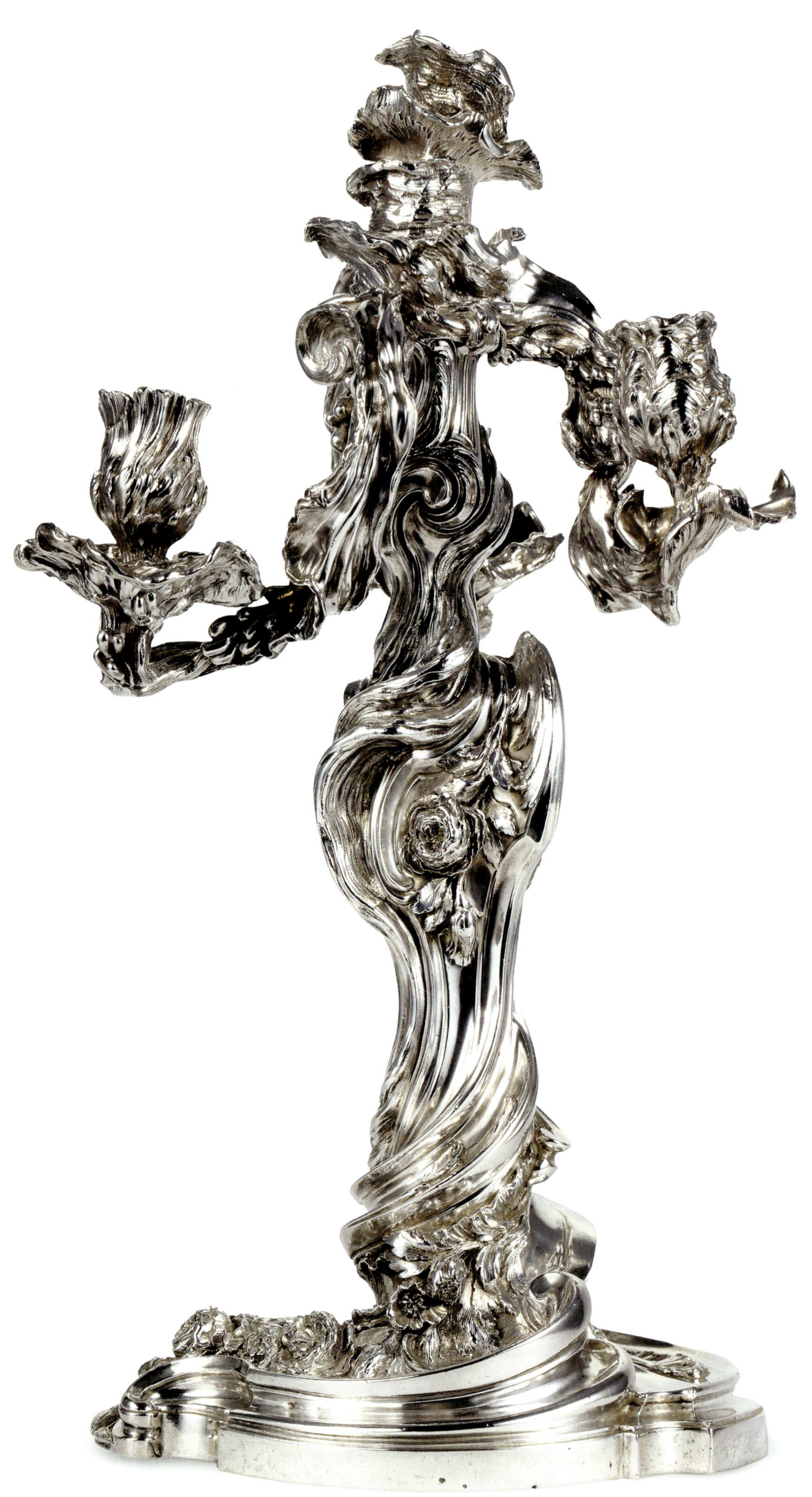

Candelabrum

French, Paris, 1734–1735
Design: Juste-Aurèle Meissonnier
(1695–1750)
Cast: Claude Duvivier (circa 1688–1747)
Silver. H. 15⅛ in. (38.5 cm)
Gift of David David-Weill, 1937

Here, the quest for dynamic and shifting movement has completely transformed the traditional concept of this type of lighting. Starting from the asymmetrical base, a spiral motion engulfs the object, heightened by the opposition of rising and descending elements. The energy of opposing forces in confrontation courses through the silver to the extremity of the branches bending in resistance.

This candelabrum is made up of three parts, which can be added one to the other to increase the level of light. The stem is a single large candlestick, into which fits a three-branch girandole. At its center, a fourth candleholder is concealed by a leaf-shaped stopper that can be removed, thus increasing the number of candleholders to four.

The candelabrum bears the coat of arms of Evelyne Pierrepont, duke of Kingston, who in 1732 ordered a table service from the most daring French designer and silversmith of Louis XV's reign, Juste-Aurèle Meissonnier. The duke furnished his own silverware to be melted down and used for the commission.

Meissonnier, who above all was an inventor of form, created a universe filled with surprises and marvels. His radical ideas were the source of the Rococo style that conquered Paris in the 1730s. He disseminated his designs across Europe through the publication of prints and entrusted their realization to other, less well-known silversmiths working under his close supervision. Among them, Claude Duvivier was responsible for casting and chasing the duke of Kingston's prestigious order. —B.R.

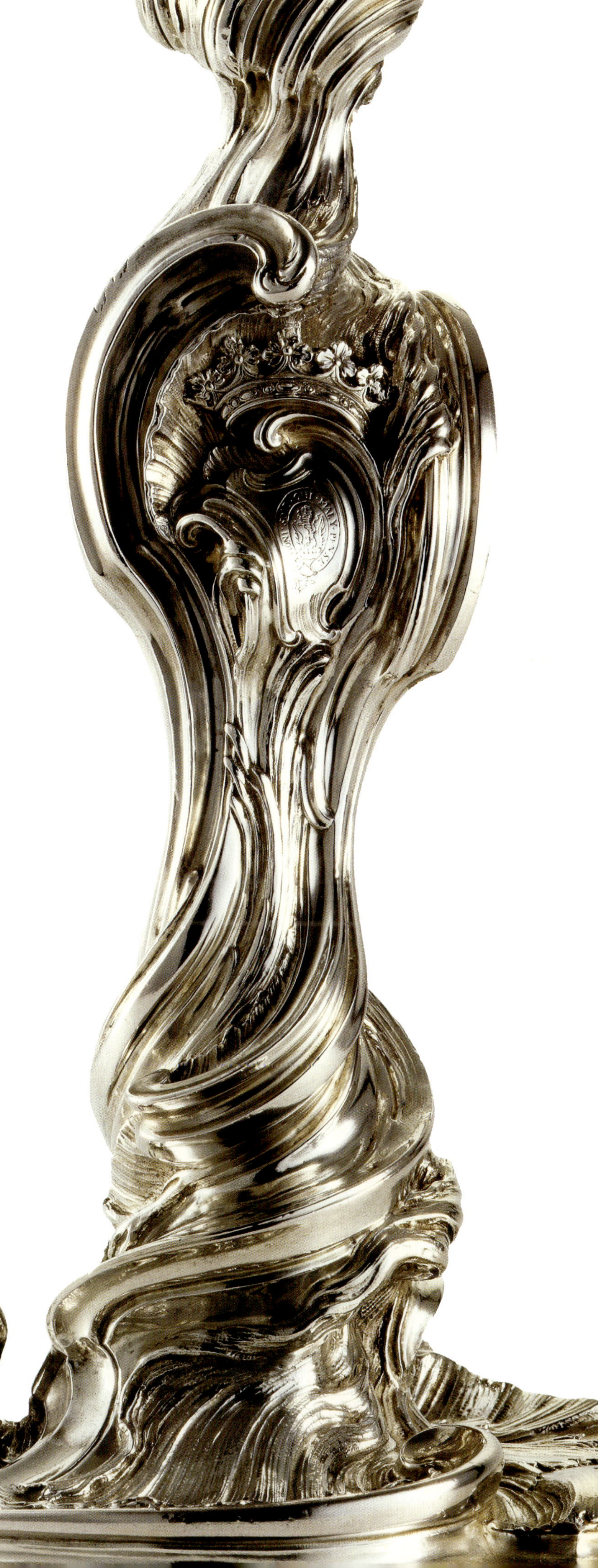

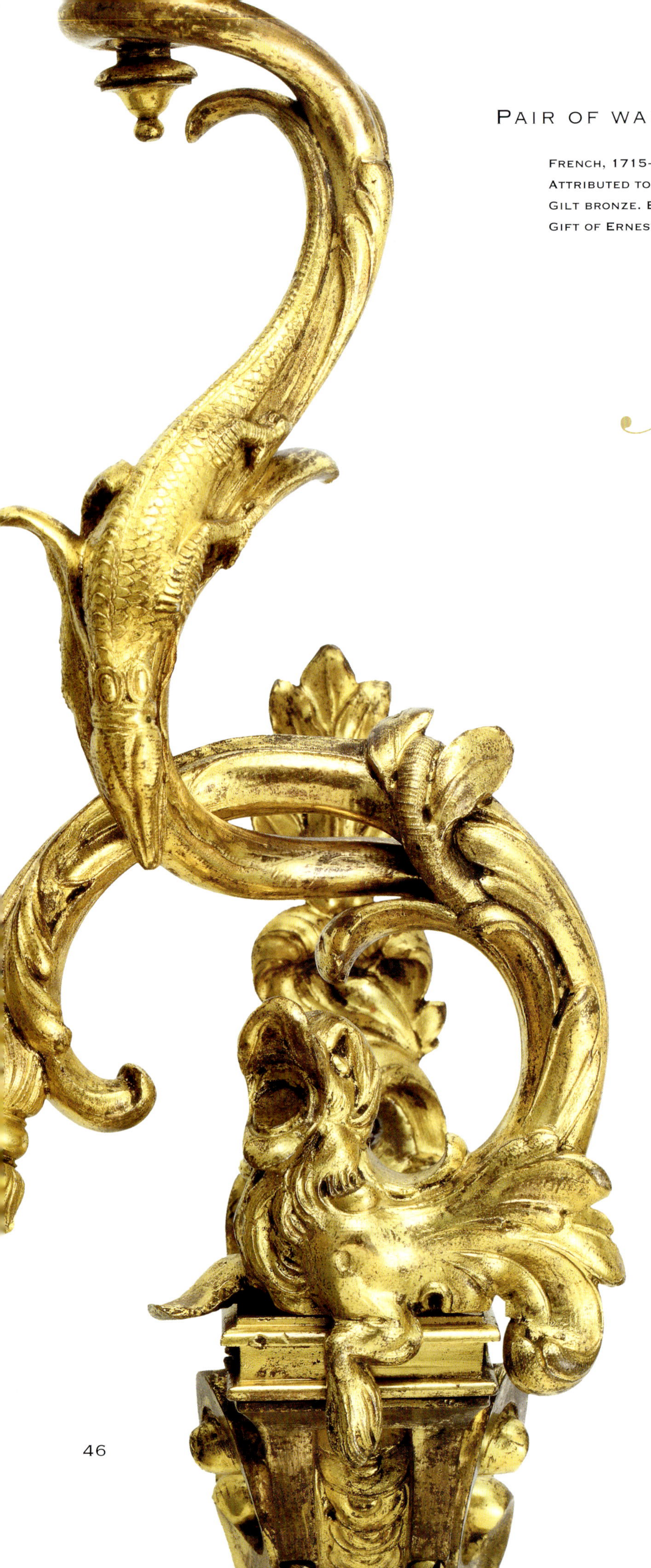

Pair of Wall Lights

French, 1715–1720
Attributed to André-Charles Boulle (1642–1732)
Gilt bronze. Each H. 20½ in. (52 cm)
Gift of Ernest Grandidier, 1906

André-Charles Boulle, cabinetmaker, chaser, gilder, and sculptor, was one of the most important purveyors to the French king and court from 1672 until his death. Between 1664 and 1732, his workshop, set up within the walls of the Louvre, employed up to twenty-six people, producing not only the furniture that earned him his fame but also bronzes of the highest quality. In the later years of his life, Boulle designed and engraved a series of plates, *Nouveaux desseins de meubles et ouvrages de bronze et de marqueterie* (New designs for furniture and bronze and marquetry works), illustrating the main features of his work.

The decoration of these wall lights consists of asymmetrically scrolling branches with different candle nozzles: one with straight fluting and the other in the form of a flower with falling petals. Symmetry was regained by placing the wall lights on either side of a mirror. The branch closest to the mirror was reflected in it, thus creating the seductive illusion of multiple lights.

Mythical animals allude to the theme of fire. A salamander on the uppermost branch hugs the curve of the arm. According to classical tradition, the salamander lived in fire, from which it drew life and protection, but was not consumed by the flames. It was also paradoxically credited with the power to extinguish fire. Is it not, moreover, playing with fire, in taunting the dragon and preventing it from spitting flames from its gaping mouth? The dragon is another imaginary beast that is closely linked with fire. Here, it is represented with wings, claws, and a serpent's tail buried in leafy ornament. The dragon is perched on a small console in the lower part of the wall light.

Lastly, at the base of the lamp, a turbaned Moor's head evokes heat and distant Africa. These features all convey the fascination with exoticism that dominated the first three decades of the 18th century. —S.M.

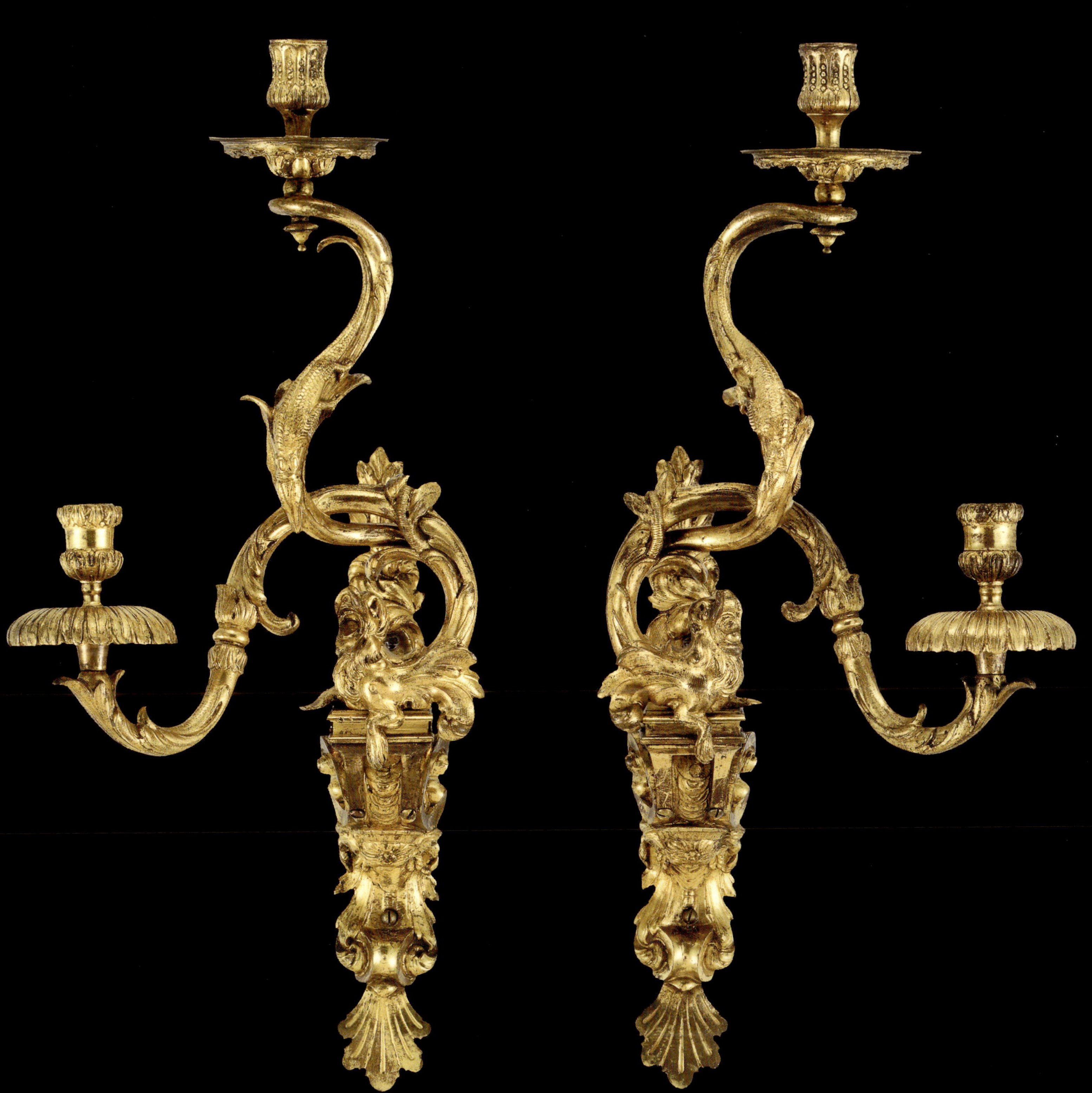

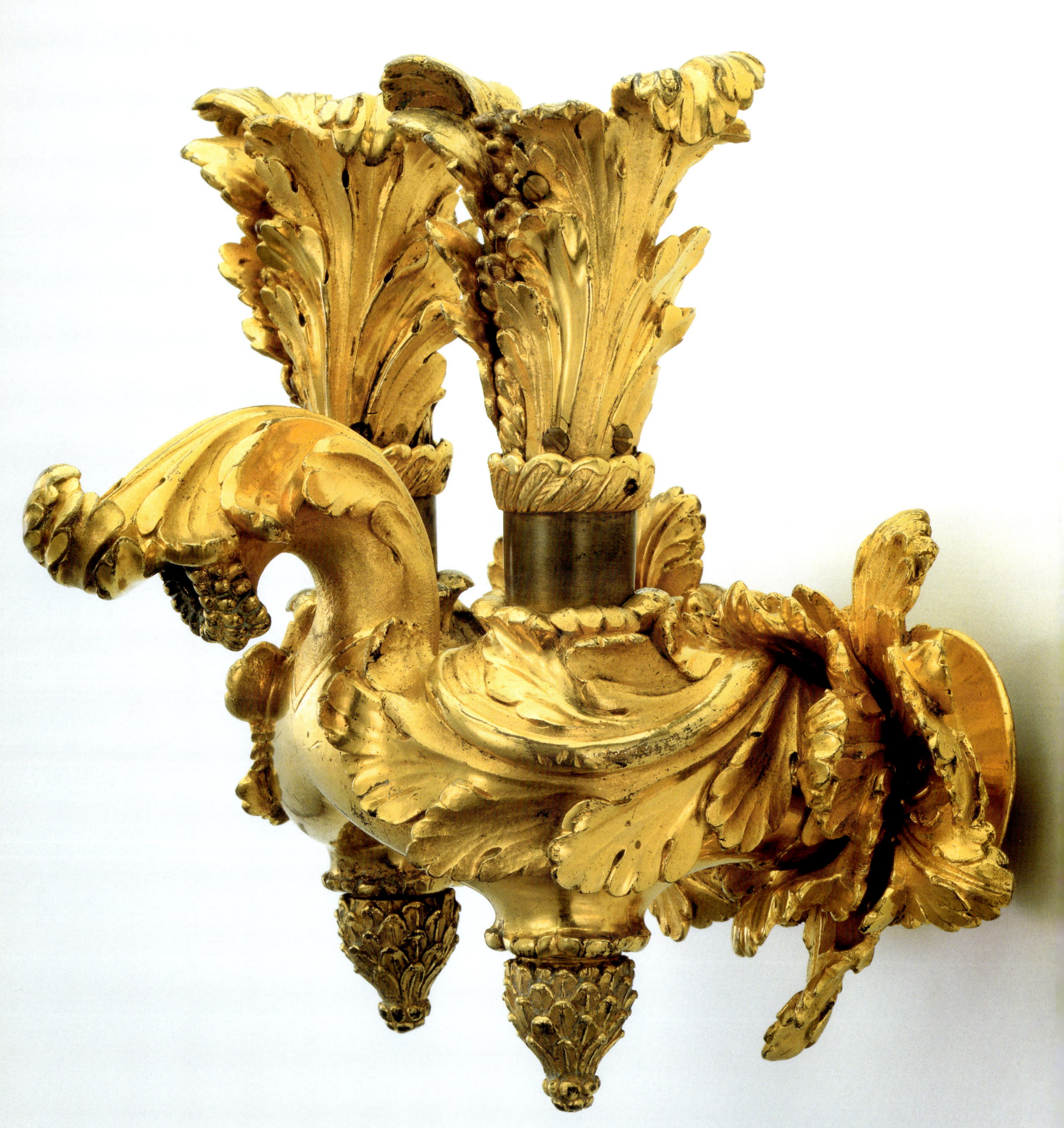

Baths, so important in the culture of classical antiquity, fell from favor in the Middle Ages because of the fear of spreading the plague, but they regained popularity during the Renaissance. In the 17th century, as a result of the practice of household porterage—renting a bathtub and having the hot water delivered—one could bathe at home. But because no particular room was earmarked for bathing, the tub was put in a dressing room or antechamber for as long as required. Bathtubs were usually made of tin or copper—good heat-conducting metals—and lined with a cloth to guard against burns. Before getting into the tub, the bather would put on a flannel shirt. In the 18th century, it was not unusual to work, have a chocolate drink, or receive friends while enjoying the delights of soaking in the tub.

Running water dates back no further than the late 19th century, but in the 18th century wealthier homes had an elaborate system of tanks and pipes installed in the mezzanine, making it possible to fill the bathtub directly through two faucets, one for cold water, the other for hot. In the palace of Versailles one can still see the device that provided water in the king's "bathroom apartment."

Using the lost-wax technique, this gilt bronze faucet was cast with elaborate foliate embellishments. Each duct passes through a cluster of leaves and ends up in the center at an outlet formed by acanthus leaves. Neither the chaser's name nor that of the person for whom the faucet was made has come down to us, but the quality of the bronzework clearly demonstrates the luxury of the residence. —S.M.

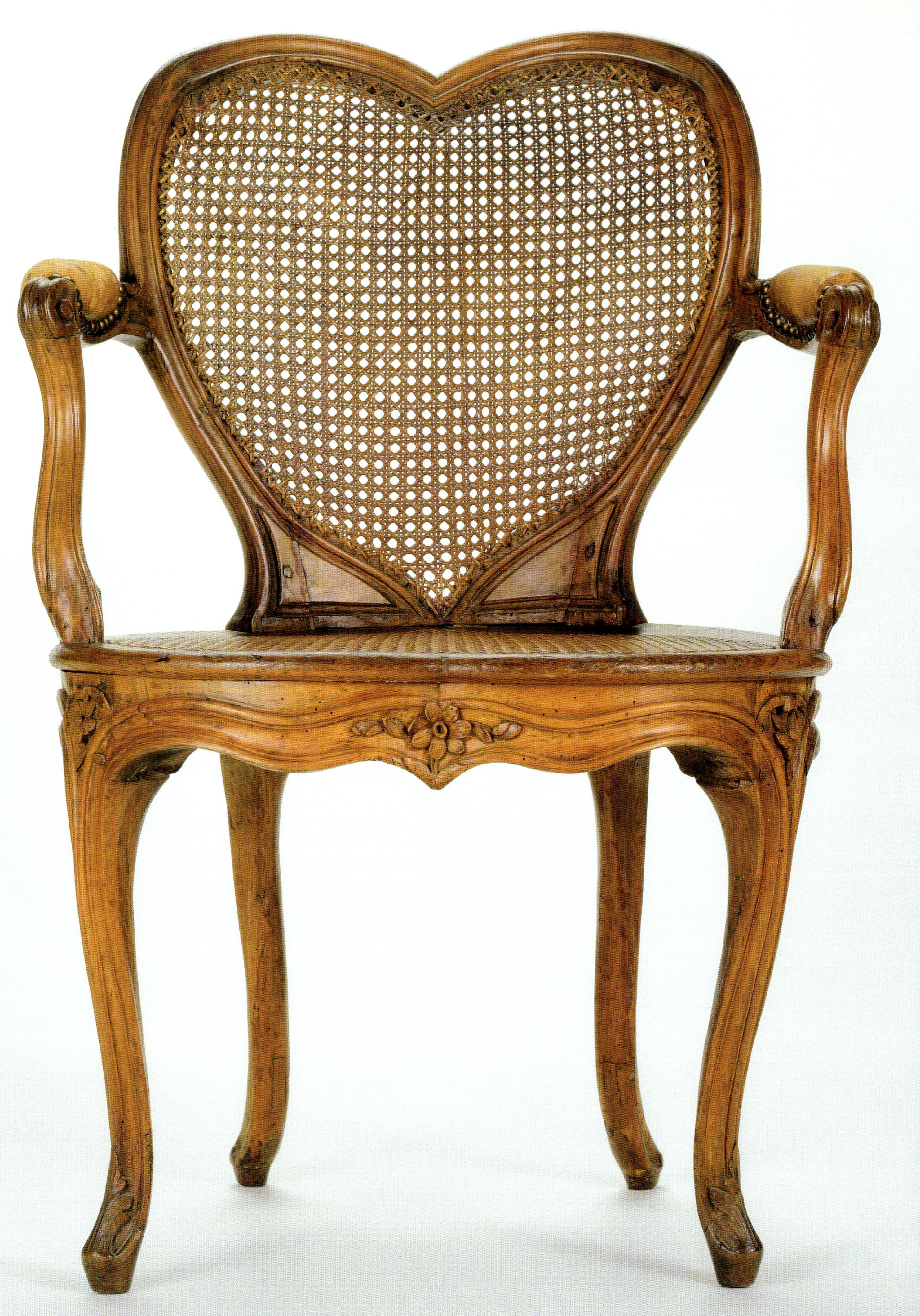

Armchair (Fauteuil en cabriolet)

French, 1750–1760
Beech wood, cane, leather. H. 33 in. (84 cm),
W. 19⅝ in. (50 cm), D. 22½ in. (57 cm)
Gift of Frederick P. Victoria, 1972, in memory of
his son Frederick P. Victoria, killed in Vietnam

The seat and back of this armchair are made of cane, a material found in tropical Asia. Narrow strips of rattan bark were anchored by passing them through holes in the seat frame and then were interwoven to form a fine lattice. In the 17th century, the Dutch encountered this technique in Indonesia and brought it to Europe through the importation of caned chairs. After the numerous campaigns waged by Louis XIV against Holland and the return of peace in 1714, the technique of caning was transmitted to Parisian chairmakers. More elegant than the straw and rushes that were used on common seats, cane resulted in chairs that were at once strong, light, and less costly than those with fabric or leather upholstery.

This airy, lightweight type of chair, called *"fauteuil en cabriolet"* (armchair with a rounded back), was especially well-suited to tropical climates such as the East Indies. Europeans found new applications in dining rooms and dressing rooms (forerunners of the bathroom). Waterproof and stain proof, cane was particularly useful for seating at the dressing table, because it was easier to keep clean than fabric and leather (only the padded armrests were leather covered for reasons of comfort).

The indentation of the back of the dressing-table chair facilitated arranging the hair or setting a wig in place. By cleverly disguising this feature in the form of a heart and repeating the shape in the seat, the joiner transformed a utilitarian consideration into a highly original design. —B.R.

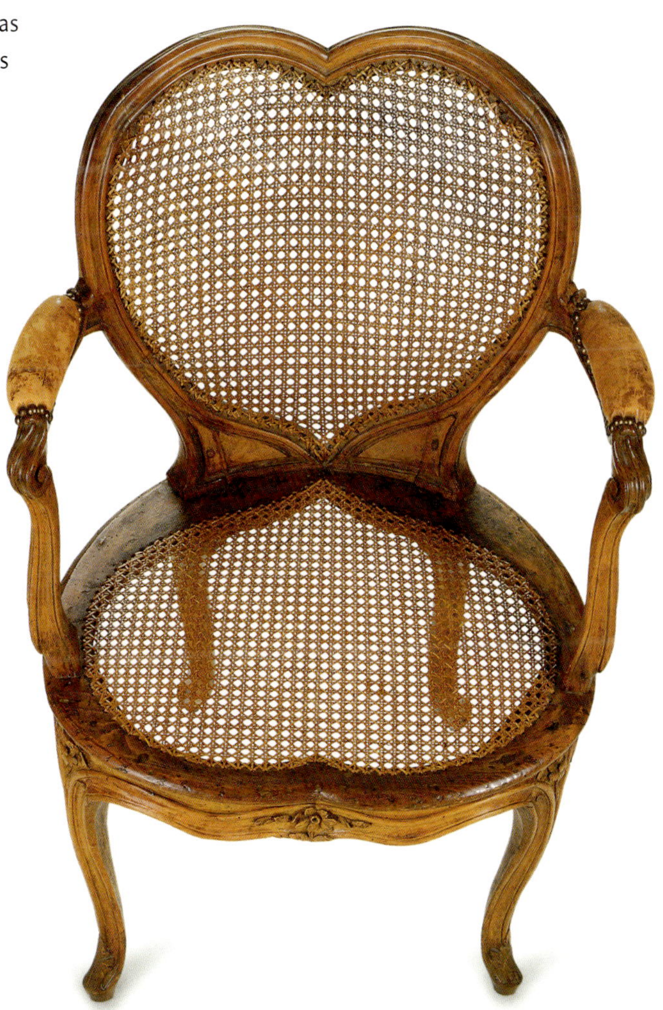

Chocolate Pot

French, Paris, 1753–1754
Antoine Bailly (master 1748, died 1765)
Silver, amaranth wood. H. 6¼ in. (16 cm)
Gift of Edouard Monod-Herzen, 1950

From the bottom of each foot of this small pot, two branches intertwine: the reed, symbolizing water, and the cacao tree, heavy with large beans, a decoration inspired by the pot's function as a jug for hot chocolate. The beverage was prepared in a small tin-plated copper pan by adding boiling water to chocolate wafers or drops. When ready, the drink was transferred to an elegant vessel of porcelain or silver, and spices, vanilla, and cinnamon were added.

For this chocolate pot, Antoine Bailly made brilliant use of all silversmithing techniques. The body of the pot was raised from a fairly thick sheet of silver, which was struck first with a wooden mallet and then with metal hammers over a rounded form to produce a hollowed piece. The silver was regularly reheated to keep it malleable and to prevent the metal from breaking. As he hammered, the silversmith also had to keep the metal sheet at a constant thickness. With this technique it was possible to fashion deep, narrow-necked vessels. Then came planishing, which removed the hammer's marks. The feet, spout, and plant decoration were all cast separately and soldered to the body of the piece. Lastly, the fine detail of the reliefs was obtained by chasing, using small hammers to strike the surface of the pot at a perpendicular angle.

The handle was supplied by a member of a different craft guild—a woodturner. To avoid burning the person serving the beverage, chocolate pots and coffeepots had straight horizontal wood handles, here made of amaranth, a precious tropical wood. —B.R.

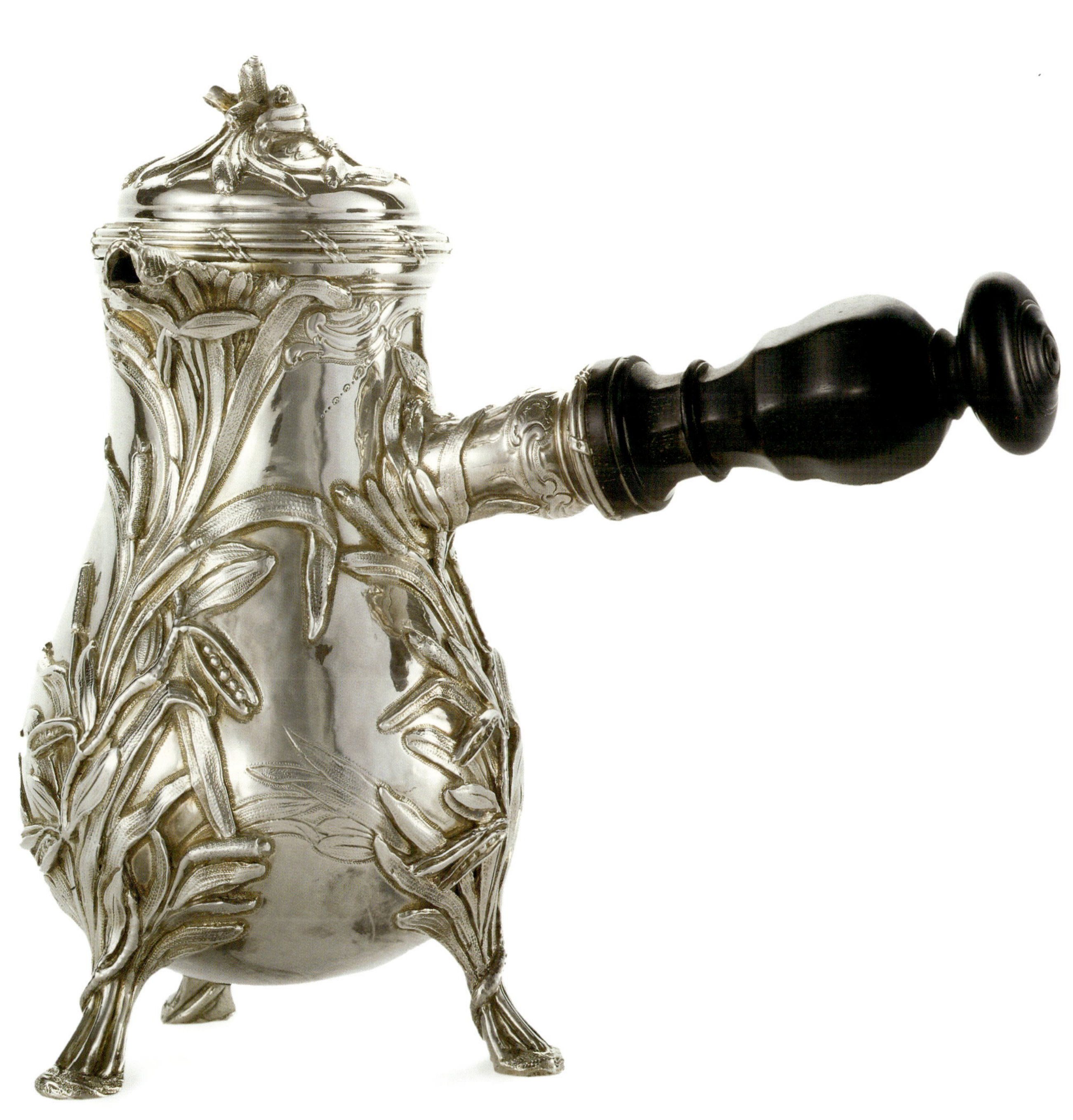

Mustard holder

French, Paris, 1753–1755
Antoine-Sébastien Durand (master 1740)
Partially gilt silver. H. 6 in. (15.1 cm),
L. 8⅞ in. (22.5 cm), D. 3¾ in. (9.5 cm)
Mrs. Louis Burat bequest, 1929

The mustard-and-vinegar vendor, a familiar sight among craftsmen plying their trade on the streets of 18th-century Paris, is traditionally depicted pushing a barrow holding the cask containing the precious condiment. In those days, mustard was used like a sauce, in a more or less liquid form.

What had been a craze for spices in the Middle Ages was followed by an almost total rejection during the 17th and 18th centuries in France. Spices lost their appeal once the trade monopoly to the Orient had been broken and competition made them affordable and readily available to all. They were employed less and less in France, leaving only the classic threesome of pepper, nutmeg, and cloves in use by the end of the 17th century, and even those in small quantity. While the rest of Europe persisted with spicy sweet-and-sour and bittersweet cuisine, French chefs swore only by sweet herbs and garden vegetables.

Seasoning had two purposes: to make food more appetizing and better tasting, and to prevent illness. In the history of taste and spices, mustard has always been a special case. It first appeared in the 15th century and has been popular with the French ever since.

> *Everyone knows about the use of mustard, which one eats with almost all kinds of roast and boiled meat, and is introduced in various sauces, & is above all a seasoning for the different dishes made with pork, and one that is as wholesome as it is pleasant. It has a powerful effect on the digestive organs; this is why it is particularly suitable for idle stomachs & cold, damp, weak temperaments; conversely, it may disagree with those whose digestion is fiery and whose temperament is hot, dry and in general loose.* (from *Encyclopédie ou dictionnaire raisonée des sciences, des arts, et des métiers,* Neufchâtel, 1765)

Antoine-Sébastien Durand fashioned this mustard-and-vinegar vendor with the features of Cupid, his quiver laid across the handle of his barrow and a greyhound jumping up to joyfully greet him. Durand, who was admitted as a master in the Paris guild of goldsmiths in 1740, had achieved fame by supplying the Portuguese court with his wares, along with François-Thomas Germain. A pair of very similar, albeit slightly larger, mustard holders was featured in the inventory of Madame de Pompadour's belongings after her death in 1764. —S.M.

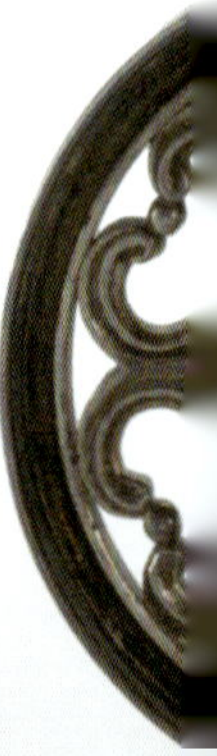

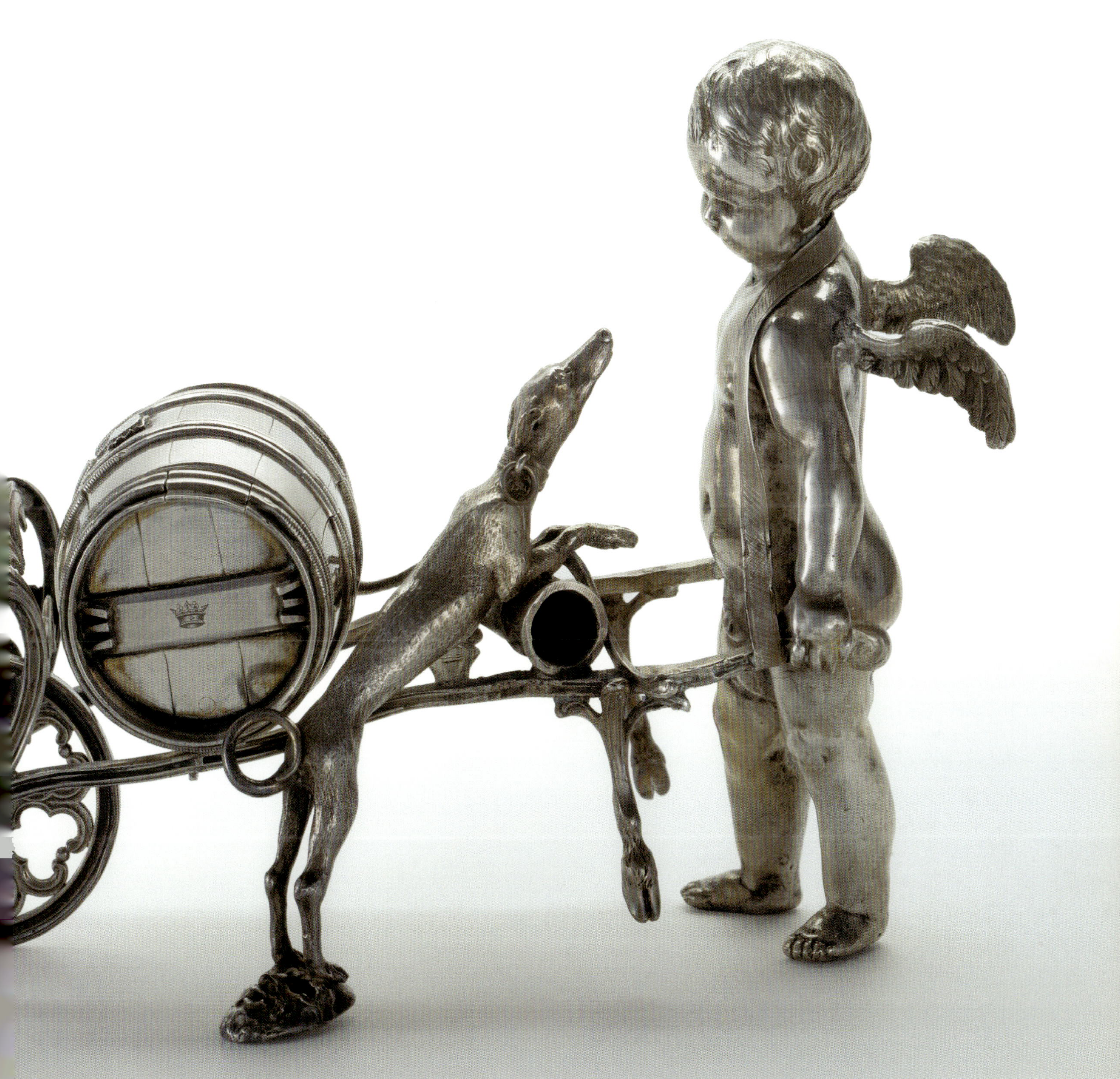

Model of the Tomb of Pastor Langhans's Wife

French, Niderviller Factory, circa 1775
Biscuit porcelain. H. 12⅝ in. (32.2 cm),
W. 8⅞ in. (22.7 cm), D. 3½ in. (9 cm)
Gift of Jules Audéoud, 1885

When Maria Magdalena, the wife of Pastor Langhans, died the day before Easter 1751 while giving birth to their first child, Langhans resolved to entrust to a sculptor the task of expressing the tragedy. Johann-August Nahl (1710–1785) depicted Maria Magdalena with her baby in marble, alive, and desperately trying to break the tombstone. The monument (since destroyed) was erected in a church in Hindelbank, in the canton of Bern, Switzerland.

The spectacularly morbid character of the work was fascinating to contemporaries, and the site soon became a pilgrimage destination. In the journals of travelers at the time, the tomb appears in counterpoint to the pre-Romantic enthusiasm for wild, dramatic landscapes of the Swiss Alps. A stop at Hindelbank became mandatory for young people on the Grand Tour—that initiatory and cultural journey that took them through Europe in search of the roots of Western civilization.

The renown of this tomb prompted several manufactories to produce reductions in terra-cotta or porcelain. These portable souvenir versions spread the fame of the image abroad. In this version, the coldness of stone is perfectly translated in the material of biscuit (unglazed) porcelain. Its author was probably Charles Sauvage (1741–1827), known as Lemire, who was the chief modeler at the Niderviller factory in Lorraine. —S.M.

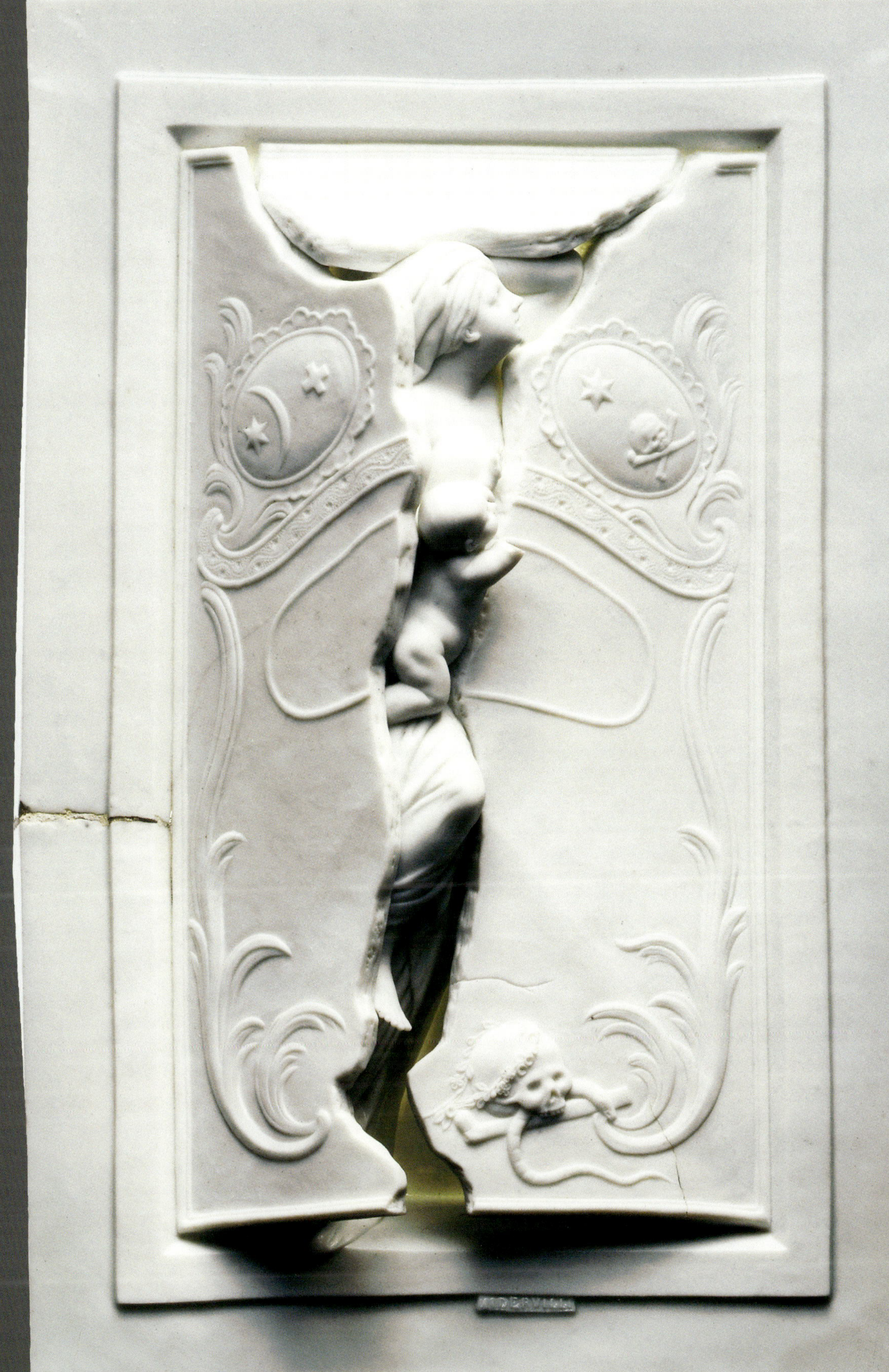

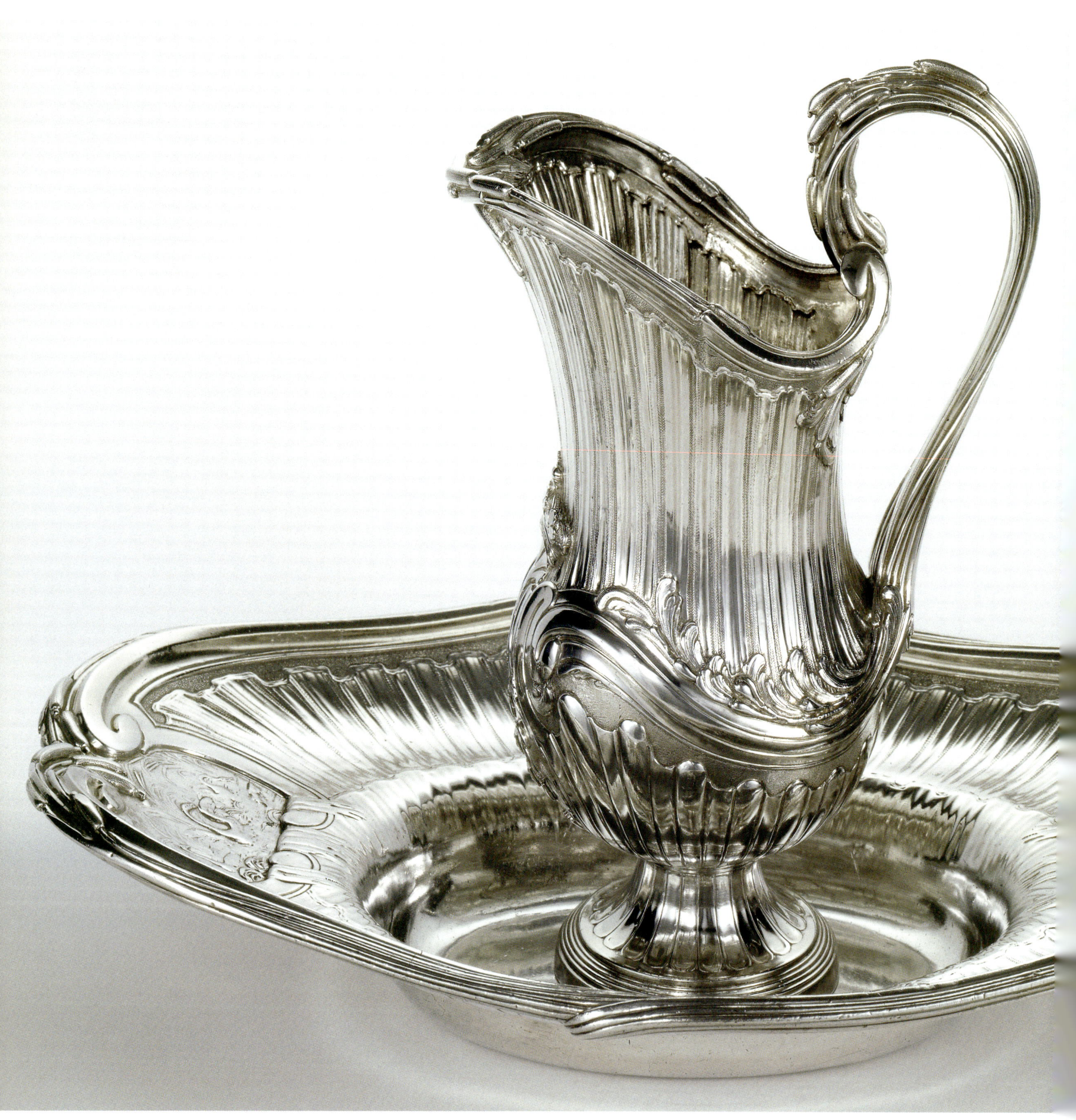

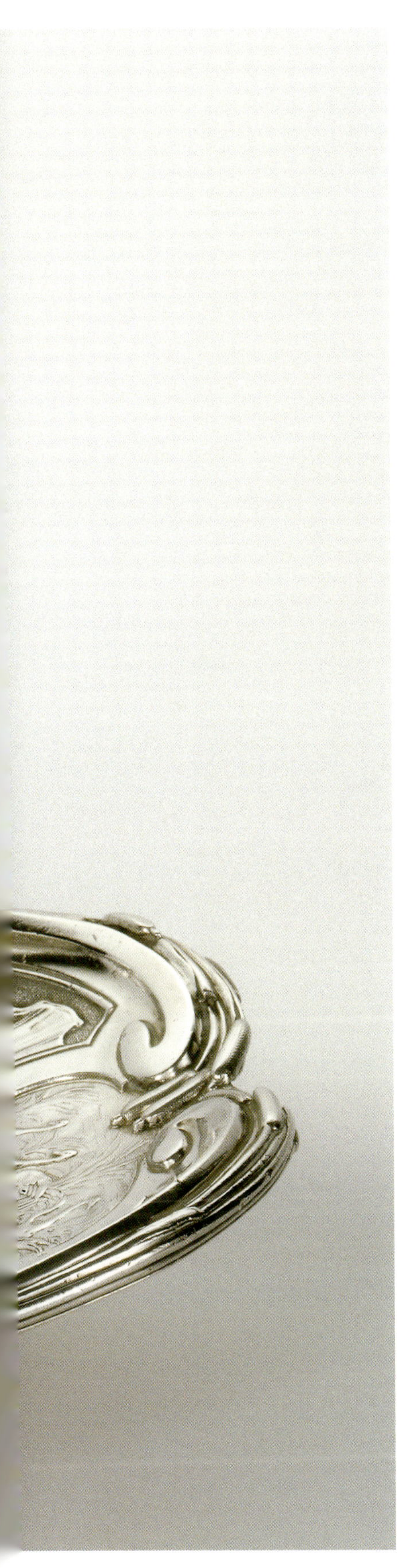

Ewer and Basin

French, Paris, 1756–1758
François-Thomas Germain (1726–1791)
Inscribed on ewer: *FAIT PAR F.T. GERMAIN SCULPTr ORF DU ROY AUX GALERIES DU LOUVRE A PARIS 1758; 64.*
Silver. Ewer: H. 10¾ in. (27.3 cm); basin: H. 3 in. (7.8 cm), L. 15⅞ in. (40.3 cm), W. 11¼ in. (28.7 cm)
Mrs. Louis Burat bequest, 1929

On 1 November 1755, a tremendous earthquake destroyed Lisbon and buried most of the royal silverware that King John V had ordered from the most renowned Parisian silversmith of the day, Thomas Germain. So it was quite natural that John's successor, Joseph I, should place an order in June 1756 with the craftsman's son, François-Thomas Germain, for four new services and various dressing table sets; eight years later, a gold service was ordered. François-Thomas had taken over from his father in 1748 and expanded the workshop into a proto-industrial enterprise. No fewer than forty workmen executed pieces to his models in a workshop housing five forges and seventeen workbenches. Joseph I's commission was the largest order from a foreign court ever received by Germain. Deliveries to the Portuguese court were staggered between November 1757 and May 1765; they were stowed in twenty-five crates and loaded onto Portuguese vessels lying at anchor in the port of Le Havre. The order included four ewers and their basins. This ewer bears the engraved number 64, part of the serial numbering required of the silversmith so that the order could be recorded on receipt in Lisbon and the sets not be mixed up.

The helmet-like shape of the ewer had been in fashion since the 17th century, and examples were made of silver, pewter, and faience. Germain's brilliance lay in the ornamentation evoking the theme of water, the liquid contained in the ewer: reeds gently unfurl to form the handle and delicately surround the mouth of the ewer, while the basin is decorated with cartouches featuring swans swimming through reeds. The interplay of broad scrolls, the delicacy of the reeds, and the generous forms all make this set a masterpiece. François-Thomas Germain created an object that combines the fluid quality of Rococo forms with a rigor and elegance that prefigure Neoclassicism. —B.R.

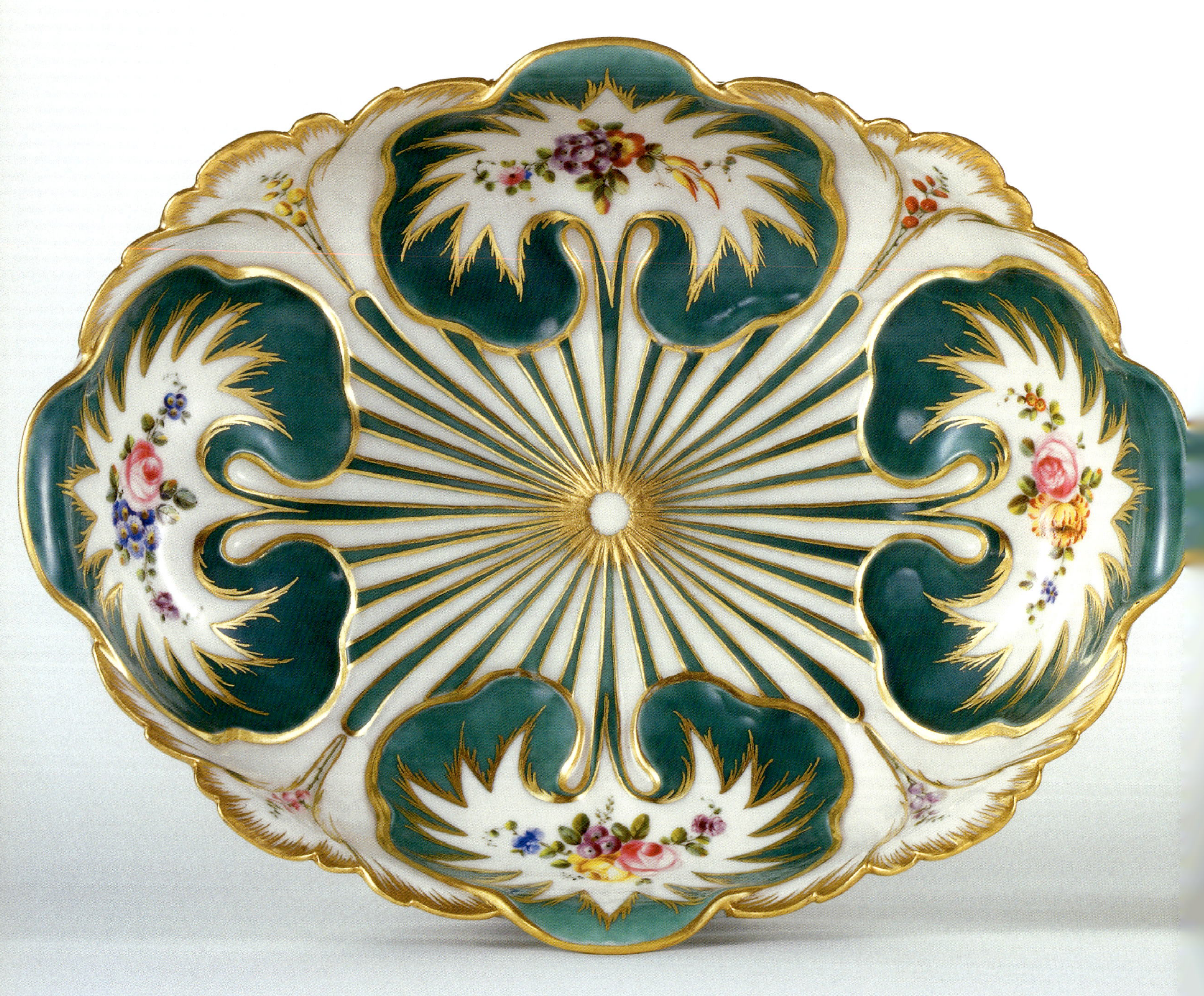

Ewer and Basin

French, Sèvres factory, 1757
Model attributed to Jean-Claude Duplessis (circa 1695–1774)
Marked D within affronted Ls for 1757
Soft-paste porcelain. Ewer: H. 7½ in. (19.2 cm); basin: H. 2¾ in. (6.9 cm), L. 11½ in. (29.3 cm), W. 8⅝ in. (21.9 cm)
Louise Grandjean bequest, 1910

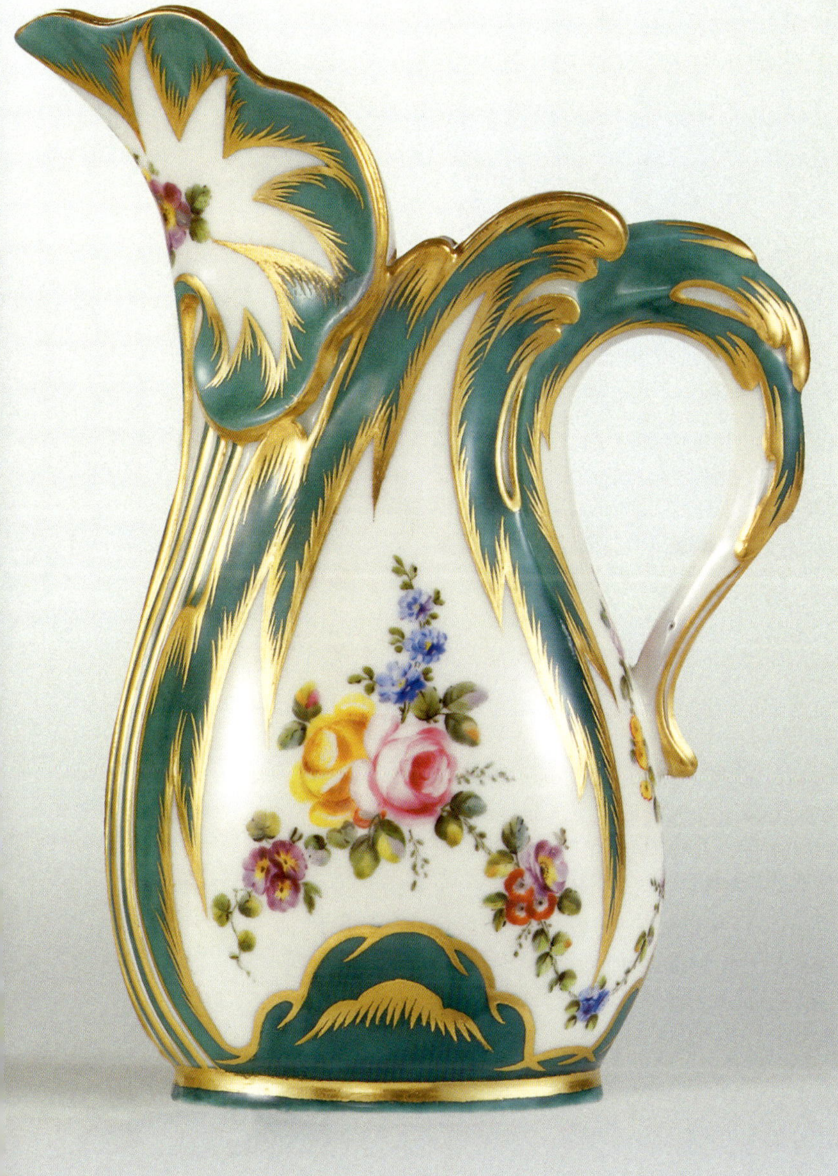

Traditionally, the water jug and its bowl were the central features of the dressing table. Known by a variety of names, the paired items were in use from the Middle Ages up until the early 20th century, when the sink with running water made them obsolete. They were used for morning ablutions and for washing the hands before and after meals. Ewers and basins could also be luxury items in silver, and at a very early stage the porcelain factory at Vincennes (founded in 1740 and moved to Sèvres in 1756) made them in porcelain.

This model, identified in the factory records as *feuille d'eau* (water leaf), ranks among Sèvres's most original works, where the actual shapes of the objects devolve from ornamental details and refer to the function. Ovoid in format, these two objects are composed of water-lily leaves in relief that also form the ewer's lip and handle. Elements painted with a green ground highlighted with gilding stand out against the soft creamy white of the porcelain, thus accentuating the dimensional effect.

The Sèvres factory produced the *feuille d'eau* pitcher in three sizes (the piece here is the largest) and in three colors: sky blue, green, and pink. The factory guaranteed its success not only through the innovation and refinement of its shapes but through the quality and originality of its colored backgrounds. Mastery of color was one of the major accomplishments in the chemistry of making porcelain. Metal oxides were used to obtain the colors and each reacted differently in the kiln, which made this stage of the process particularly tricky. Sky blue was developed in 1751 and was immediately chosen by Louis XV for the table service he ordered. Green ground color appeared in 1753. Pink was achieved in 1757, but the extremely high cost of production limited its use.

Factory records reveal that the first pitcher of the *feuille d'eau* model was sold at the end of 1757 and had a green ground and flowers, as does this piece. The following year, Louis XV presented two Sèvres pitchers with basins of different-colored grounds to the Empress Maria Theresa of Austria—sure proof of the esteem in which the model was then held. —B.R.

Sauceboat

French, Sèvres factory, 1756
Soft-paste porcelain. H. 4¾ in. (12 cm),
W. 10⅛ in. (25.7 cm), D. 7⅝ in. (19.5 cm)
Purchased with funds from David David-Weill, 1924

A veritable manifesto of the Rococo style, this sauceboat resembles an unfurling wave sweeping seaweed and coral in its path, as its fringe of spindrift hemmed with blue and gold plays out in a scrolling rim. The inherent motion of the object invites our somewhat disoriented eye to rove across the surface and discover the surprising harmony in its refinement of detail and asymmetry of curves. Ornament alone seems to have dictated the form of the boat, altogether overwhelming considerations of function.

This sauceboat represents a technical triumph in that its medium of soft-paste porcelain is difficult to work and is ill-suited to complex shapes. The results were most uncertain, with successive firings and repeated failures when the kiln was opened.

The model, which translates into the soft-paste porcelain the sharply defined lines and bravura movement of virtuoso metalwork, was probably created by goldsmith Jean-Claude Duplessis.

In 1745 Vincennes granted the privilege of "manufactur[ing] in France porcelain items of the same quality as those made in Saxony to relieve consumers in this kingdom from having to transfer their monies to foreign lands in order to come by this kind of curiosity." The factory at Meissen in Saxony (Germany) had in fact been producing porcelain with the key ingredient of kaolin, which made it hard-paste like the treasured imports from the Orient. The secret of kaolin was unknown to French manufacturers, and they produced only soft-paste with a lead-rich glaze until 1769. It was in 1756, at the urging of Madame de Pompadour, that Louis XV took over Vincennes as an official royal factory and transferred the operation to new premises on a site at Sèvres near the château of the royal mistress and closer to Versailles. —S.M.

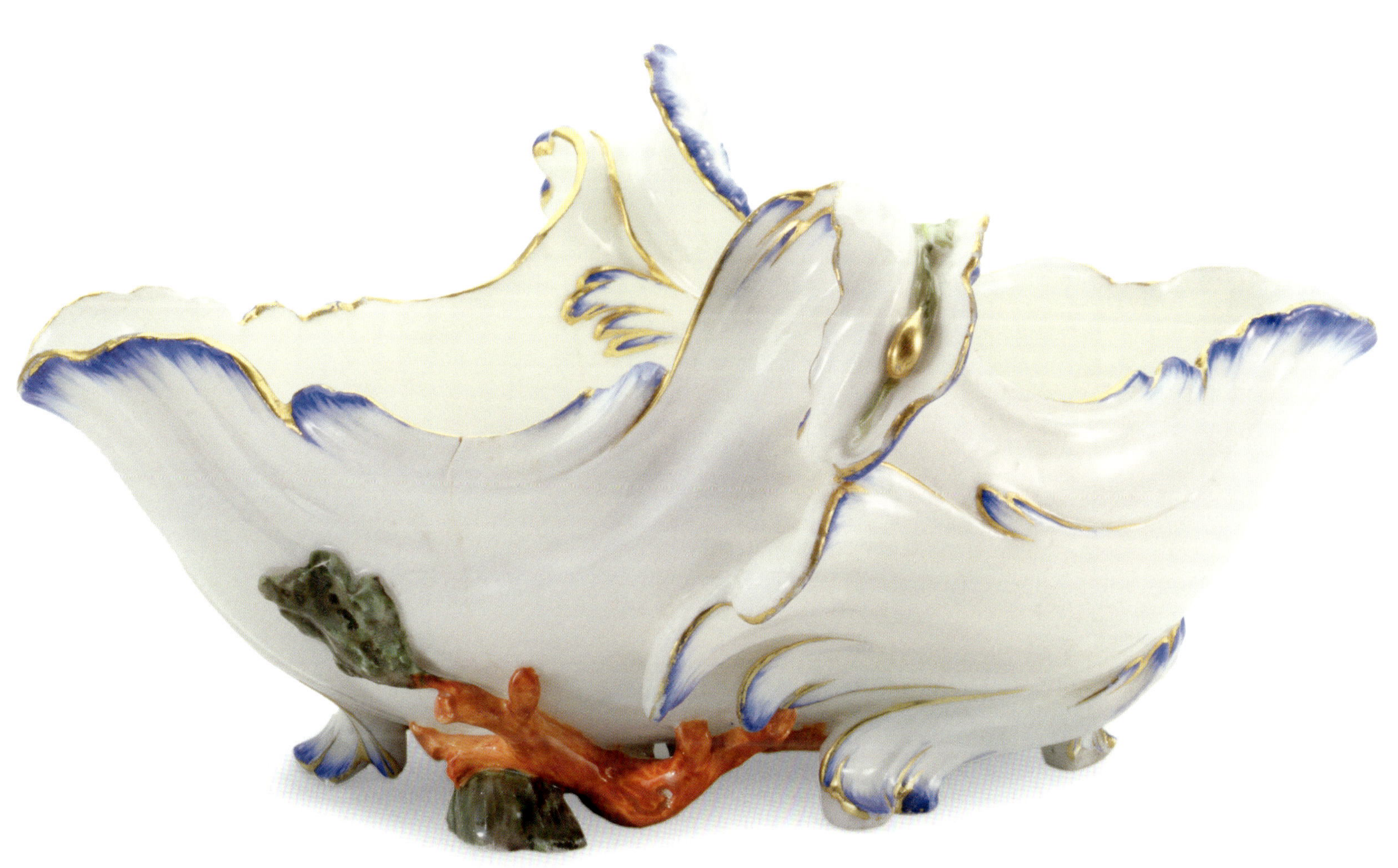

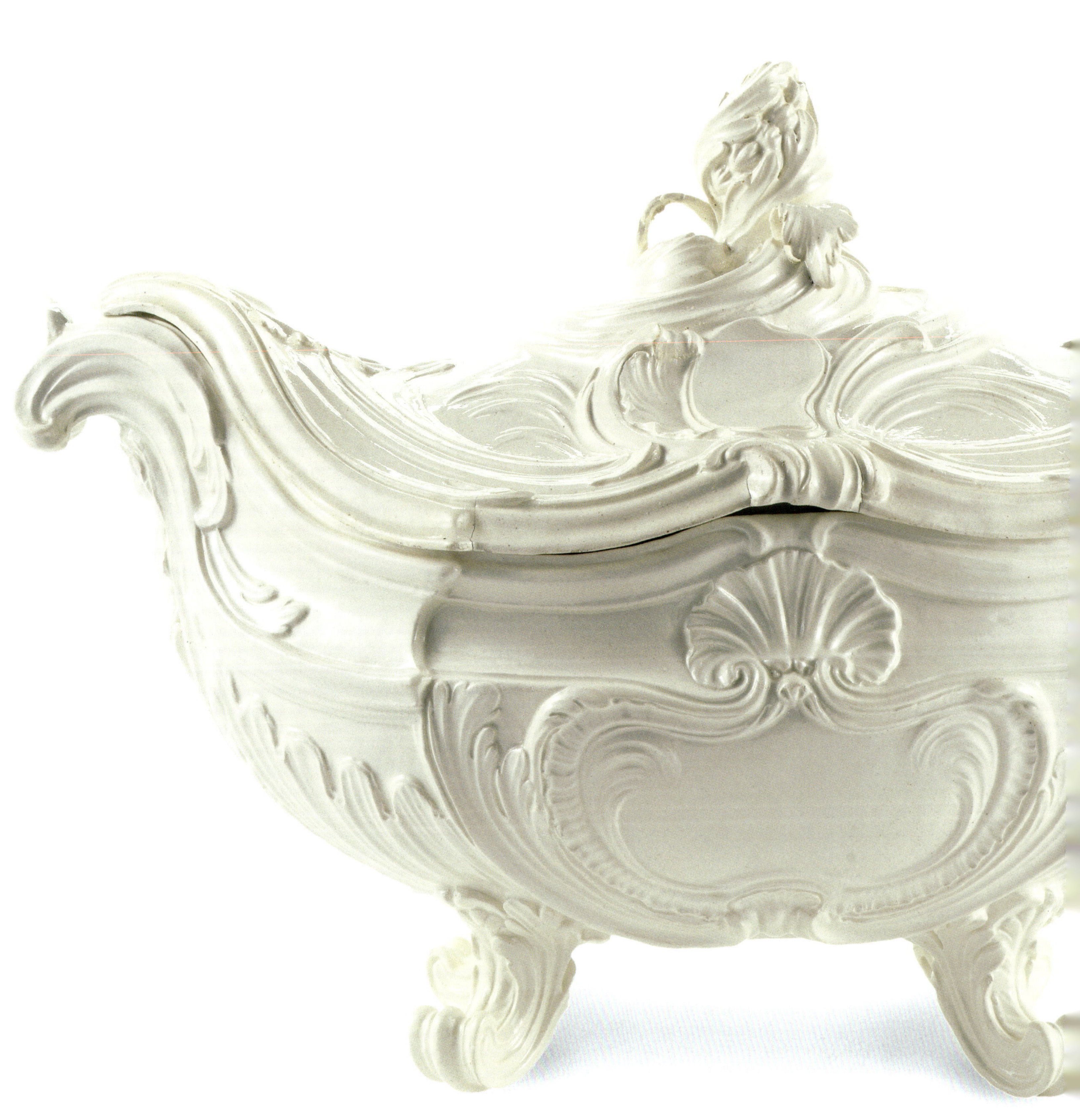

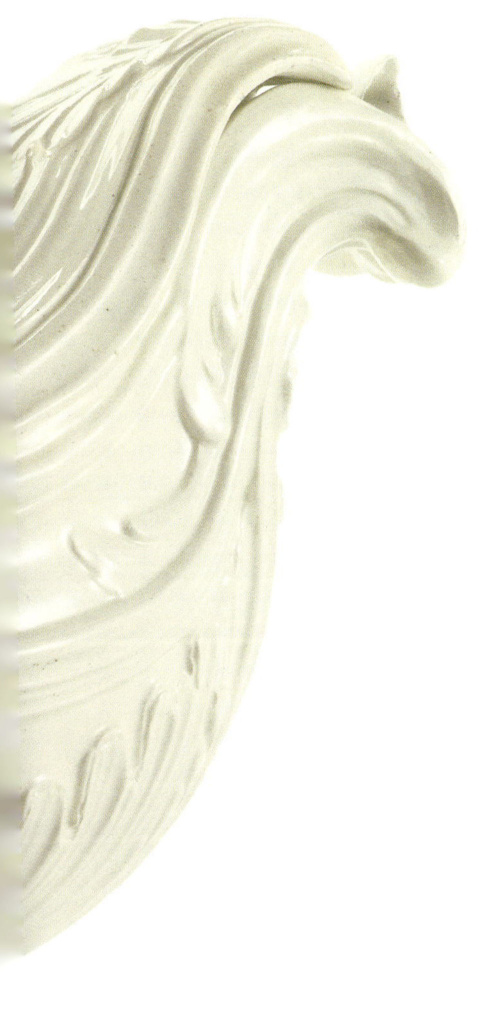

Tureen

French, Pont-aux-Choux factory,
circa 1750–1770
Creamware. H. 11¾ in. (30 cm), W. 18½ in. (47 cm), D. 10⅜ in. (26.5 cm)
M. Allain purchase, 1906

The form of this large ovoid tureen used for serving meat dishes is based directly on silverware models, for which it provided a more economical substitute. We know from the archives that the Pont-aux-Choux factory made casts of silver pieces for producing replicas in white earthenware, or creamware.

Of the many factories that were established in France in the wake of the success of English creamware between 1720 and 1725, none came so close in its approximation of porcelain as Pont-aux-Choux.

This Parisian factory was founded in 1743, and five years later it was awarded a twenty-year monopoly on the manufacture of creamware in France, receiving the title of Manufacture royale des Terres de France à l'imitation de celle d'Angleterre (Royal French Earthenware Factory in the Manner of English Earthenware). Pont-aux-Choux used a clay body that lent itself to molding and, when covered with a transparent glaze, was perfectly adapted to the complex relief shapes of the Rococo style. In 1788, when fashion moved away from Rococo to Neoclassicism, the factory closed down completely.

The products of Pont-aux-Choux, ivory-colored and bold in form, were designed for a less affluent clientele that was nonetheless keenly aware of the beauty of shapes. The line included various pieces intended for table service—terrines, sauceboats, ewers, and bowls—along with decorative elements such as busts, statuettes, and trompe l'oeil. —S.M.

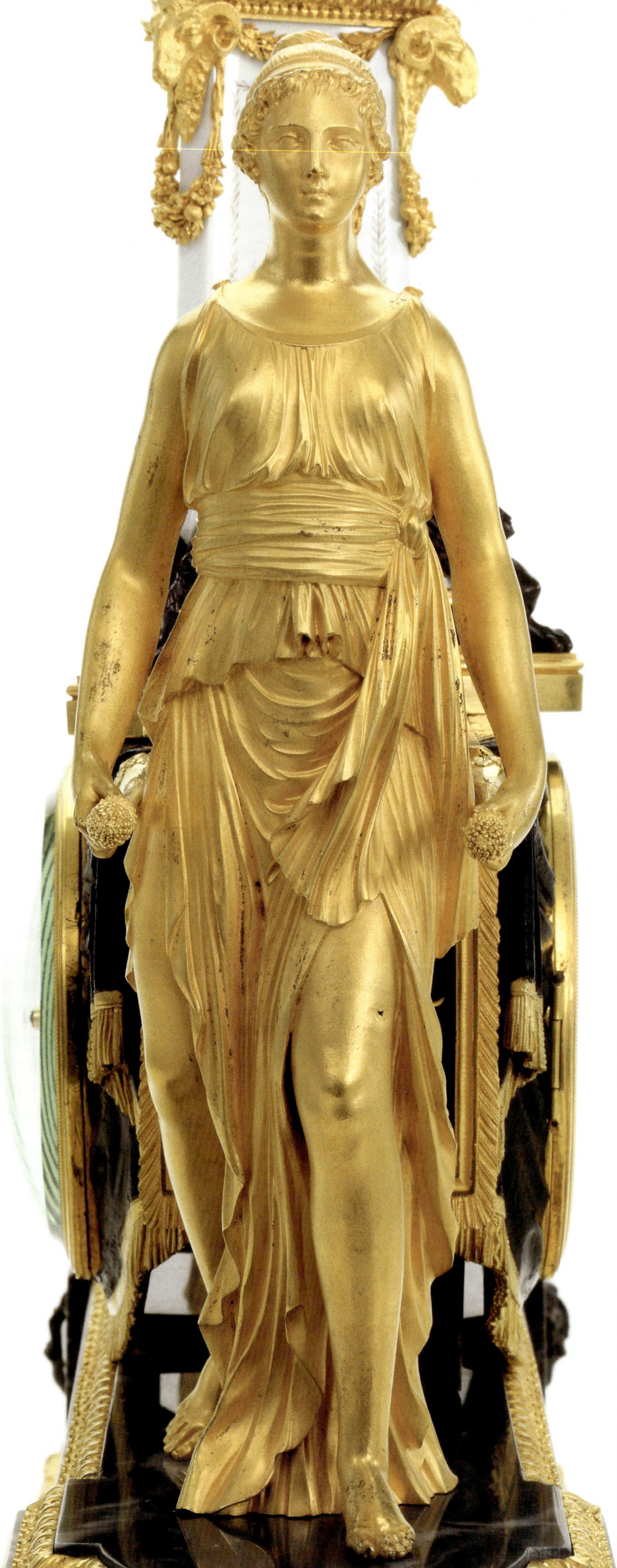

Clock

Paris, 1788
Bronzes: Pierre-Philippe Thomire (1751–1843)
Clockworks: Robert Robin (1742–1799)
Gilt and patinated bronze, Sèvres porcelain, marble. H. 19⅞ in. (50.5 cm), W. 25⅝ in. (65 cm), D. 7 in. (18 cm)
Loan from the Ministère de l'Intérieur, 1907

In the mid-17th century, it was customary to decorate the tops of mantelpieces with sets of ceramic vases. Around 1775–1780 this practice gave way to a new type of decoration: a clock flanked by candelabra. With the fashion for clocks depicting allegorical subjects, the dial became a secondary element encompassed in a sculptural program. Form took precedence over function.

This clock originally graced Marie Antoinette's bathroom in the Tuileries palace. The composition as well as the manufacture of its bronzes are believed to be by Pierre-Philippe Thomire, one of the queen's favorite bronzemakers, whose mark appears on several clocks of this type. His inspiration was an engraving by the painter Hubert Robert, published in 1771–1773 in a collection titled *Griffonis.*

The unusual subject is two vestal virgins, in the robes and upswept banded hairstyle of classical antiquity, carrying a draped litter supporting a porcelain altar with sacred fire and offerings of a goblet and ewer set before it. On the base, supported by four panthers, are two medallions made of Sèvres biscuit porcelain, in the "manner of Wedgwood," depicting Urania, muse of Astronomy, and Clio, muse of History. These flank a long porcelain plaque decorated with a frieze in the Pompeiian style. —S.M.

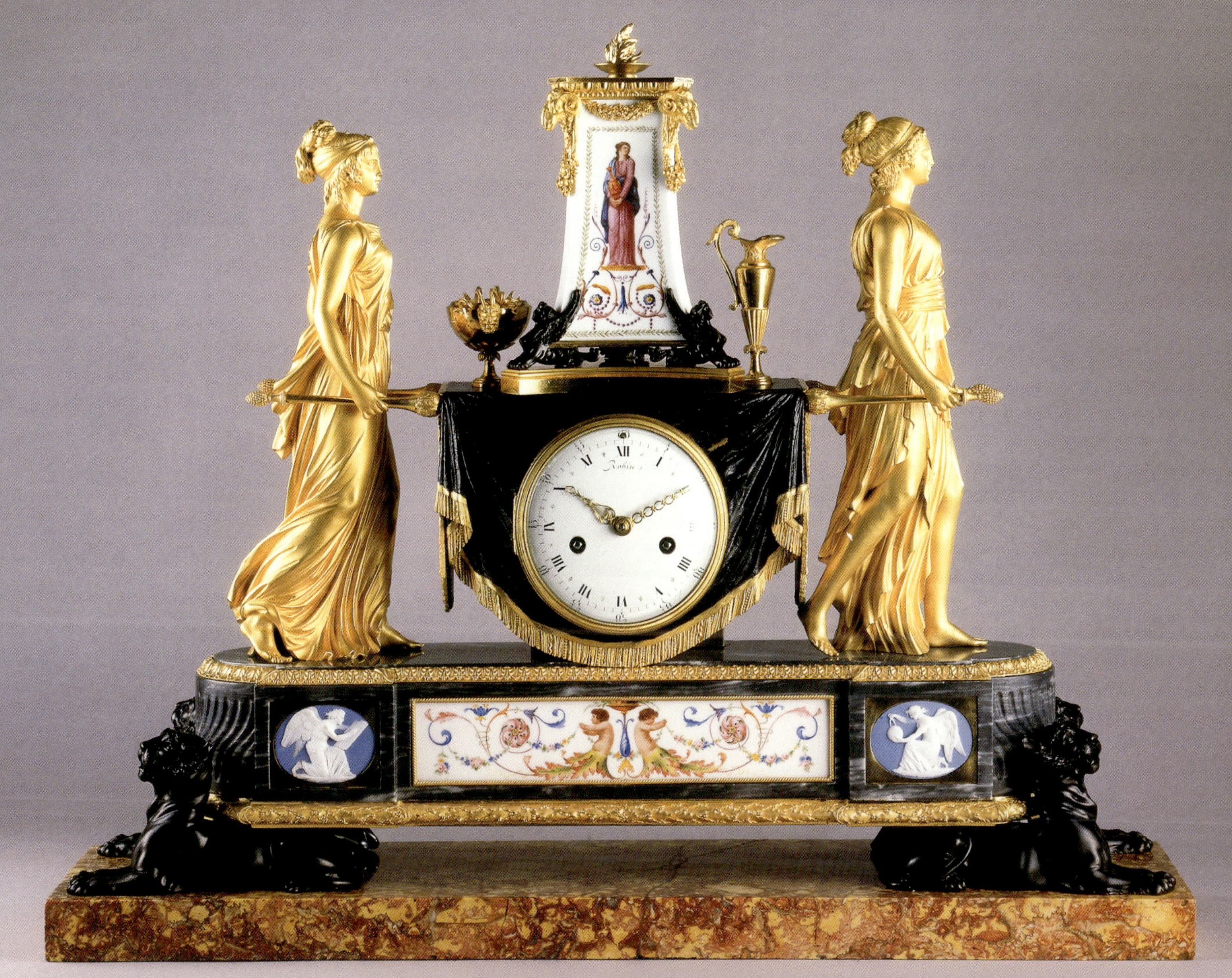
Robin

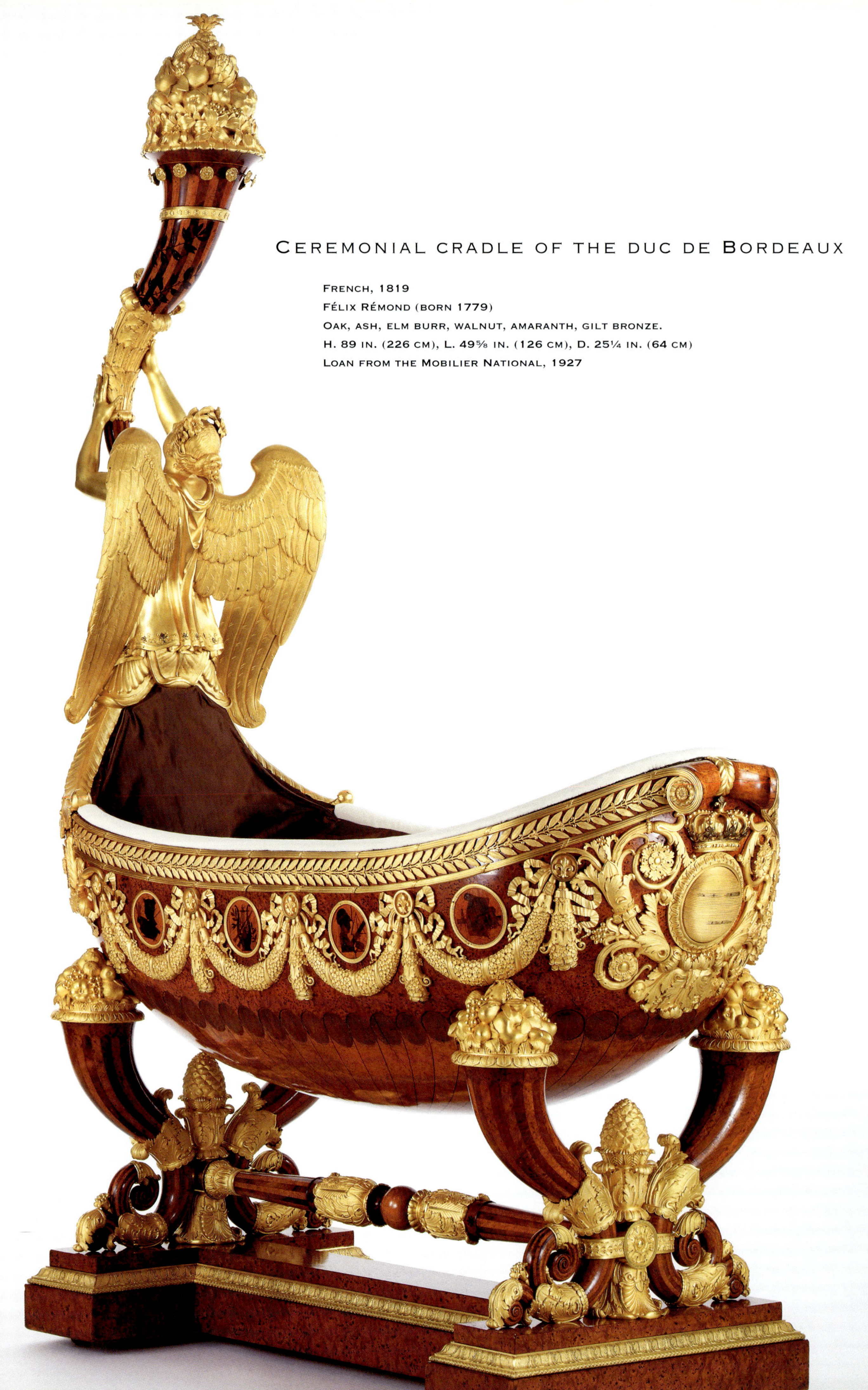

Ceremonial cradle of the duc de Bordeaux

French, 1819
Félix Rémond (born 1779)
Oak, ash, elm burr, walnut, amaranth, gilt bronze.
H. 89 in. (226 cm), L. 49⅝ in. (126 cm), D. 25¼ in. (64 cm)
Loan from the Mobilier National, 1927

Mythological tales of birth, fertility, and death have often used the image of a frail boat sailing on perilous waters. The best-known example may be Noah's ark in the biblical flood, but perhaps the most moving image of life's frailty is the basket floating on the Nile, carrying an abandoned infant Moses before he was rescued by the pharaoh's daughter. Paradoxically, the gondola-like cradle, with its rounded forms, has also been associated with a spirit of protective intimacy and the soothing rocking of an infant.

So it is not surprising that on the occasion of the birth of royal heirs, cradles were fashioned as precious vessels. These so-called ceremonial cradles were used during official visits to mother and child. They usually included a figure of Fame, a winged woman representing the clamor of public opinion, holding a crown above the infant's head and watching over her charge.

When the duc de Berry, son of King Charles X, announced the imminent arrival of an heir (the duc de Bordeaux), the royal Garde Meuble (furniture administration) decided to commission a cradle that would express the victory of the Bourbon dynasty over the Napoleonic Empire. Here, Fame's back is turned to the infant as she takes the position of the figurehead on the prow of a ship. She seems to take flight as she raises high into the air a cornucopia overflowing with fruits and vegetables, symbolizing the wishes for success and prosperity addressed to the young prince.

The body of the cradle has been fashioned like a boat's hull, and its sides decorated with a series of wreaths and medallions representing the Arts and Sciences, part of the child's destiny. Oddly enough, this boat is not designed for rocking the child. It is fixed, supported on four cornucopias set solidly on the floor, as if it were moored to the earthly wealth of France—the very image of the regime's restoration of stability. —O.N.

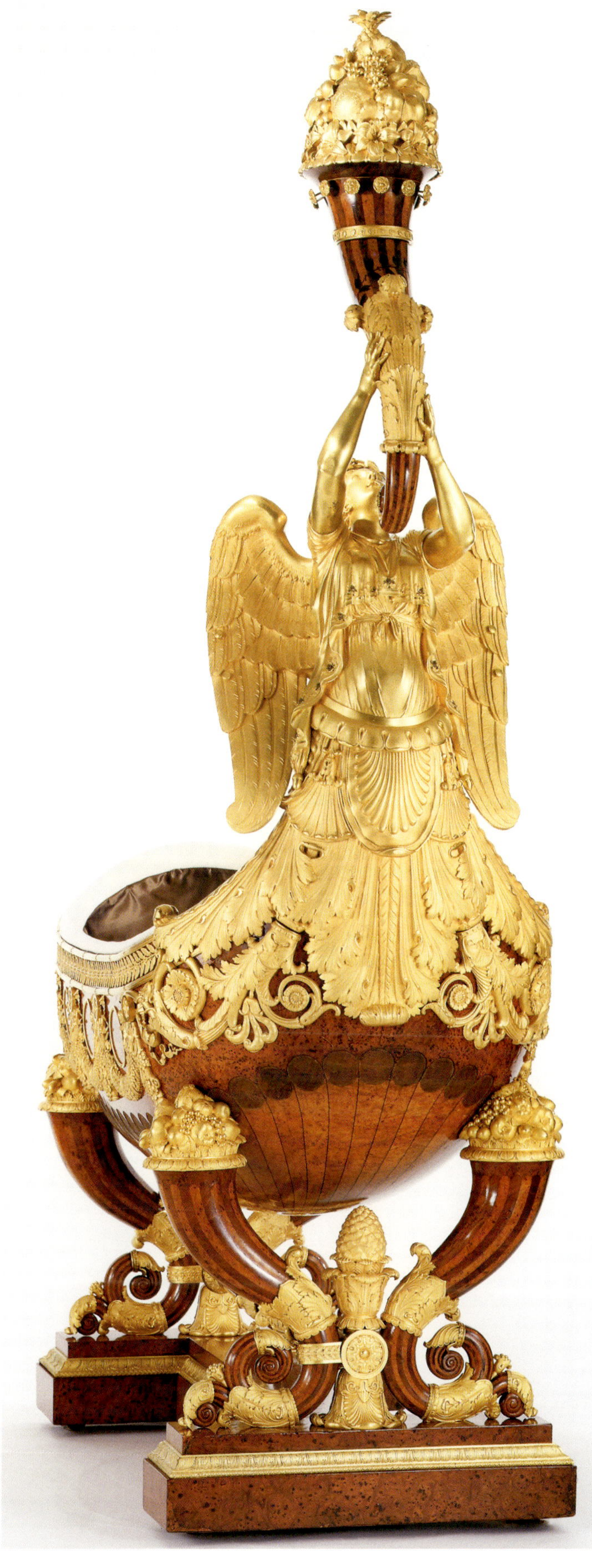

Gondola Bed

French, 1827
François Baudry (1791–1859)
Gray poplar, ash, olive-ash, elm burr, amaranth,
Santo Domingo lemon, mahogany. H. 53⅞ in. (137 cm),
L. 83⅞ in. (213 cm), D. 66⅞ in. (170 cm)
Gift of Mr. and Mrs. de Galéa, 1963

The form of bed known as a "boat," "gondola," or, in America, "sleigh" became fashionable at the beginning of the 19th century. These beds' novelty lay in their curved silhouette with down-scooped sides, calling to mind a boat floating on water, but they retained the rectangular format of more conventional beds.

François Baudry was keen to push the naval comparison to the point of inventing this extraordinary completely oval bed, whose sophisticated design represented an enormous technical challenge. The bed's supple contouring recalls principles of shipbuilding. There is a stunning brilliance about the bed's curves and countercurves: the ends round like sails filled by the wind, then taper, expiring like waves into refined scrolling flanges. Oddly enough, the perfectly straight head- and footboards conform to convention, except that they conjure up the supporting crossbars of a sailor's hammock, as if emphasizing the metaphor of rocking oneself to sleep. They are decorated with oak branches and garlands of ivy, laurel, and myrtle. In the middle of each end, a delicate crown of rosebuds is placed as if to form a halo around the sleeper's head.

Baudry produced this extraordinary piece for the Exposition des Produits de l'Industrie in 1827. The bed was accompanied by a fall-front desk, a chest of drawers, and an armchair, all with the same blond woods and curving lines. His approach was a manifesto of modernity, reacting against the traditional models dominated by the use of straight lines and dark mahogany.

Produits de l'Industrie exhibitions were inaugurated by Napoleon Bonaparte at the end of the French Revolution, with the aim of stimulating the French economy in general and the luxury goods industry in particular. They were organized like competitions for each arts and crafts sector, and medals were awarded to the best craftsmen. King Charles X personally presented Baudry with a bronze medal for his furniture. —O.N.

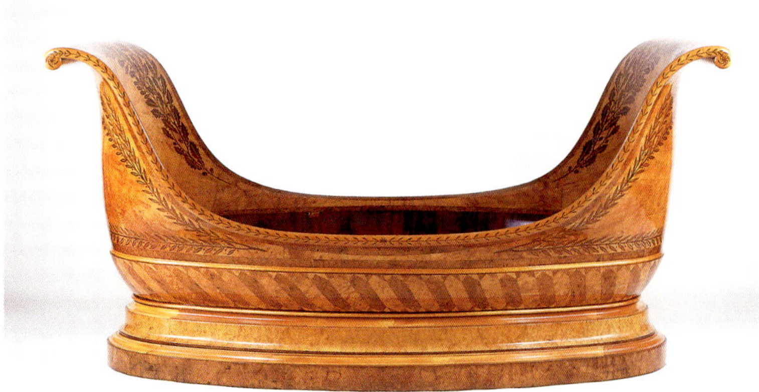

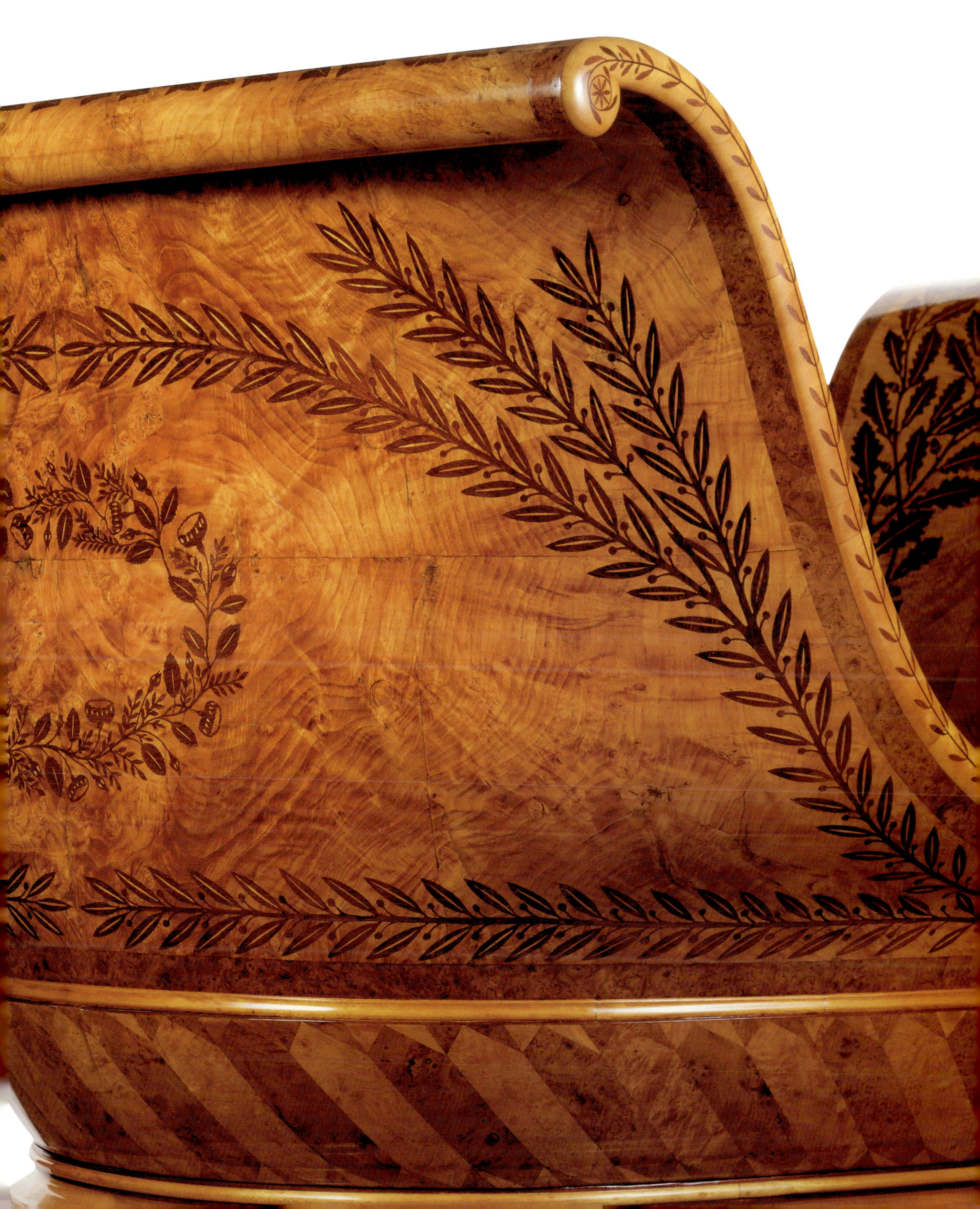

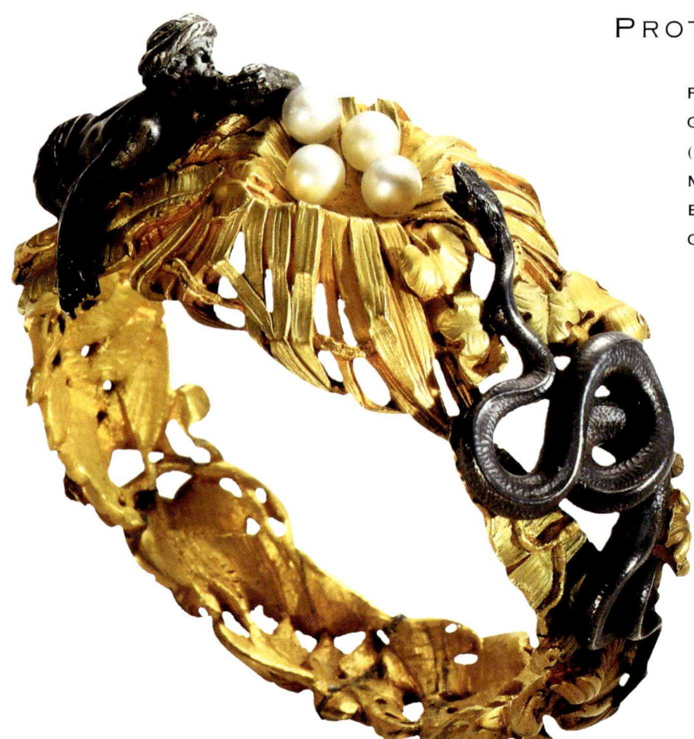

Prototype bracelet

French, 1842–1848
Goldsmithswork: Morel & Cie; Jean-Valentin Morel (1794–1860) and Henri Duponchel (1794–1868)
Model: Jean-Baptiste-Jules Klagmann (1810–1867)
Bronze, gold. Diam. 2¾ in. (7 cm)
Gift of Jules Brateau, 1901

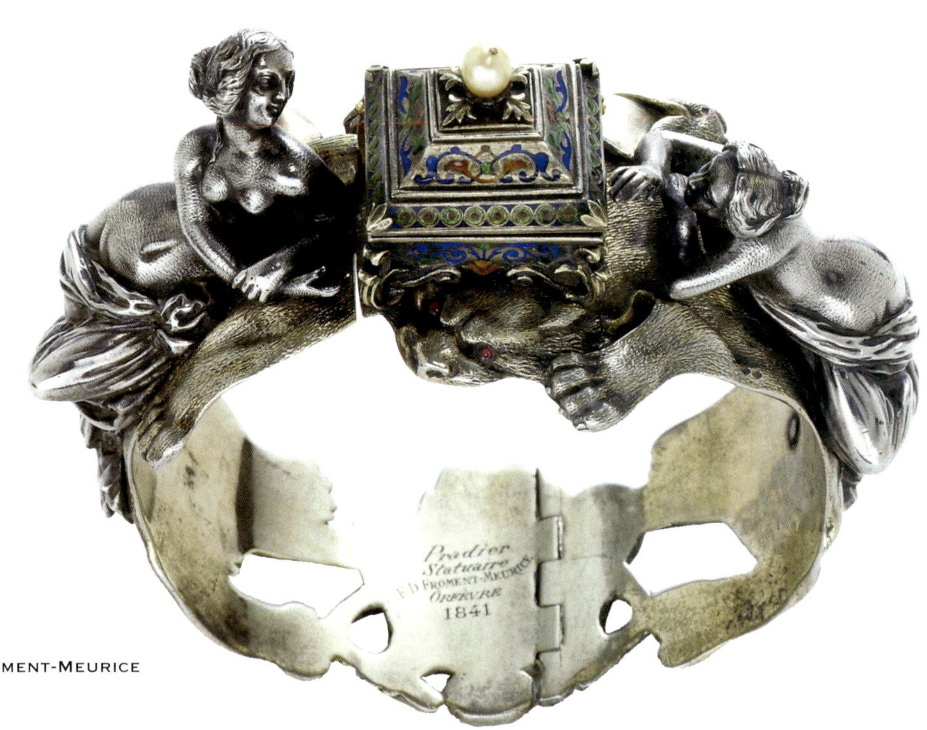

Bracelet

French, 1841
Goldsmithswork: François-Désiré Froment-Meurice (1802–1855)
Model: James Pradier (1792–1852)
Silver, gold, pearls, rubies, enamel. Diam. 3⅛ in. (8 cm)
Gift of Henri Vever, 1924

For this bracelet, the sculptor Jean-Baptiste-Jules Klagmann fashioned an egg-filled nest about to be ravaged by a turbaned figure on one side and a snake on the other. This nest theme, brainchild of the jeweler Petiteau, symbolized love of hearth, home, and family and was very popular for more than twenty years. It was adopted by many jewelers and came in several versions. The bird defending its nest, either alone or with its mate, might be attacked by various predators, such as man, snakes, or lizards.

The Romantic movement in art and literature took pleasure in depicting the workings of the heart and soul. Artists liked showing figures whose actions and sentiments were morally uplifting and in tune with the values championed by the bourgeoisie during the reign of Louis-Philippe (1830–1848).

This piece, a prototype and not the finished bracelet, helps us visualize the design and production phases of a piece of jewelry. To adapt the subject to the form of the bracelet, Klagmann made many drawings on tracing paper, and a watercolor or gouache with instructions as to the materials to be used. A modelmaker then produced a two-dimensional plaster or wax maquette, on which any requested alterations were made. Next a three-dimensional metal model was chased and cast, based on this maquette. The jeweler kept this model, which was the basis for making any number of finished bracelets cast by the lost-wax technique. —E.P.

This silver bracelet features two women reclining on lion skins on either side of a small enameled box, known as a "vinaigrette." With its perforated top, this tiny box held a sponge saturated with aromatic fragrances, smelling salts, or vinegar, and was used by elegant ladies to prevent swooning and fainting fits. The scent contained here on the bracelet was more usually in a hollow finger ring or in a vial attached to the ring and held in a lady's palm or secreted in her glove.

The jeweler François-Désiré Froment-Meurice was the first to reintroduce the female form into jewelry, thus triggering a major debate about using depictions of the human body. But in so doing, he was merely drawing inspiration from Renaissance artists. These two half-naked female figures, lying languidly on animal hides, are based on the figures Michelangelo sculpted for the Medici tomb in Florence, and their long-limbed shapes derive from Mannerist models introduced by the Renaissance Italian painter Primaticcio.

Through Romantic art, the French became reacquainted with their national history, in particular that of the Middle Ages and the Renaissance. Subjects taken from the novels of Victor Hugo and Alexandre Dumas invaded jewelry and other decorative arts. Goldsmiths and jewelers like Froment-Meurice, as well as Fauconnier, Morel, Rudolphi, and Wagner, called on the services of sculptors such as Cavelier, Feuchères, Jean-Baptiste-Jules Klagmann, and James Pradier to breathe life into all these fictional characters. This bracelet is one of the finest illustrations of the collaboration between sculptors and goldsmiths. It is also one of the rare pieces of jewelry to be signed by both artists and dated like a full-fledged sculpture. —E.P.

Egg-and-Snake Teapot

French, Sèvres factory, 1833
Hard-paste porcelain. H. 7½ in. (19 cm)
Gift of Jules Audéoud, 1885

Since the 18th century, teapots, coffeepots, and chocolate jugs, all designed for holding exotic beverages, have given artists a chance to draw their inspiration from Nature in exotic lands as distant as they were full of surprises. The spouts of these vessels were fashioned to resemble the mouths of more or less imaginary animals such as chimeras, griffins, lions, and dolphins.

Here, a threatening snake raises its head, hissing with anger. It is coiled twice around the egg, the way certain boas do to hatch their young and protect them from danger. Its rings and scales, all meticulously depicted in dark green and gold, contrast with the white egg, decorated with gilt rosettes evenly distributed in gilt latticework. A classical stylized flower forms the finial.

The decorative conceit is such that the snake, winding its path from spout to handle, is the sole motif giving both structure and strength to the pot. The artist did not want to make a realistic reproduction of a natural scene; rather, he strove for visual elegance. Here the creature seems in thorough control of its strength, giving an impression of contained force, and the egg looks all the more fragile in its formal perfection. This evocation of ideal Nature tallies well with the highly controlled aesthetic rules of the Empire style.

The teapot was part of a service whose naturalistic decoration contained allusions to the source of each foodstuff: a cream jug in the form of a cow's head, a sugar bowl in the shape of a pineapple, an herbal teacup in the form of a flower, and a chocolate cup with the same motif as the teapot. The snake brings to mind Asia, the source of tea.

The model was made at Sèvres only until 1833, and in very small numbers. One was bought by the duc d'Orléans, son of King Louis-Philippe, and a keen collector.

—O.N.

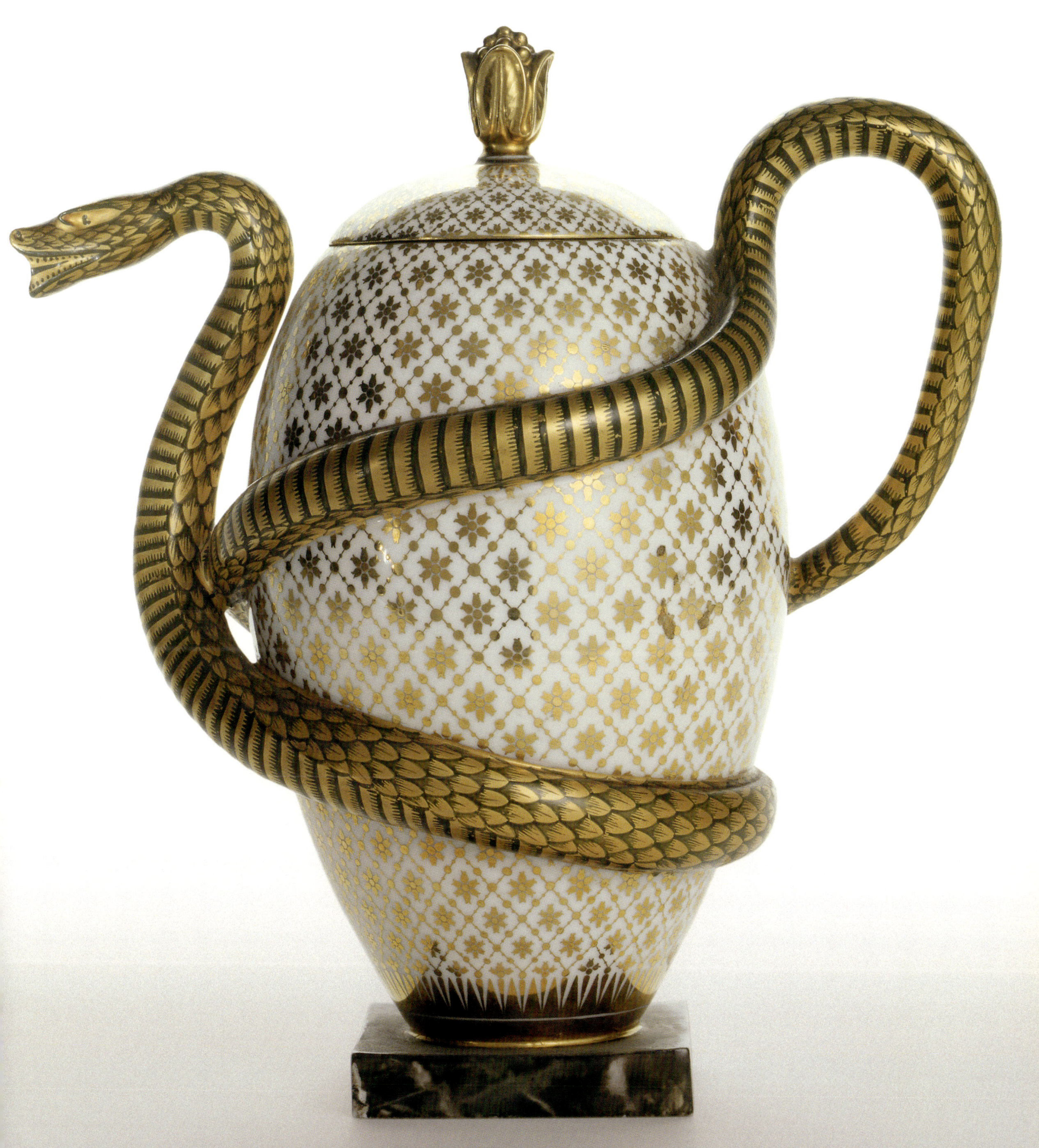

Centerpiece

French, Christofle factory, 1852–1856
Electroplated bronze, silver-plated bronze.
H. 39⅜ in. (100 cm), W. 115 in. (292 cm), D. 41⅜ in. (105 cm)
Gift of Paul Christofle and Henri Bouilhet, 1891

Beginning in the 17th century, it was customary to decorate banquet tables with a series of objects collectively known as the "centerpiece." The principal element could take the most varied forms, inspired by Nature or featuring allegorical figures, and made of silver or, later, of porcelain. It was often accompanied by secondary, functional pieces like saltcellars, pepper pots, cruets, and sugar bowls.

This centerpiece was the main decorative element of the service commissioned by Louis Napoleon Bonaparte (nephew of Napoleon I and soon to be Napoleon III). It was designed for a table one hundred feet in length, seating one hundred guests, and included fifteen sculptural decorations of electroplated metalwork. This brand-new technique, to which Christofle (manufacturer of silverware) then owned the exclusive rights in France, involved coating a piece of bronze with gold or silver by electrolysis. Electroplating made possible the low-cost production of pieces with the appearance of solid gold or silver. Napoleon III justified his choice by saying that most centerpieces made of precious metals and commissioned by French monarchs had been melted down to help finance wars. History had a new twist in store for this service, however. In 1871, during the civil war of the Commune, the centerpiece survived the fire that destroyed the Tuileries palace. Had it been solid silver, it would have perished. Henri Bouilhet, vice president of the Christofle factory, rescued it from the smoldering ashes, and his successors gave it to the Musée des Arts Décoratifs. The violence of the fire is evidenced to this day by the centerpiece's damaged and blistered surfaces.

In the central section, winged France, standing on the vault of the heavens, hands out crowns of glory to War, personified by a warrior in an Etruscan chariot drawn by four horses, and to Peace, represented by a young woman in a Gallic chariot drawn by four bulls. The figure of France is surrounded by the allegories of Justice, Harmony, Religion, and Might.

The urn, surmounted by an imperial crown that is half-hidden behind France, symbolizes the political changes occurring in the country. When Louis Napoleon Bonaparte ordered the centerpiece, he was prince-president; by the time it was delivered, he had become Emperor Napoleon III. —O.N.

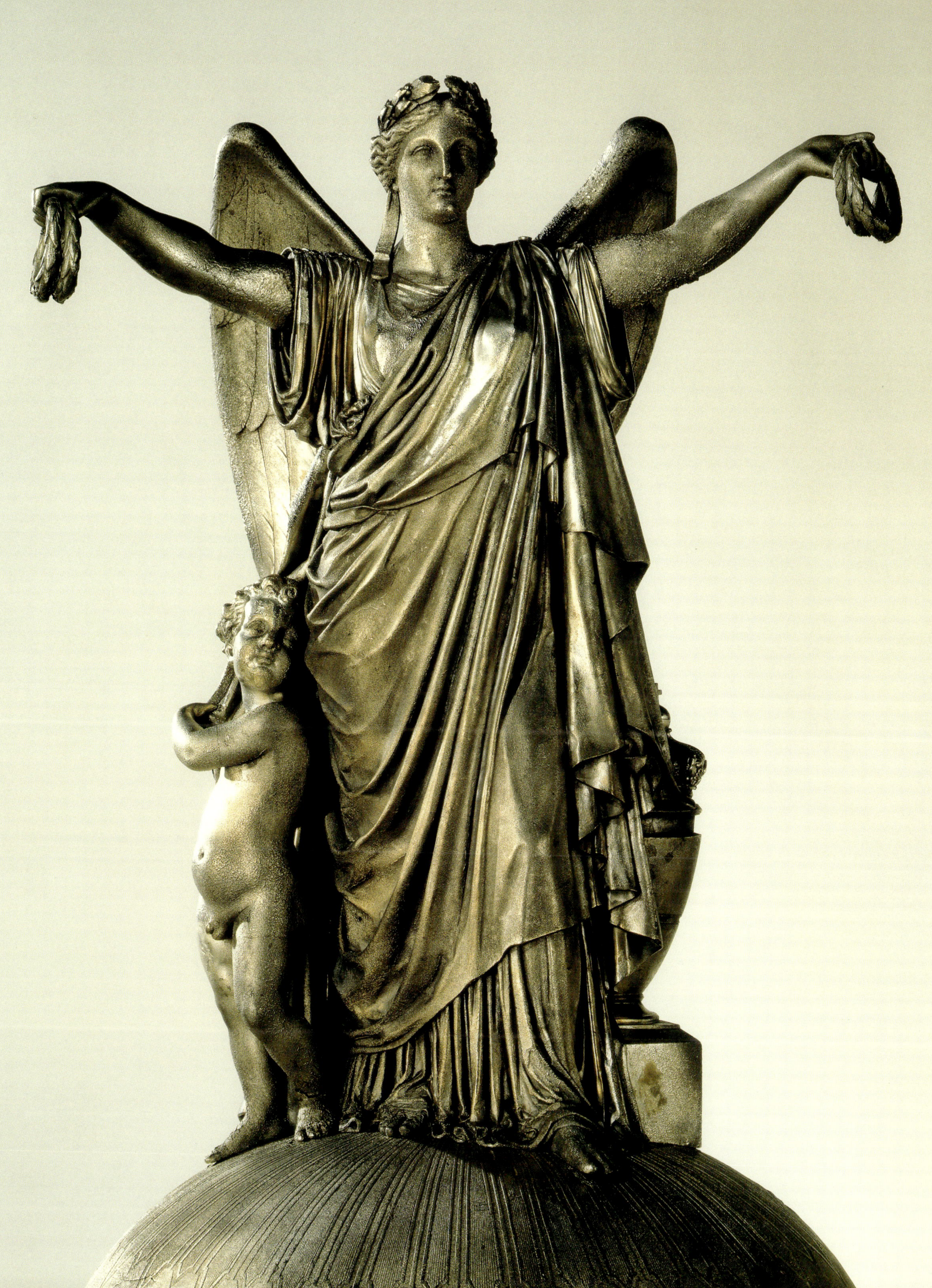

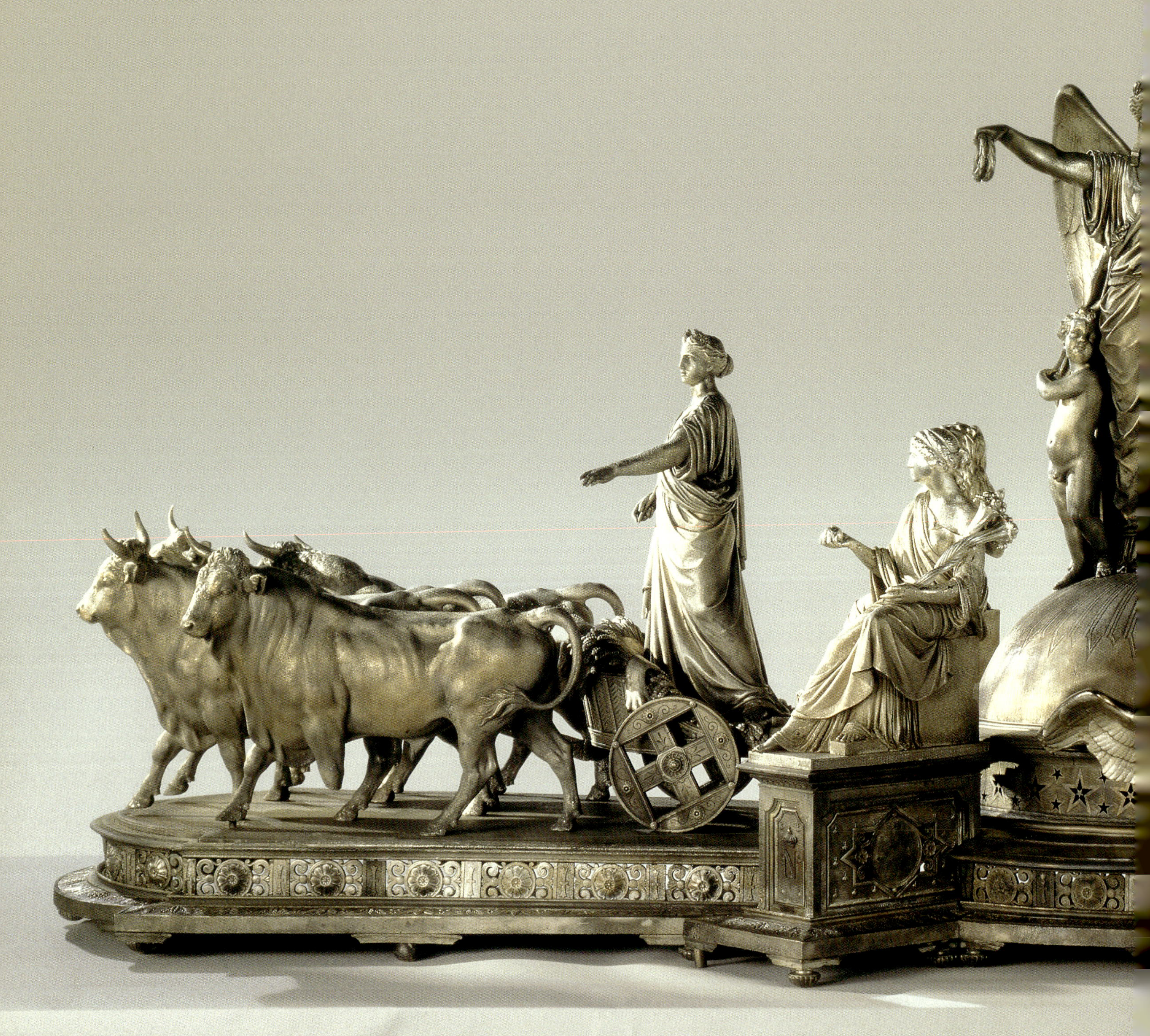

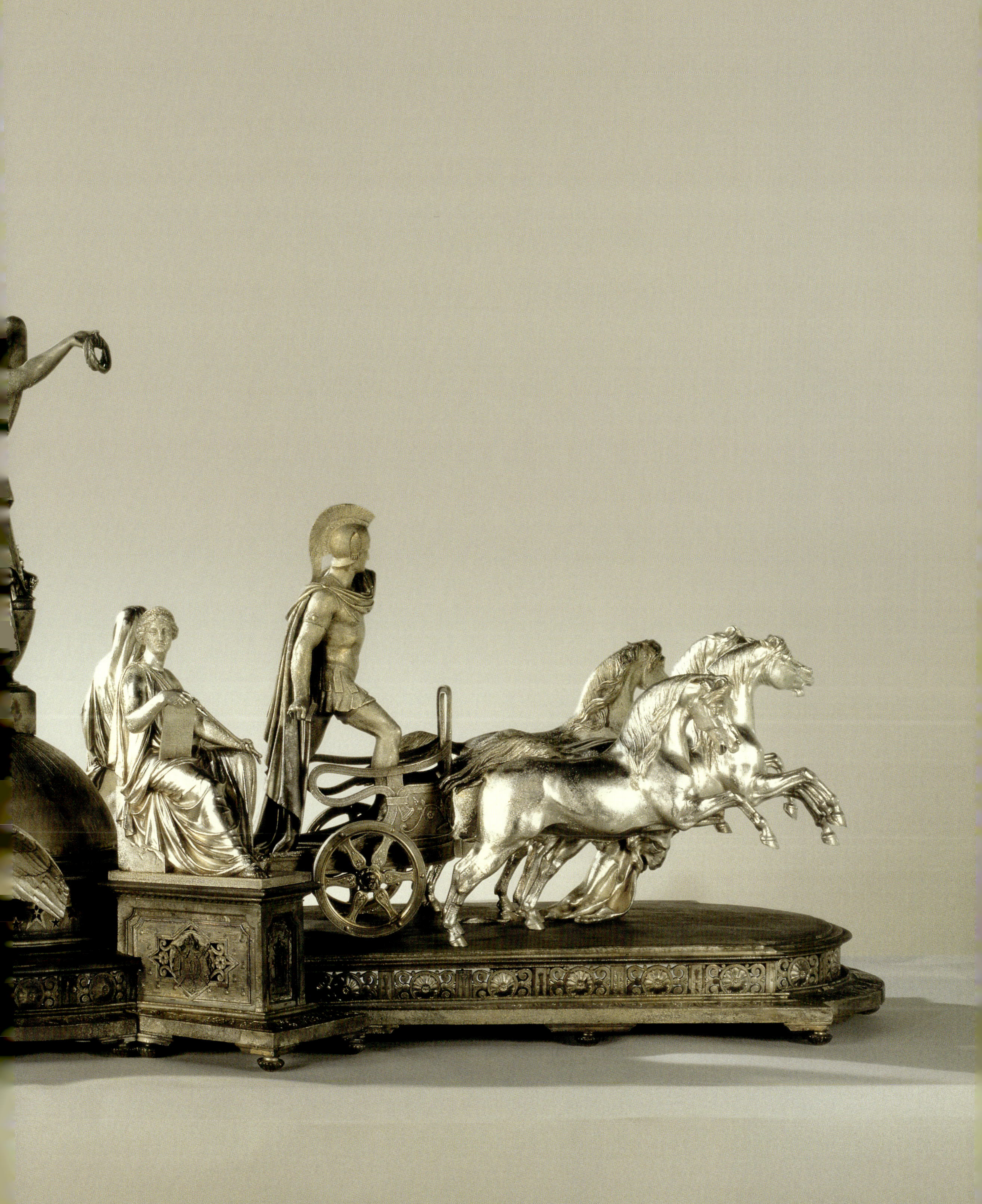

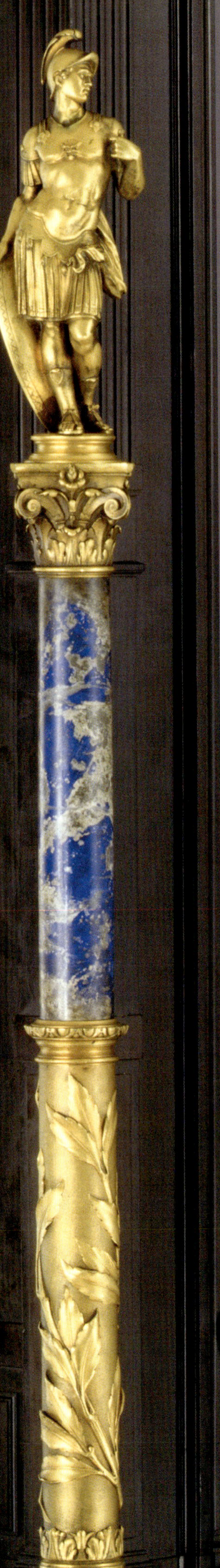

Cabinet

French, circa 1856
Pierre Manguin (1815–1869)
Ebony, ebonized pear wood, gilt bronze, enamel, lapis lazuli.
H. 118⅛ in. (300 cm), W. 61 in. (155 cm), D. 27½ in. (70 cm)
Gift of Mrs. Loiseau, widow of Mr. Loiseau, and
Mr. Paul Baubigny, grandchildren of Pierre Manguin, 1919

This cabinet belonged to one of the most ambitious and scandalous courtesans of the Second Empire, Thérèse Lachmann, who came from the Moscow ghetto and converted to three different religions as her love affairs dictated. In 1855 she had become a wealthy socialite and had just married the marquis de Païva, her third husband, when she was offered a sumptuous mansion on the Champs-Elysées by one of her lovers, Count Henkel of Donnersmark, cousin of Bismarck and Prussian ambassador in Paris. As both were suspected of spying, the marquise (known simply as la Païva) and her paramour Donnersmark left Paris after France's defeat by Prussia in 1870.

La Païva made her staggeringly luxurious mansion one of the most sought-after venues for anyone who was anyone among the Paris smart set and artistic circles, as she dared to rival Princess Mathilde, the emperor's cousin.

This cabinet reflects la Païva's fondness for power as well as her unabashed narcissism. The architect Pierre Manguin took his inspiration from Renaissance furniture in designing the severe black construction, which serves as a frame for the central theme of female seduction and eroticism. In gilt bronze medallions on the sides and doors of the upper section, four of the most famous women in mythology are depicted in conjunction with the four elements, thus among them encompassing the universe: Juno is associated with water, Venus with fire, Leda with air, and Diana with earth. In addition, reclining, half-clad women decorate narrow rectangular cartouches. Plaques on the lower section doors are based on the *Aeneid:* Venus, at her most appealing, beseeches Jupiter to arm her son Aeneas; then she kisses her son and urges him on to victorious battle. All this sensuality is displayed beneath the sober but doubtless approving gaze of Fame, who stands above the busts of the twelve Caesars in the superstructure. Mars and Minerva perch on slender columns at the front corners, and a lion's mask guards access to the central drawer.

The cabinet's interior, lined in trimmed sky-blue silk, is a tactile invitation, and inside each door is mounted an enamel medallion painted with a naked woman doing her hair or putting on a necklace. A steel safe is secreted in one of the small interior drawers, while the central drawer, lined with dark red velvet, can be opened out to make a writing desk. —O.N.

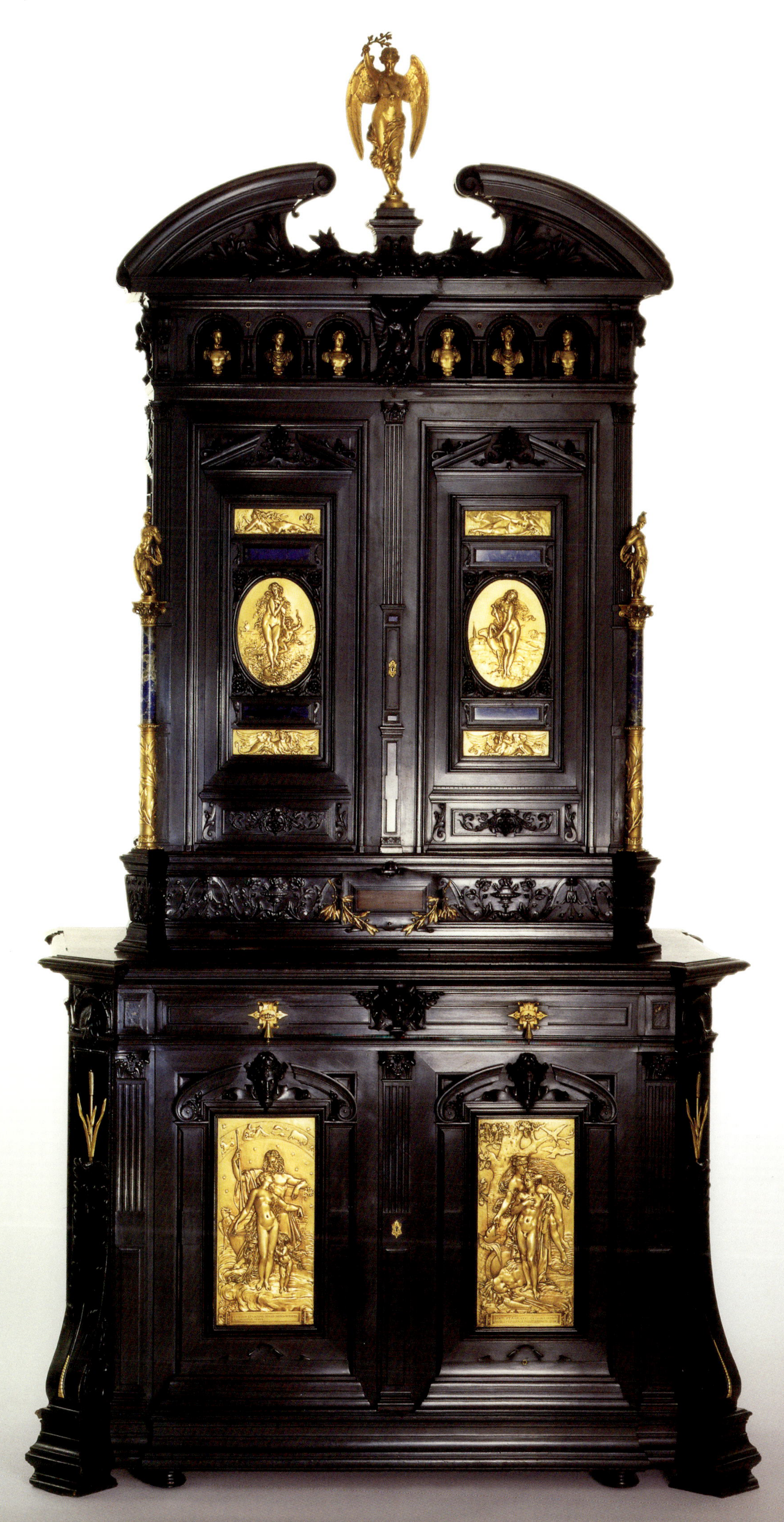

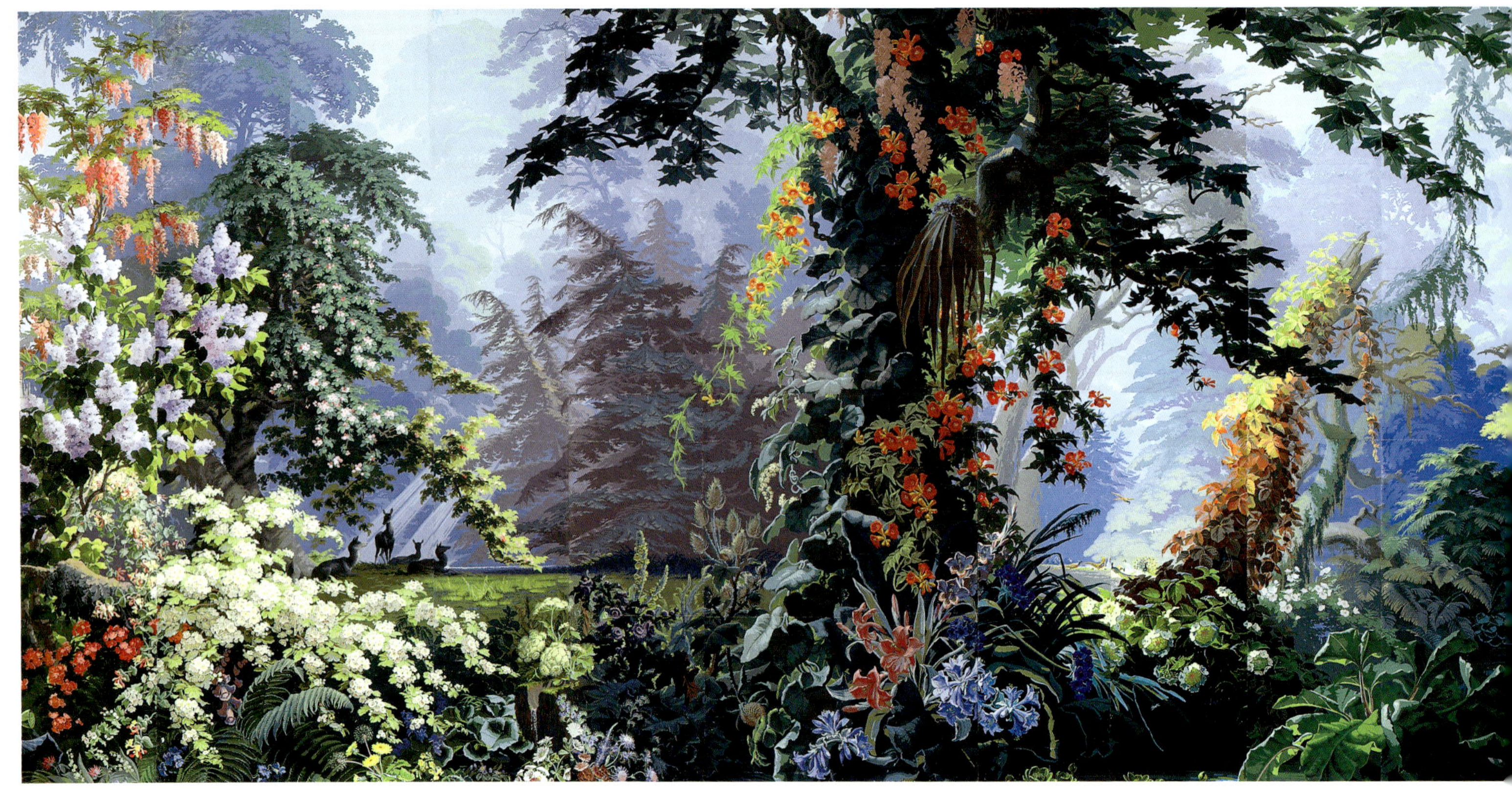

Eden scenic wallpaper

French, Paris, Jules Desfossé factory, 1861
Design: Joseph Fuchs (1814–1888)
Block printed paper. Six panels, each H. 107½ in. (273 cm), W. 78⅛ in. (198.5 cm)
Purchase, 1982

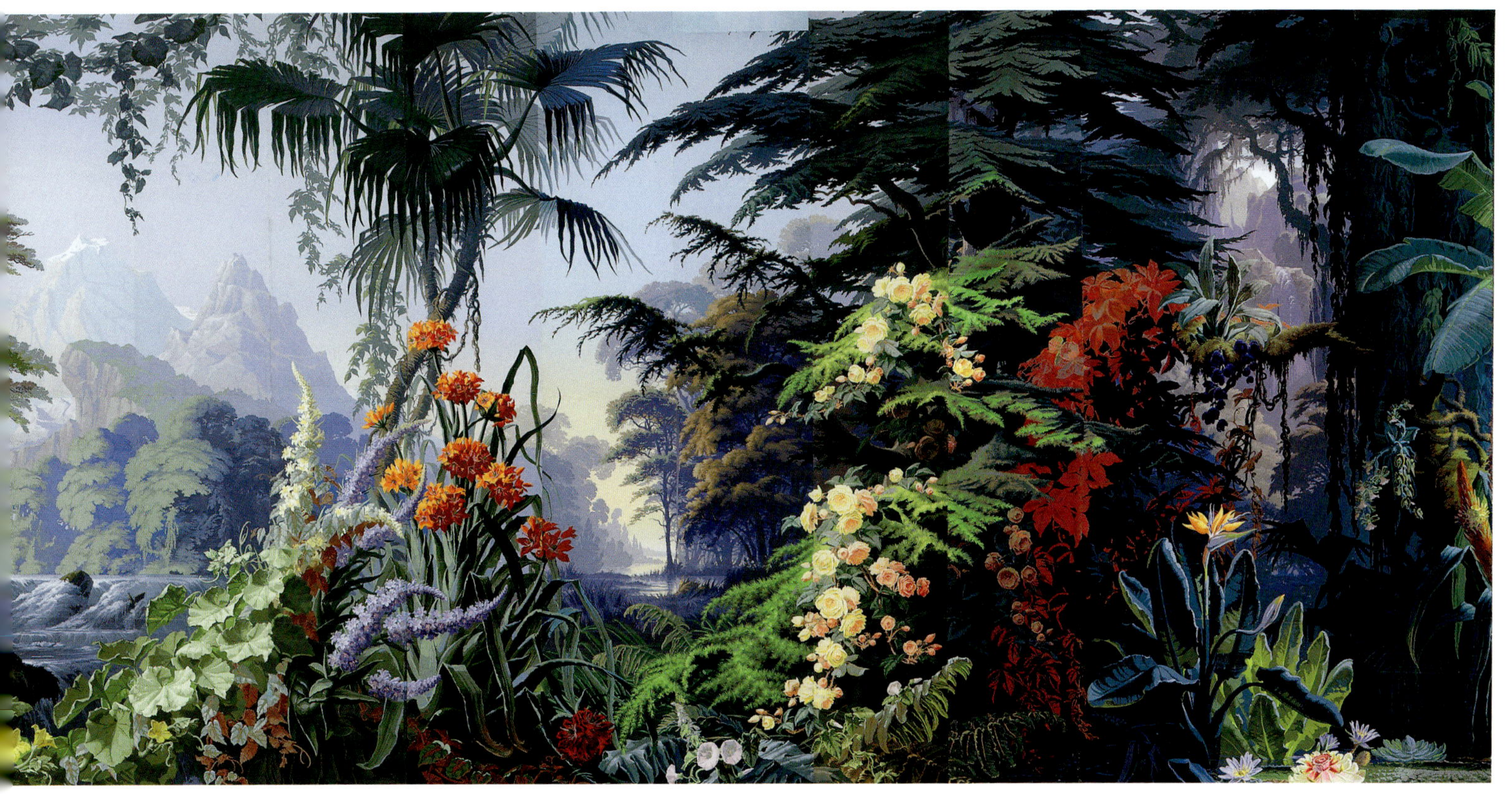

Scenic wallpaper originated in France at the very end of the 18th century. In this genre, a continuous landscape, wherein no scenes or motifs were ever repeated, was block printed on a series of several lengths of paper joined together and designed to cover all the walls of a room. Initially, these landscapes included narratives drawn from mythology, the Bible, or literature. They depicted feasts and festivals, hunts, or an historical event, or they might describe a land near or far enlivened by figures and animals. The narrative element was subsequently dropped, and these scenic wallpapers became pure landscape.

This paper, named Eden, belongs to the latter category. It is characterized by the absence of any narrative feature and by the extremely discreet presence of animals. It glorifies Nature in a virgin and idyllic state, describing a paradisaical land where all plants bloom at the same time. There is no sky, and the viewer is plunged into the vegetation.

Although the maquette (a lithograph with watercolor, also in the collection of the Musée des Arts Décoratifs) shows a design filling twenty-six lengths, Eden was printed on only twenty-three. It included 1,099 colors and required 3,642 wood blocks to print on widths of paper precolored by brush.

The composition is by Joseph Fuchs, an outstanding flower painter, who created the first scenic wallpaper without a story element, Isola Bella, for the Zuber factory in 1843. This was followed by Eldorado (1849), a grand landscape vision of the four main continents. After Eden, Jules Desfossé asked Fuchs to produce another panorama titled Brazil (1863). —V.L.H.

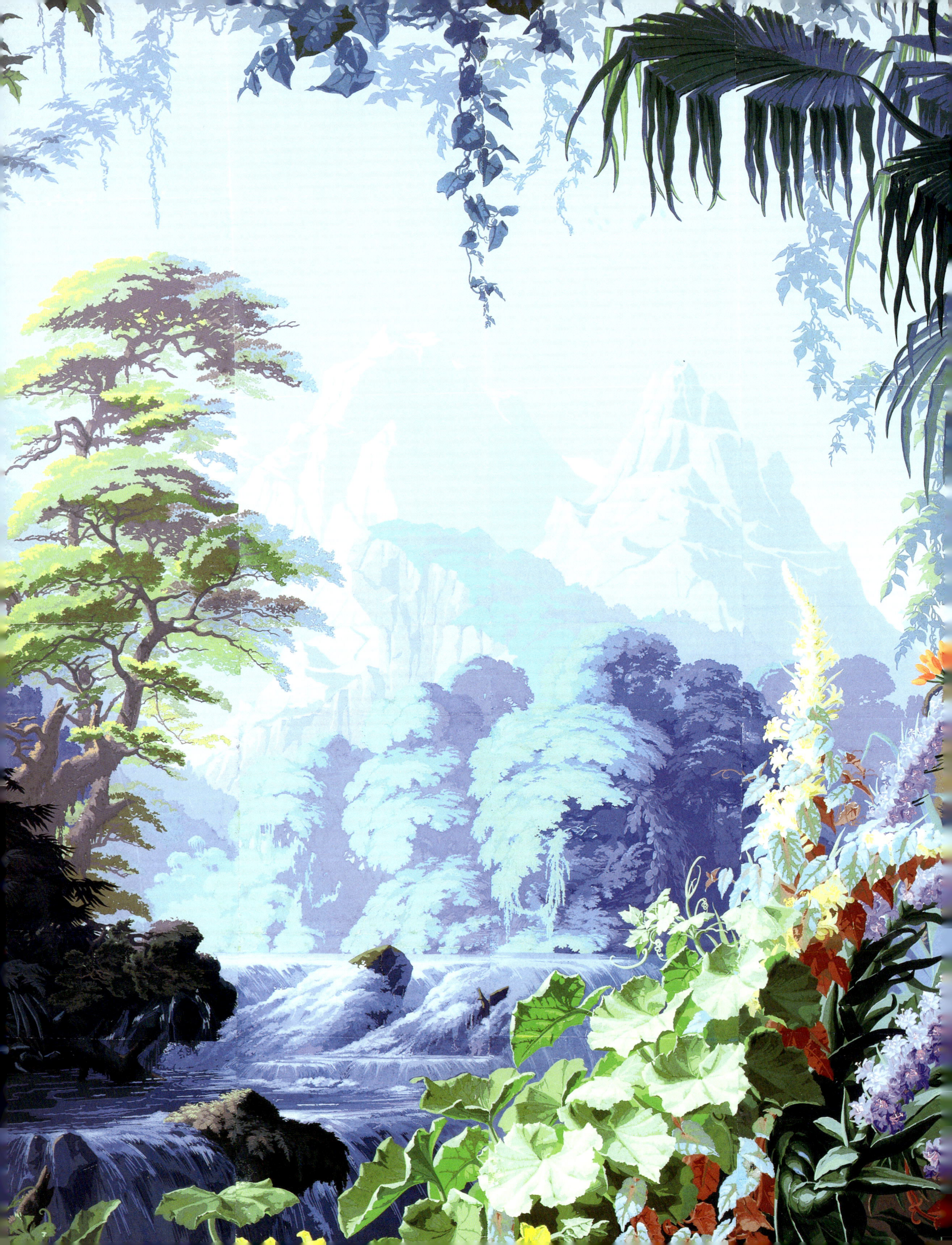

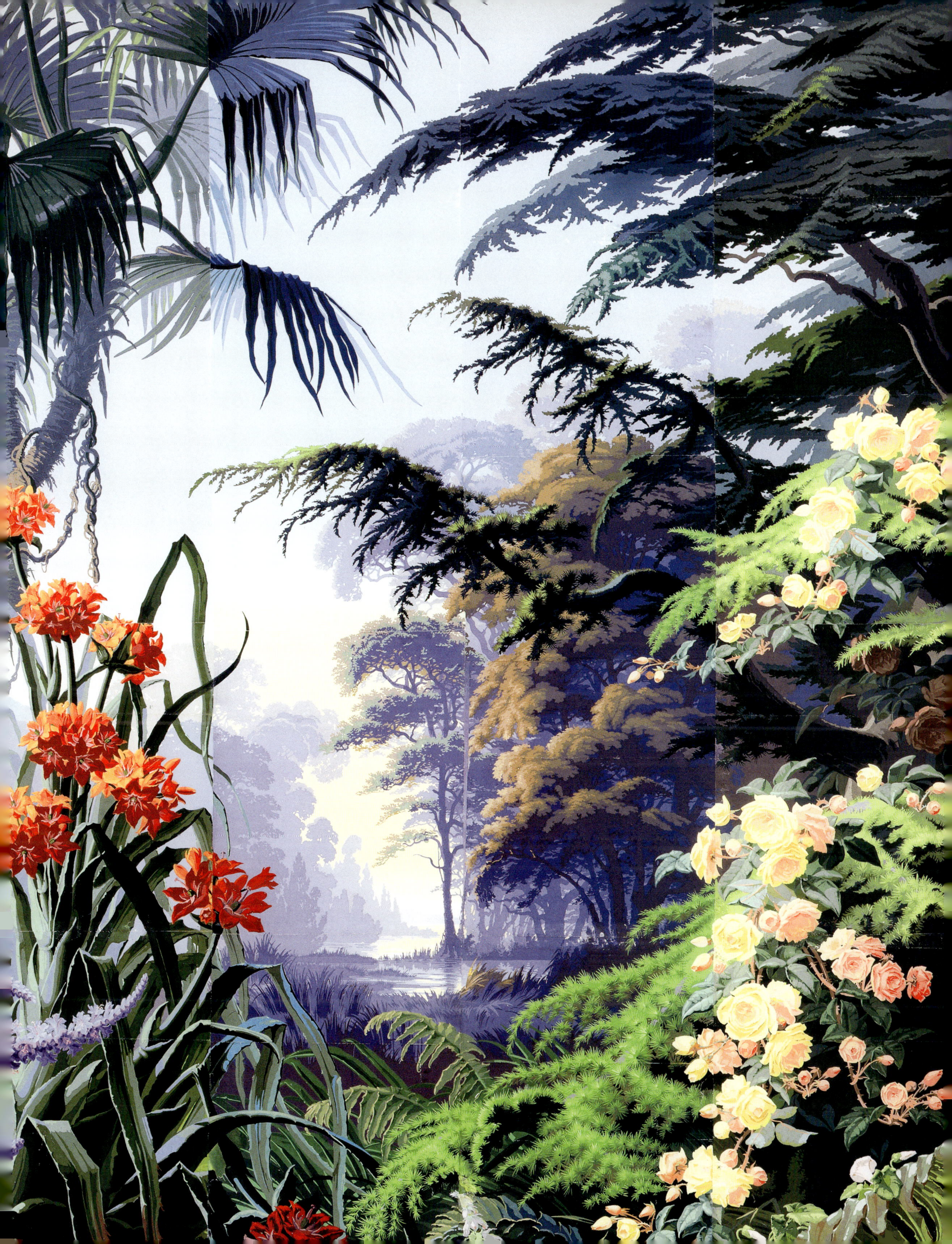

Corner cabinet

French, Christofle factory, 1878
Design: Emile Reiber (born 1826)
Ebony, rosewood, ebonized pear wood, electroplated gilt and patinated bronze, copper, silver, gold, cloisonné enamel.
H. 76¾ in. (195 cm), W. 37⅜ in. (95 cm), D. 24¾ in. (63 cm)
Gift of André and Tony Bouilhet, in memory of Henri Bouilhet, 1930

This strange piece of furniture was created as an example of goldsmithswork. The Christofle factory, which specialized in silver and gold and pioneered the use of electroplating, also manufactured a small number of spectacular pieces of furniture on an unheard-of level of luxury for exhibition at world's fairs. The aim was to show that the various electroplating techniques could be extended to furniture, giving it the brightest of colors, which could not be obtained with traditional wood marquetry.

Christofle chose to create a corner cabinet for the 1878 Paris World's Fair to play off an 18th-century furniture form that so successfully solved the problem of decorating the corners of drawing rooms. As was often the case with items made for world's fairs, Christofle's corner cabinet became something of an encyclopedic demonstration piece. To the traditional format was added a Far Eastern theme, very much in vogue at that time, and a broad range of electroplating techniques. The geisha decoration on the door was created with deposits of gold and silver painstakingly electroplated on the convex surface of a chased bronze panel; the bordering plaques with little flowers were made of cloisonné enamel using electroplated inlays. The framing of black wood enhanced the impact of the colors of the décor.

Emile Reiber, nicknamed "the high priest of Japonisme," had been fascinated by the items Japan sent for the first world's fair in 1867. He subsequently specialized in making gold and silver objects and small tables of cloisonné enamel. He discovered that electroplating techniques made it possible to obtain industrially the same effects achieved by the master craftsmen of Asia. —O.N.

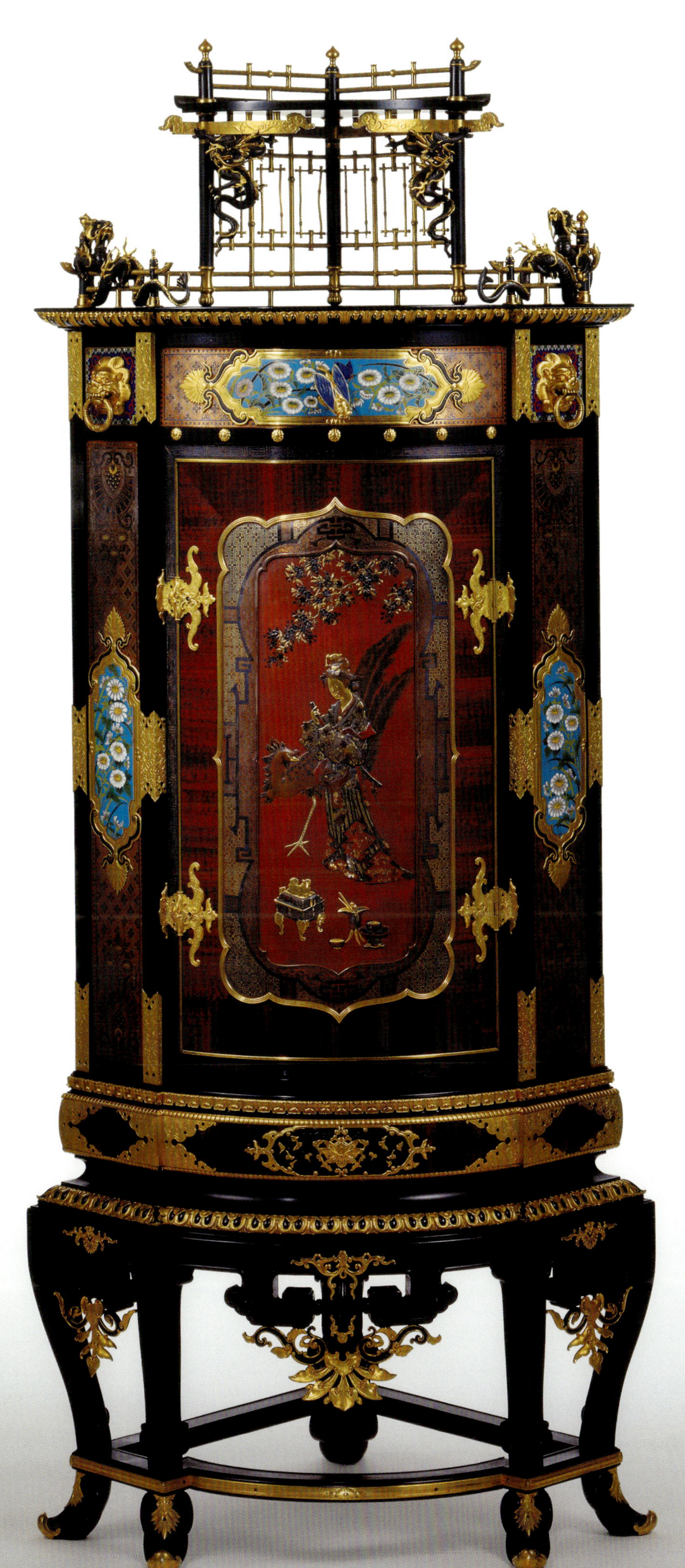

Sphinx chatelaine and watch

French, 1878
Alphonse Fouquet (1828–1911)
Chased gold. H. 5 in. (12.7 cm)
Gift of Alphonse Fouquet, 1908

A chatelaine is a short chain attached to a belt from which the wearer can hang a watch and its key and small personal items, such as a small flask for smelling salts, a pair of scissors, or a seal. Worn by a man or a woman, this piece of jewelry would be engraved with a coat of arms to display social rank.

This example is fashioned as a sphinx seated in profile upholding a chain to which a pocket watch is attached. The goldsmith endowed it with an aura of mystery by invoking the Greek myth of Oedipus and the sphinx, a subject then favored by Symbolist painters, especially Gustave Moreau. (The sphinx, with its lion's body, bird's wings, and woman's face and bust, assailed all passersby with riddles and devoured those unable to answer. Oedipus had all the answers, and so silenced the sphinx.) In the chatelaine, the sphinx seems to be posing the riddle of time's passing.

Alphonse Fouquet was awarded a gold medal when he exhibited this chatelaine at the 1878 Paris World's Fair. Starting as an apprentice, he worked his way up through the ranks to head one of the leading jewelry establishments in Paris, producing goldsmithswork marked by the outstanding quality of its chasing. While Egypt, Greece, and the Renaissance served as inspiration for the jewelry he exhibited in 1878, Fouquet's predilection was for fantastic creatures, such as chimeras, doing battle with serpents, griffins, and animals with women's bodies. —E.P.

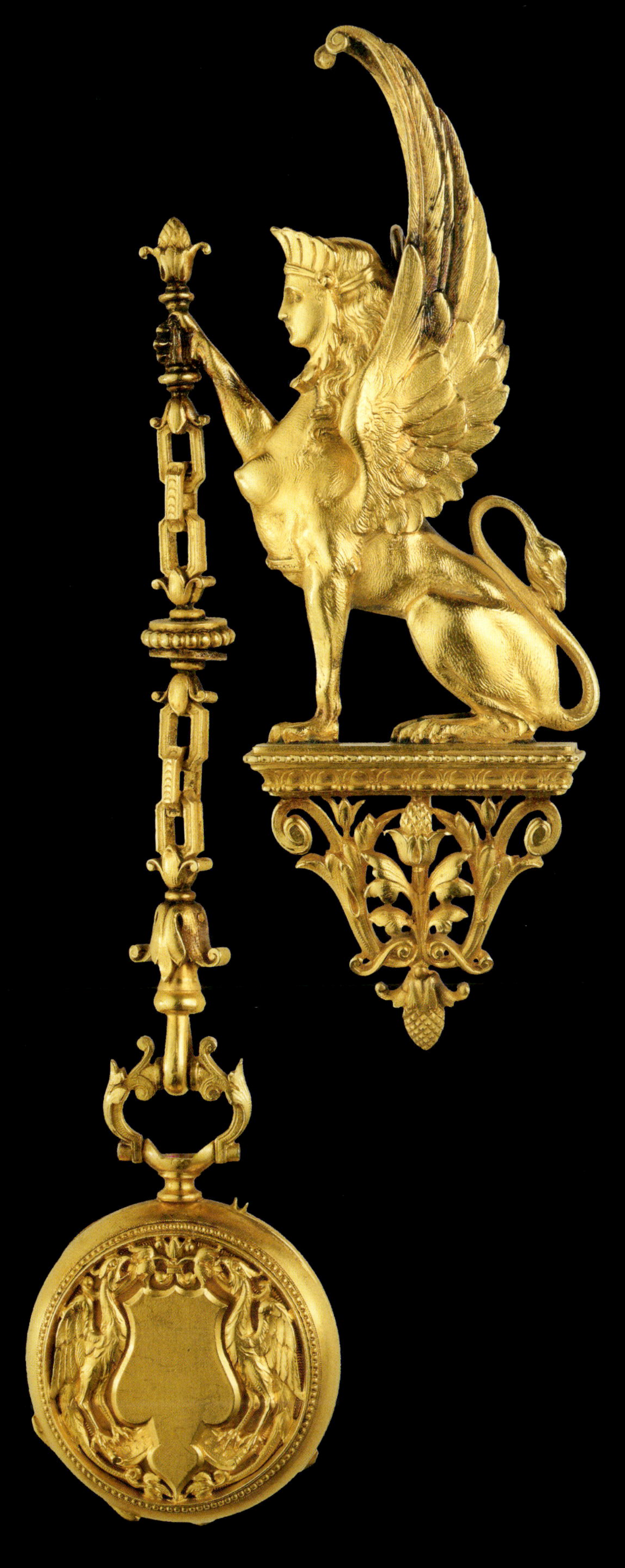

Bed of Emilie Valtesse de La Bigne

French, circa 1875
Edouard Lièvre (1829–1886)
Varnished bronze. H. 161⅜ in. (410 cm),
L. 102⅜ in. (260 cm), W. 78¾ in. (200 cm)
Emilie Valtesse de La Bigne bequest, 1911

This gigantic bed was made for Emilie Valtesse de La Bigne, one of the most prominent courtesans in Paris in the late 19th century. It conforms to the tradition of the *lit de parade,* or ceremonial bed, facilitating a custom of distinguished persons receiving visitors in the bedchamber which dates back to the Middle Ages. In the 17th century, Louis XIV drew up a very precise ritual for his awakening and bedtime ceremonies at Versailles. To impress visitors, ceremonial beds from then on were raised on a dais and separated from the rest of the room by a balustrade.

In Valtesse's bedchamber, the concept of the balustrade was treated quite differently. Here it was incorporated as part of the bed itself, wrapping around the foot and sides, with two flaming lamps, symbols of ardent passions, at the corners as boundary markers of the territory of licentious lovemaking.

On the headboard, two small cupids, naked and chubby, hold a coat of arms bearing the letter *V,* surmounted by a crown indicating the nobility of the courtesan (a misrepresentation, since she had simply appropriated the name of an old aristocratic family). A rectangular canopy amplifies the monumentality of the ensemble.

Valtesse was especially fond of the motif of the faun, which she called "the clever little god." Masks of grimacing fauns watch with sardonic smiles from atop the baldachin, and their fantastic profiles recur on either side of the coat of arms. At the foot of the bed they mischievously hold the flaming lamps of the balustrade.

Ceremonial beds were traditionally made of sumptuously gilt wood, while brass and iron beds, which appeared in the late 18th century, were developed during Napoleon's military campaigns. In the mid-19th century, they were manufactured industrially at low cost. Valtesse's architect, Edouard Lièvre, combined two traditions: he chose bronze, which could be varnished to approximate the brilliance of gold and was stronger than wood in providing the structural support required for his monumental design.

The writer Emile Zola used this bedchamber as the basis for his description of the bedroom of Nana, the courtesan heroine of his most scandalous novel.

Valtesse amassed a large collection of art objects but decided to bequeath just the most celebrated of them—her bed—to the Musée des Arts Décoratifs. —O.N.

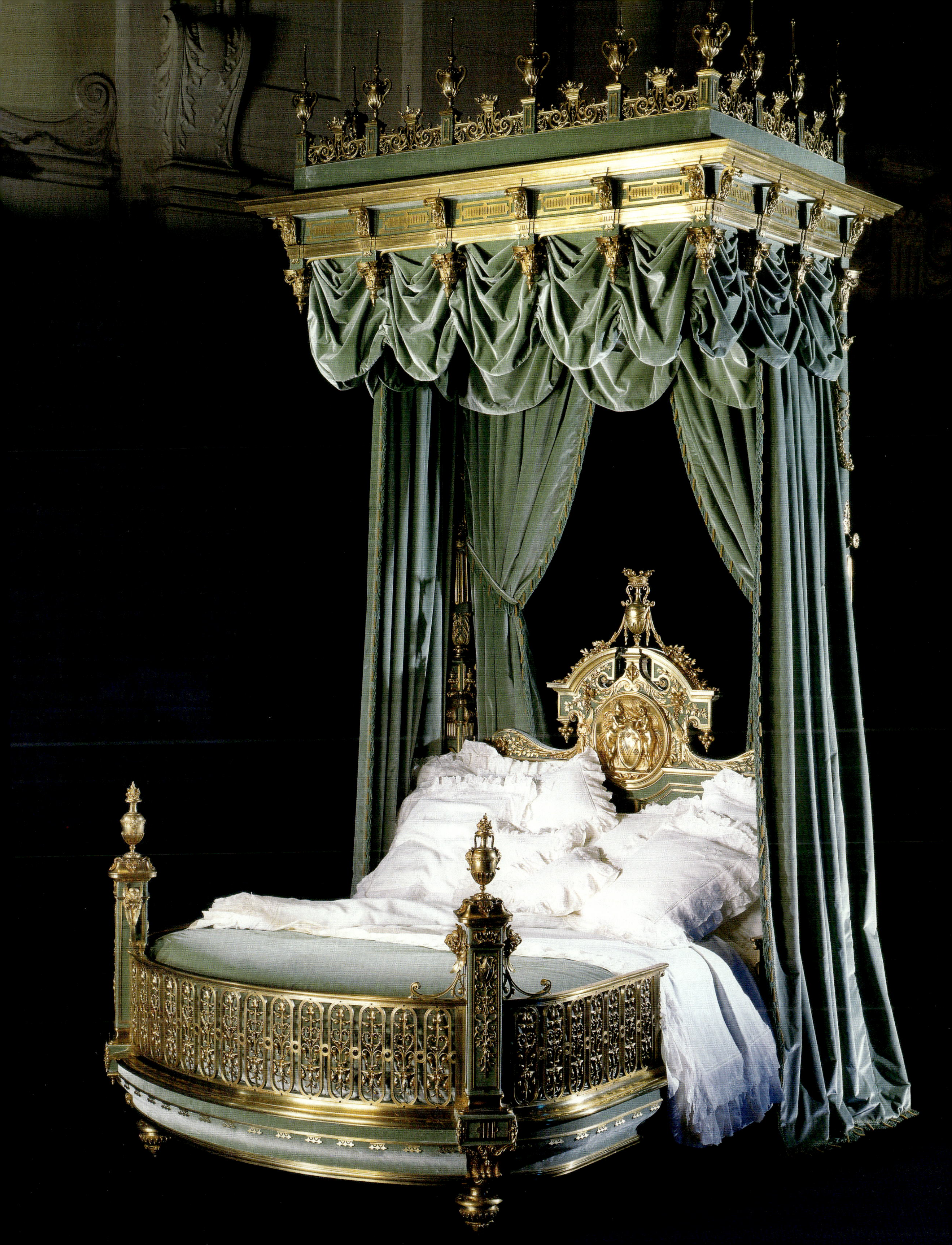

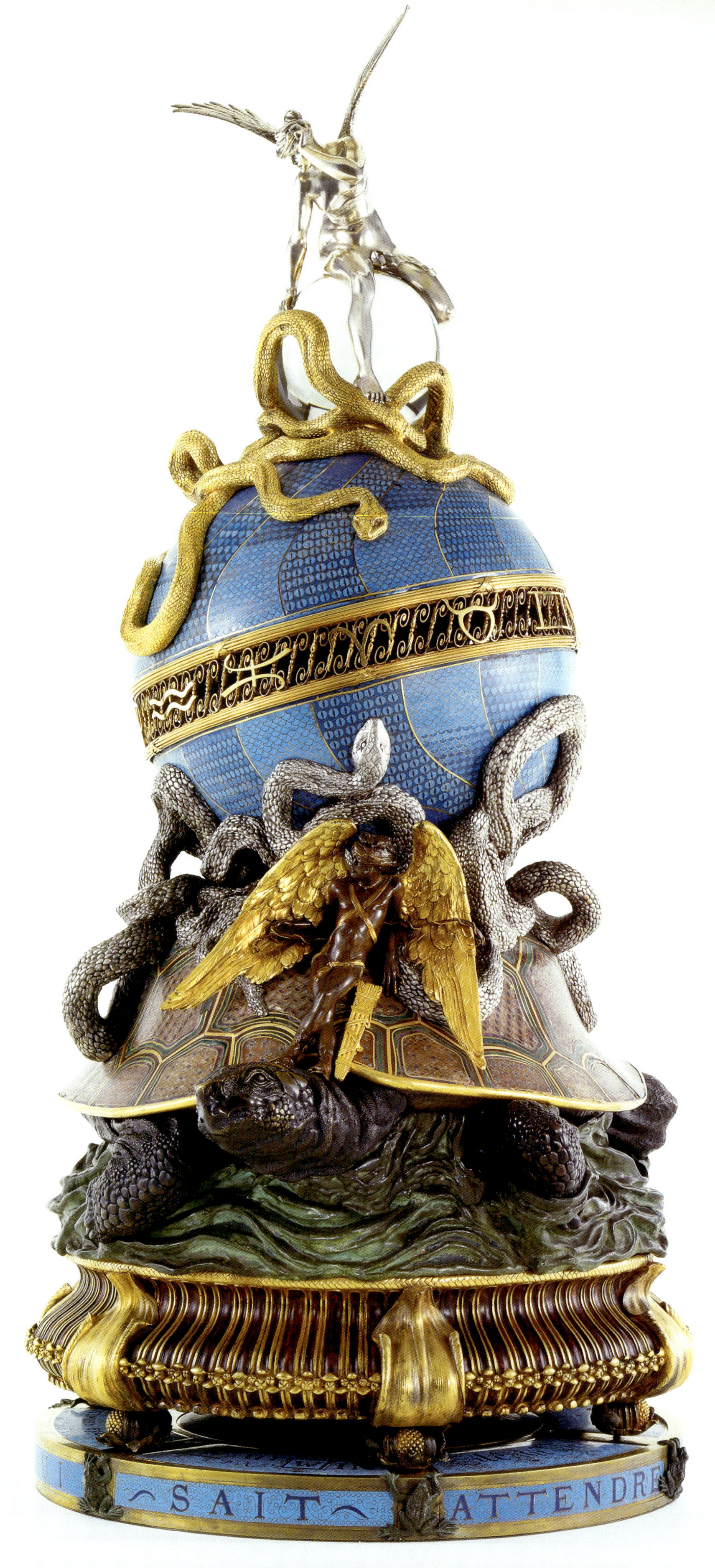
SAIT ATTENDRE

FORTUNE (MODEL FOR A MONUMENT)

French, 1878–1882
James Tissot (1836–1902)
Silver-plated bronze, silver, cloisonné enamel, walnut, glass.
H. 53⅛ in. (135 cm)
Gift of Albert Bichet, 1908

The English painter James Tissot designed this eclectic object at a time when he was planning to produce mystical cycles depicting major moral issues. This monumental project encompasses ancient, biblical, Buddhist, and Chinese myths in an astounding cosmogonic vision of Good and Evil.

The tortoise, a cosmic symbol, holds the World on its shell as it swims in primordial waters, in which it regenerates and stabilizes the World. Tissot made the tortoise the symbol of Patience, root of all success. The World is represented by a blue sphere, around which are placed the signs of the zodiac, which symbolize Time flying. It is inhabited by three figures that express human passions: Fortune, naked and winged, is sitting on the soothsayer's crystal ball, lifting the blindfold covering her eyes. Love/Compassion, a youth leaning against the tortoise's shell, has also removed his blindfold and has laid down his weapons. Lastly, Ambition/Selfishness, a young woman who, like Hercules, has donned the Nemean lion's skin, clambers upon the heavens. Three serpents grip the World and the crystal ball in their coils. A lotus blossom containing the primordial waters is supported by six open pomegranates, fruit of hell, which condemned Persephone to return to Hades once she had consumed its seeds there. The motto "Tout vient à point pour qui sait attendre" (Everything comes to those who wait) runs around the base. A radiating solar disc is hidden under the tortoise. It centers on a laurel-wreathed skull representing Fortune/Victory, encircled by the inscription "Wait & Win," which is punctuated by yin and yang symbols.

Tissot's rapture is fueled by myths that he has inextricably bound together. Among them, pride of place goes to the serpent. Love resembles Fortune in their mutual refusal to accept blindness, and the two reptiles associated with them crawl toward each other. Solitary, all-consuming Ambition, her head in the lion's mouth, slithers belly down along the ground in the direction of the third reptile toward a narcissistic encounter that would be lethal were she not protected from all onslaughts by the Nemean lion's skin. Like the tortoise, the serpent is at once male and female, Good and Evil, life and death. It assures the fragile balance of Fortune, who might take wing at any moment should the unpredictable movements of animals and human passions cause the World to crumble.

At the end of the 19th century, an era steeped in esoteric theories meant to be understood by only a privileged few, Tissot and his circle felt themselves part of a decadent world, in which only a return to origins could provide regeneration.

—O.N.

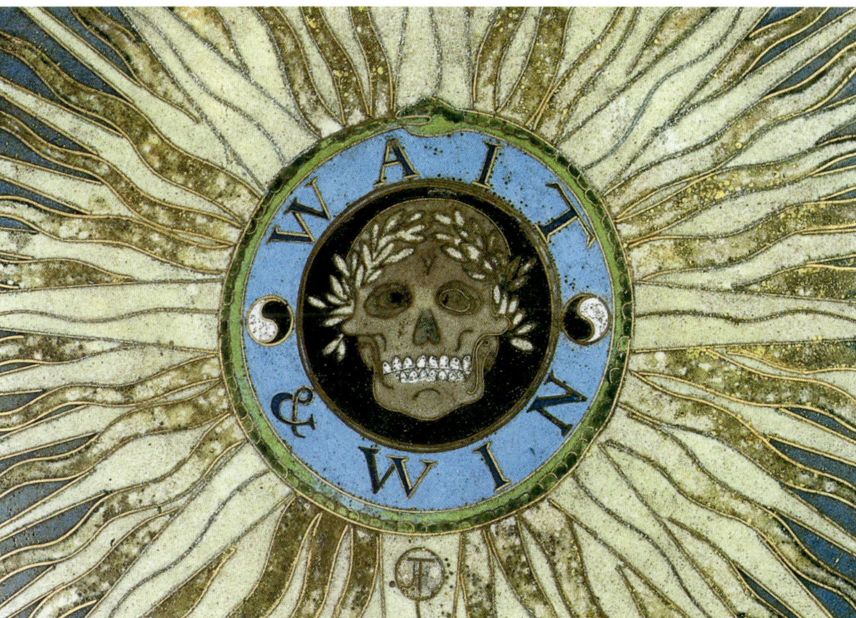

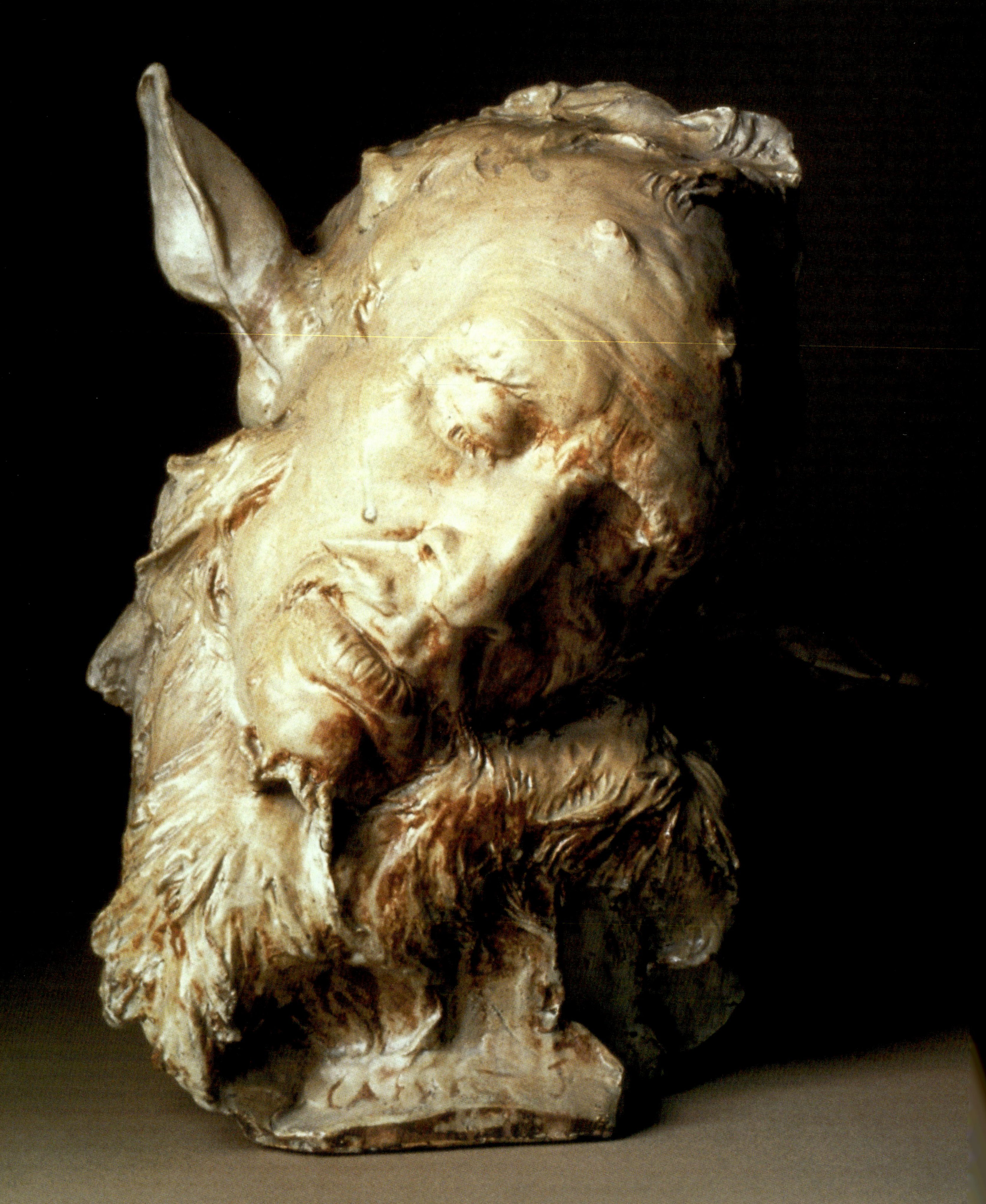

Head of a Faun

French, 1890–1891
Jean-Joseph-Marie Carriès (1855–1894)
Glazed stoneware. H. 12 in. (30.5 cm)
Gift of Eugène Soubiran, 1939

The sculptor Jean-Joseph-Marie Carriès belonged to the generation of Symbolist artists that portrayed a spiritual vision of the world in which the themes of death, evil, and decadence were central. To begin with, Carriès produced statuary and was little known among his contemporaries. At the 1878 Paris World's Fair, he was intrigued by the Japanese pottery and glazes on view and, without abandoning sculpture, oriented his work toward ceramics. In 1888 he decided to move to Saint-Amand-en-Puisaye, a traditional village of potters, in order to work in stoneware. His *Head of a Faun* is one of the earliest pieces he made there.

The Romans regarded Faunus—half-man, half-goat—as a rustic deity who protected Nature and nurtured fertility. Though reckoned to be benevolent, Faunus was nevertheless feared for his unpredictable onslaughts and his terrifying prophetic pronouncements delivered by night in the woods. He was depicted with horns on his forehead, large mobile ears, and goat's feet.

Here Carriès offers an unusual version of the faun. His head is bowed, his eyes closed, and he is caught napping, as it were, in a state of relaxation, possibly slumber, possibly contemplation, possibly due to some kind of suffering. His ears, forming a thrusting diagonal, seem to quiver at the slightest sound. They call to mind the bestial nature of the deity, as do the waves of his profuse hair, sketched with a savage, nervous energy. By contrast, the refined and sensitive face captures the impalpable split second when sadness is overtaken by a feeling of calm. On the wrinkled, almost worried brow there is just a hint of horns, as if this symbol of virile strength had given way under the pressure of an accepted renunciation. Though it comes from the hairline, the drop of glaze Carriès allows to slip down the cheek suggests a tear, full of humanity.

Carriès probably attached special importance to this *Head of a Faun,* for he first made it in wax in 1888 (his first year in Saint-Amand-en-Puisaye) and then in bronze, before producing this more sensitive version in stoneware with enamel glazes. —O.N.

Les Métiers d'Art (The Crafts of Art) Covered Cup

French, 1895
Goldsmithswork: Lucien Falize (1839–1897)
Gold, enamel. H. 8¾ in. (22.3 cm), Diam. 3½ in. (8.9 cm)
Purchased from Lucien Falize, 1896

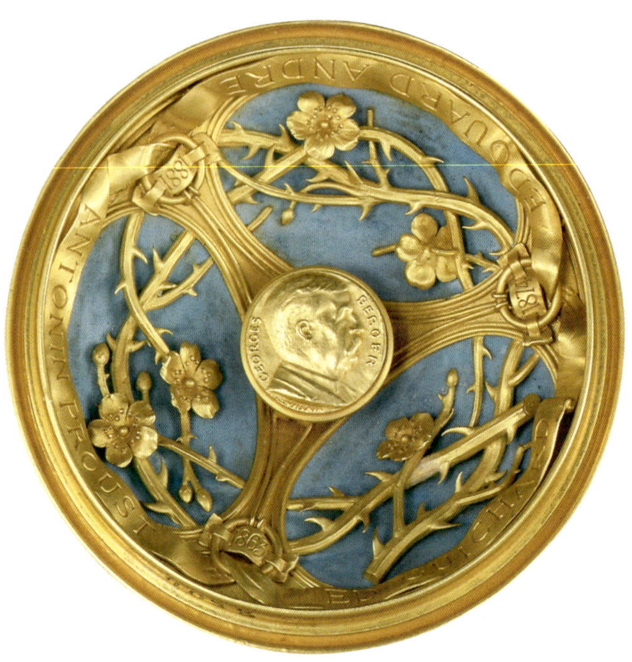

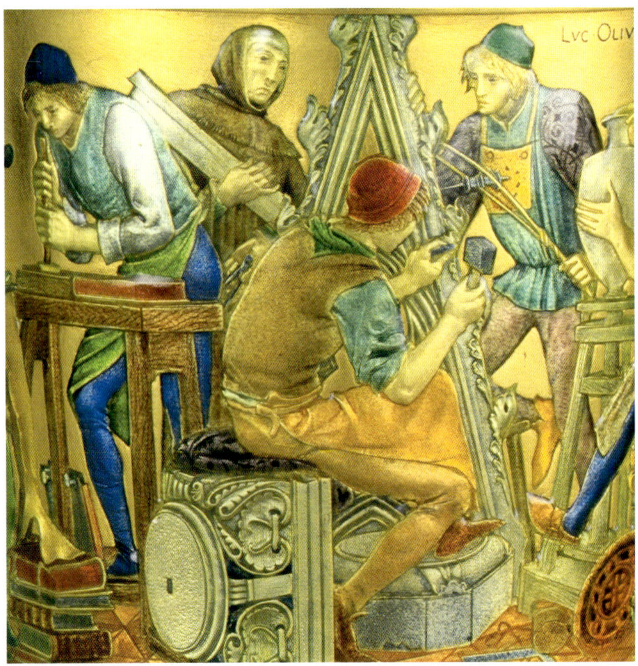

This work was the symbol of the goal established in 1864 by the Union Centrale des Arts Décoratifs. The UCAD members, who had chosen "le Beau dans l'Utile" (Beauty in utility) as their motto, dedicated themselves to promoting the decorative arts by founding a comprehensive library, presenting temporary exhibitions devoted to different media, such as fabric, paper, wood, stone, glass, and metal, and organizing competitions for craftsmen and art-school students. In 1895 the UCAD Committee asked Lucien Falize, one of the most admired goldsmiths at the 1889 Paris World's Fair, to make an enameled work of art for the Musée des Arts Décoratifs, giving him free rein in the choice of form and theme.

Falize decided to make a golden goblet for ceremonial use by the association's chairman in the tradition of the medieval guilds. This inspired the two principal ideas for the decoration: the grapevine and arts and crafts. Two-thirds of the way up the body of the tumbler, an enamel frieze (detail, bottom left), designed by the painter Luc Olivier Merson, shows Renaissance craftsmen working stone, wood, clay, metal, glass, fabric, paper, and leather. Below, interlaced grapevine branches stand out in relief against the red champlevé enamel ground. On the underside of the cup, the goldsmith and his engraver are depicted in Renaissance costume. The lid is decorated with the emblem of the Union Centrale des Arts Décoratifs, an oak branch surrounded by a laurel crown, and cartels defining the UCAD's program: Art, Science, and Craft. Inside the lid the names of the society's presidents are inscribed around a portrait medallion of then-president, Georges Berger.

Like the true virtuoso he was, Falize turned his work into a demonstration of the most sophisticated enameling techniques: champlevé enamel (enamel fills engraved part of design); cloisonné enamel (enamel fills wire-enclosed areas), which he used from 1869 on; and bassetaille enamel (translucent enamel covers engraved designs of varying depth), which had not been used since the late 15th century but which he had rediscovered. To accomplish this amazing and outstanding technical feat, Falize fired the piece forty times.

This cup is historicizing in character because it was conceived by Falize as a tribute both to his illustrious predecessors and to the historic collections assembled by the Musée des Arts Décoratifs. But most of the great goldsmith's works show him to have been a precursor to Art Nouveau. —E.P.

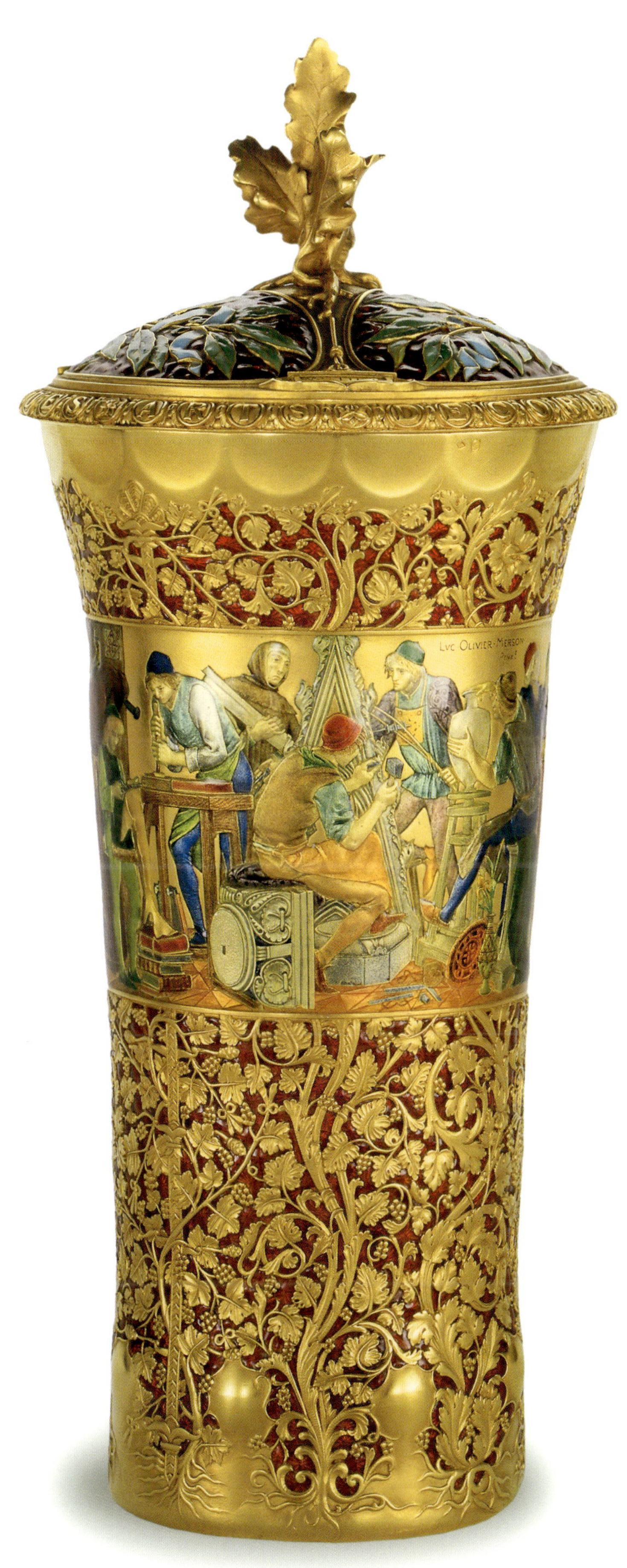
LVC OLIVIER-MERSON

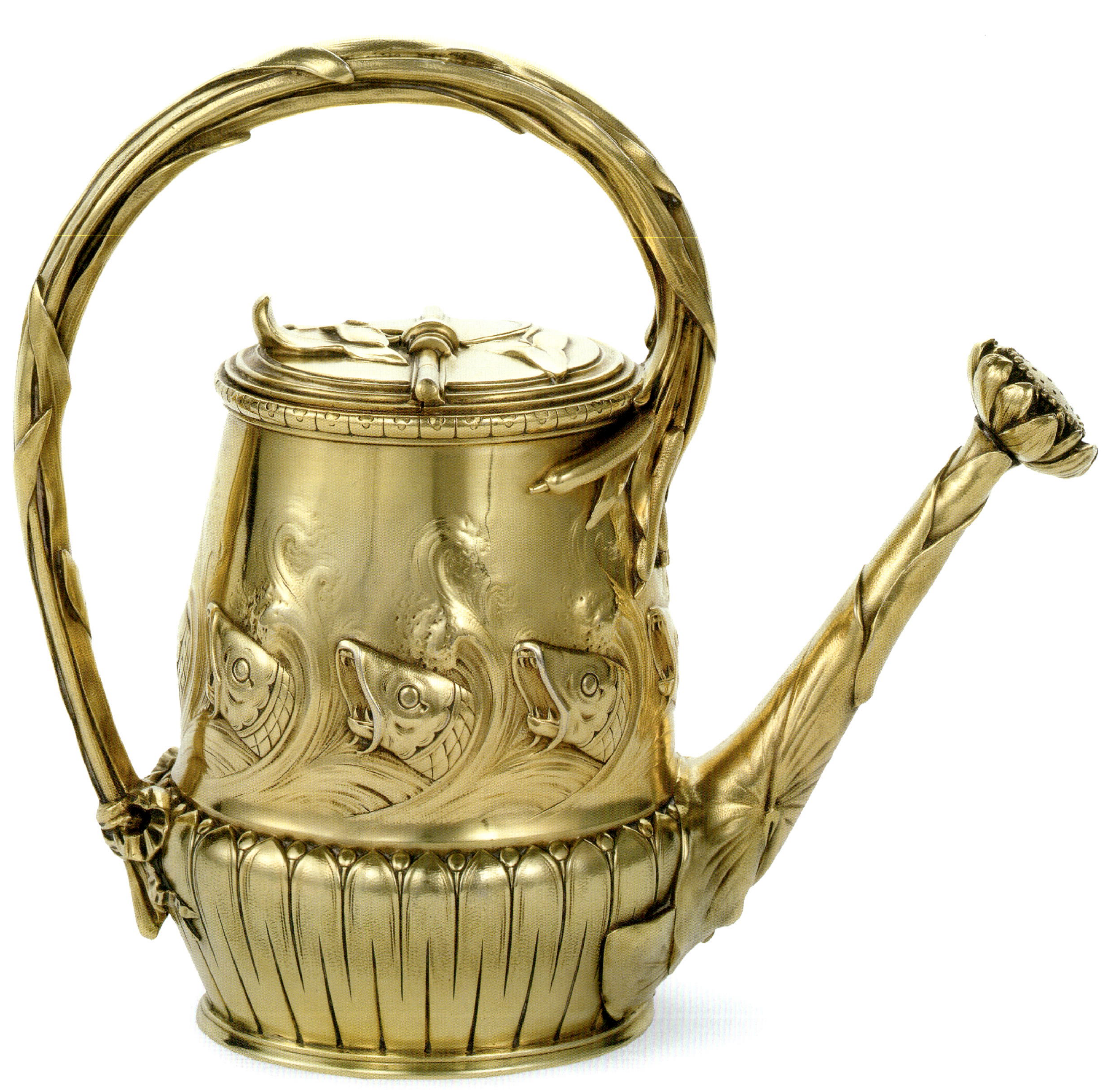

Watering can

French, Boucheron, circa 1896
Design: Lucien Hirtz (1864–1928)
Silver gilt. H. 7½ in. (19 cm)
Purchased from F. Boucheron, 1895

In tandem with its work in gold, silver, and gems, the famous house of Boucheron also made modern silverware, employing renowned craftsmen. From 1893 on, Lucien Hirtz, formerly assistant to the goldsmith Alexis Falize (founder of the Falize firm and father of Lucien Falize), and a gifted enamelist, became Boucheron's designer and foreman. He remained with Boucheron for thirty years, during which time he designed a large number of objets d'art: vases, cups, clocks, and jewelry items. His work drew mainly from the world of nature in the Japanese manner and played on flowing lines and the theme of the flower-woman.

On this watering can the décor is aquatic, as befits the object's function. The handle is decorated with reeds, while the bottom of the can is shaped like water-lily leaves and the spout like a water-lily flower. A chased frieze of carp's heads breaking through ripples decorates the body of the can. With little room left for flat surfaces, Hirtz made the motifs stand out by bold chasing.

Borrowings from different periods and cultures are mingled to make an original piece: the reeds are depicted in a naturalistic way, like 18th-century examples, and the carp are taken directly from Japanese motifs. The harmonious combination of patterns and forms is regarded as one of the aesthetic successes of Art Nouveau. —H.A.

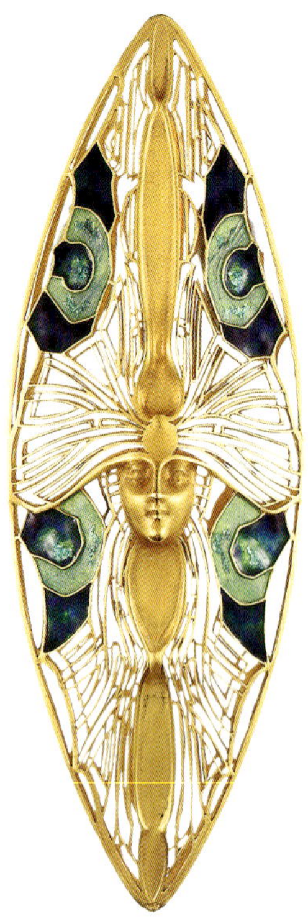

Shuttle

French, 1900
René Lalique (1860–1945)
Gold, gemstones, enamel.
H. 3¾ in. (9.6 cm)
Jean-Jacques Reubell bequest, 1933

The tool known as a "shuttle" is designed here as a luxurious and sophisticated thread-carrying device to be used by high-society ladies for their minor needlework tasks. Repeating the traditional lozenge form, this shuttle has a woman's face on each side surrounded by her flowing hair executed in gold openwork, along with four peacock plume motifs in colored enamel. On one side of the shuttle the woman's eyes are open while on the other side they are closed, symbolizing day and night.

The decoration of the shuttle alludes to the story of Penelope, faithful wife of Ulysses, as told by Homer in *The Odyssey.* Besieged by suitors eager to marry her and assume the throne, Penelope promised to make her selection when she finished her large weaving. But the queen's task was never done; by night she would undo what she had woven during the day.

The decoration chosen by René Lalique perfectly accords with the function of this piece of jewelry, showing us that the culture of classical antiquity continued in Art Nouveau. —E.P.

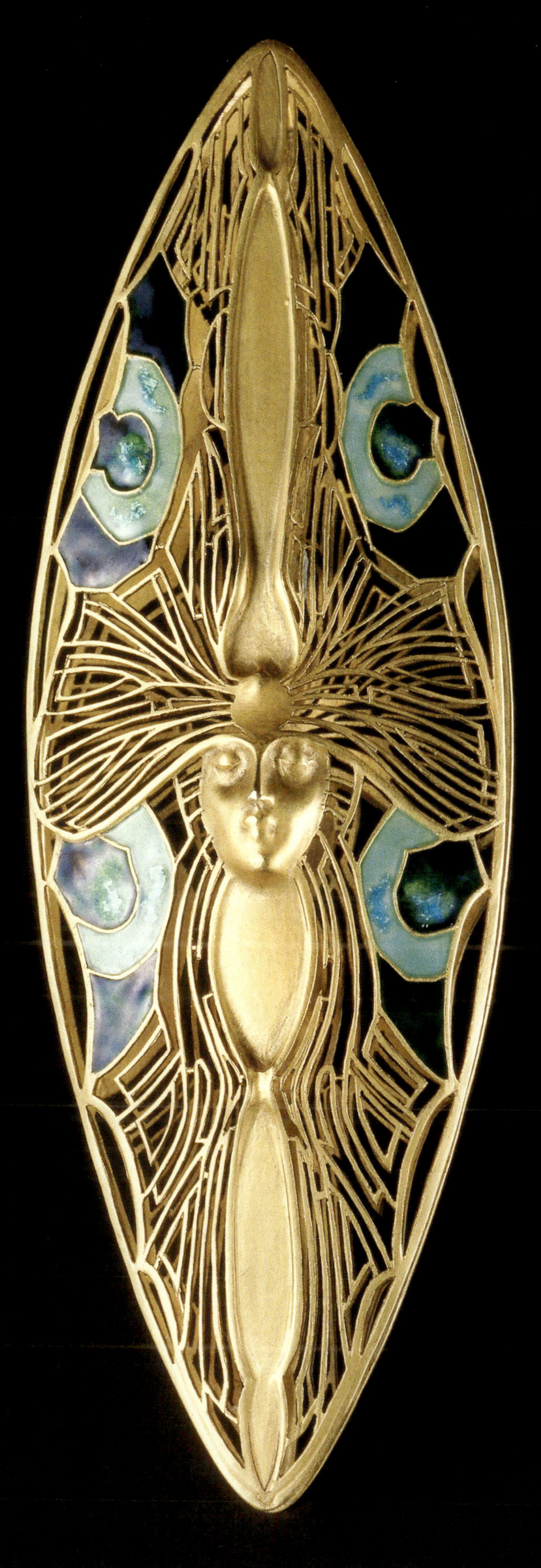

Mermaid Tiara

French, circa 1900
René Lalique (1860–1945)
Bronze, gold, opals, translucent enamel.
H. 3⅞ in. (9.7 cm)
Gift of Comte de Ganay, in memory of
Comtesse de Béhague, 1939

This tiara depicts a mermaid holding high a fire opal, or girasole. Her forked tail spreads left and right, clasping at each end an opal medallion with fish carvings. Placed on the wearer's temples, these carvings outline a kind of open helmet on the head. To the back, the mermaid's hair divides into three broad tresses, forming the teeth of a comb to secure the tiara in the woman's coiffure. The art of René Lalique is peopled with hybrid female figures, of which this mermaid is a mythic representation.

The metal, a green patinated bronze accented with gilding to disguise the welding joins, is a sculptor's material, rarely used in jewelry. Apparently Lalique used it three times in his work, but only the mermaid tiara seems to have survived.

This extraordinary piece of jewelry belonged to Martine de Béhague, comtesse de Béarn, a blue-blooded aristocrat and a great collector of art, from antiquities to Impressionist paintings. She was renowned for her taste, which was as wide-ranging as it was unerring. —E.P.

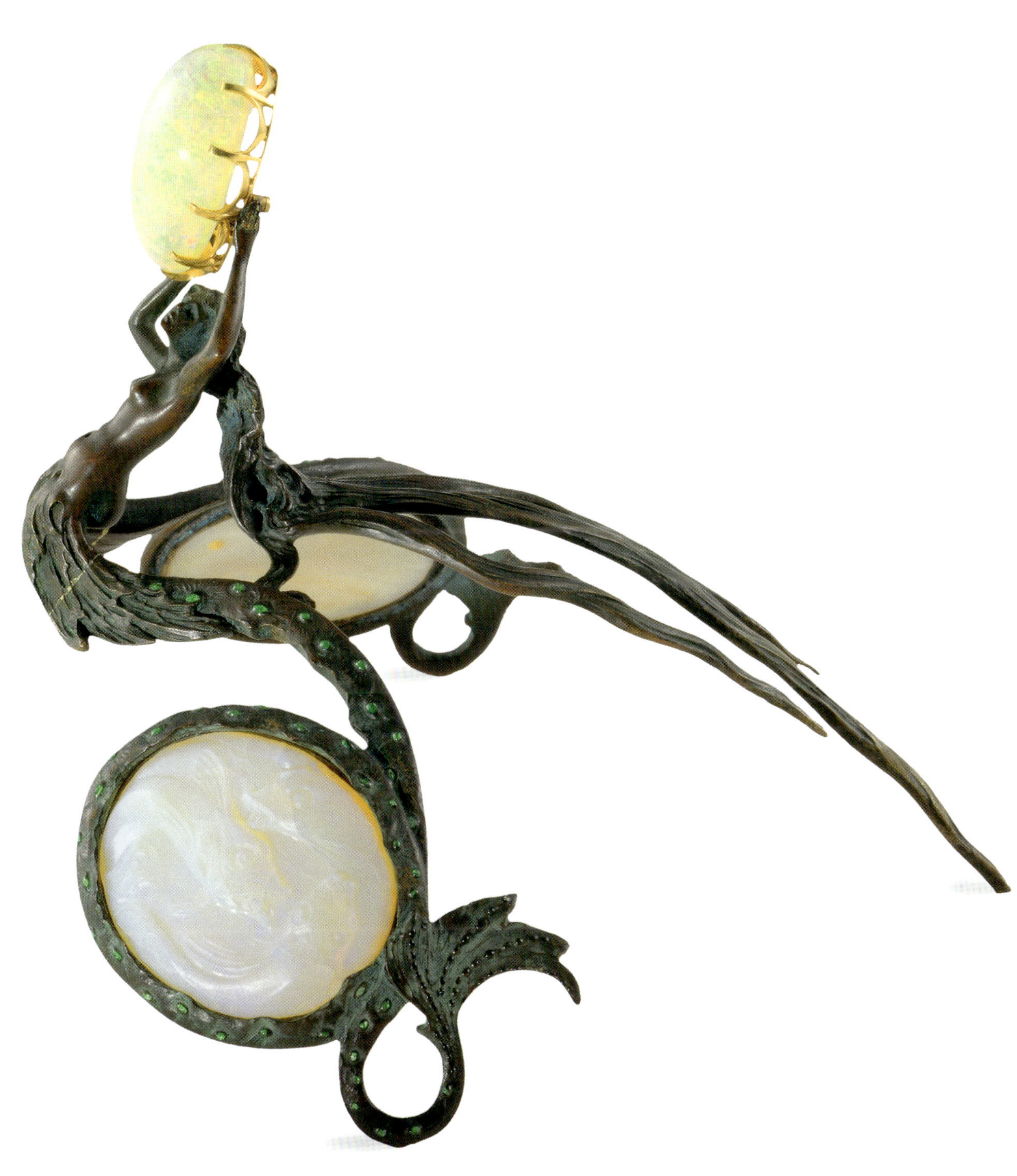

Fighting Roosters Pendant

French, 1901–1902
René Lalique (1860–1945)
Gold, cabochon-cut sapphire, rose-cut diamonds.
H. 2¾ in. (6.9 cm)
Gift of Mrs. Dreyfus-Barney, 1966

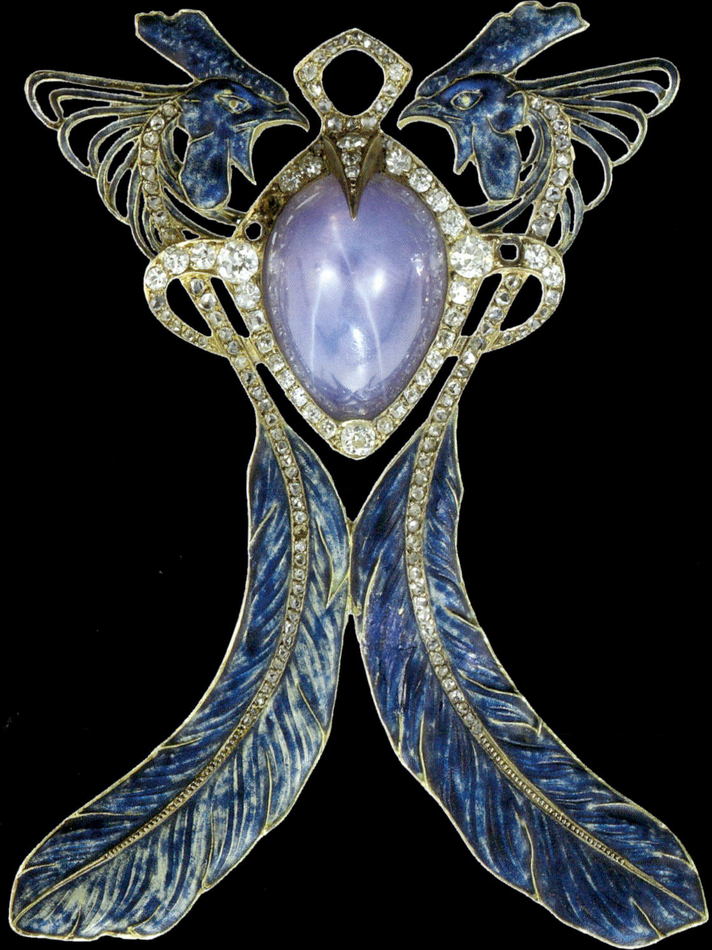

The theme of this cerulean-hued jewel, with its blue enamel and cabochon-cut star sapphire, is a cockfight. The subject is of Japanese origin and served as the décor on sword-guards, called *tsuba.* These *tsuba*—round pieces of metal with openings for the sword blade to pass through—were highly prized by Western collectors at the turn of the century, when the ornamental ingenuity of Japanese craftsmen was much appreciated.

French jewelers were fascinated by the formal and technical sophistication of these sword-guards and borrowed some of their motifs for jewelry. René Lalique chose the cockfight, an unusual theme in Western art. While Japanese craftsmen tended to depict the fight in a realistic way, with the two birds confronting each other, feathers ruffled, Lalique sets them back to back, craning to face each other in a very hieratic position.

This pendant belonged to an extremely wealthy young American, Natalie Clifford Barney, who discovered Lalique's art during her affair with Liane de Pougy, a courtesan. De Pougy offered her a ring with bat motifs, made of blue enamel and moonstone, engraved on the inside with the inscription "Tant me plaît que tu souffres de me comprendre et de m'aimer" (It pleases me so much that you put up with understanding me and loving me). Then it was the turn of the poetess Renée Vivien to cover her Barney with jewelry, which was invariably set with opals and sapphires and enameled blue—the color of Natalie's eyes. —E.P.

In this pendant, the woman's face is carved in purest white chalcedony and set in a pierced aureole of tresses of gold, from which a large Baroque pearl is suspended. Two opium poppies in blue enamel decorate the woman's hair and recur on the chain made of poppy seedpods, gold links, and Baroque pearls. Through his repeated use of Baroque pearls in pendants, René Lalique acknowledged his debt to Renaissance goldsmithswork, which, for him, represented the high point in the history of jewelry.

The women with flower-bedecked hair favored by Lalique became a popular motif in Art Nouveau jewelry. Like most of his contemporaries, Lalique perceived a strong link between Woman and Nature. The mythical figures in his landscapes bring a spiritual presence to the realm of plants. Be they flower-women or women hidden in trees, the dreamlike vision of these nymphs inhabiting Nature conjures up the existence of an alternative, emotion-filled world, where people can weave supernatural bonds with the earth's dark forces.

For the Symbolist movement, the opium poppy—a narcotic plant—evoked the idea of sleep and dreams. Lalique's women, often with opium poppies in their hair, are sometimes depicted with their eyes shut—sleeping, mysterious women, deep in a slumber through which they will achieve a dream state, source of imaginative creation. —E.P.

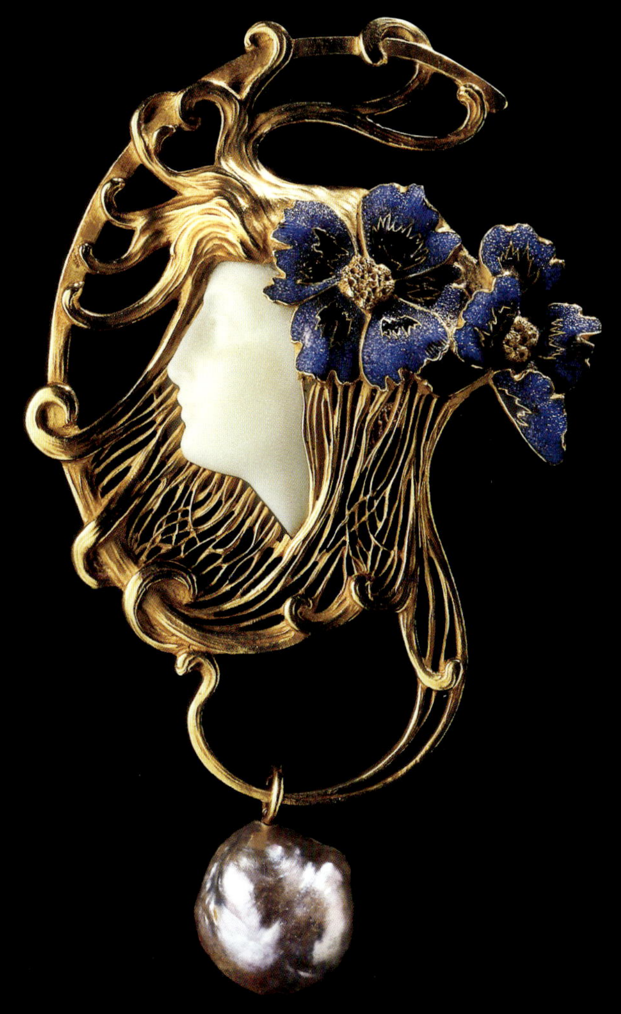

Woman with Opium Poppies Pendant and Chain

French, 1898–1899
René Lalique (1860–1945)
Gold, chalcedony, translucent enamel, opaque enamel, pearl. Pendant: H. 4 in. (10.2 cm); chain: L. 28⅛ in. (71.6 cm)
Gift of Baronne Félix Oppenheim, 1933

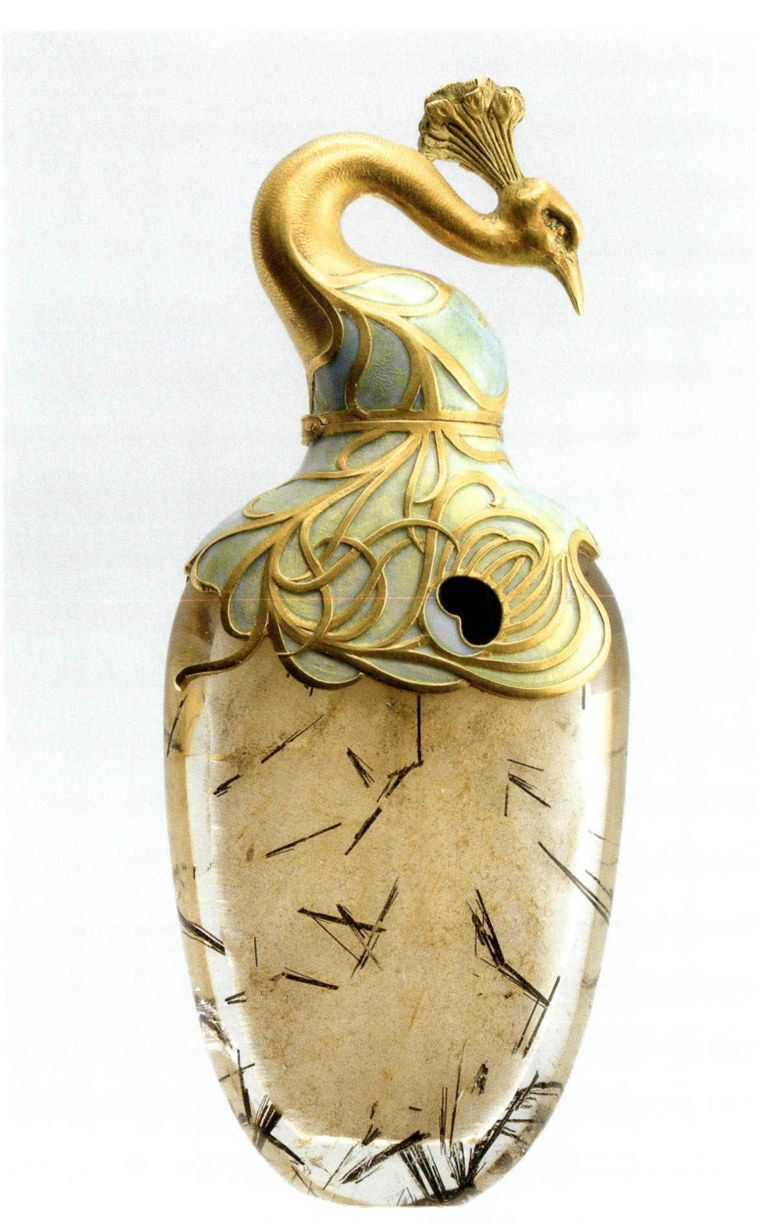

Peacock scent bottle

French, 1900
Paul Vever (1851–1915) and Henri Vever (1854–1942)
Enameled gold, quartz with tourmaline. H. 3¾ in. (9.5 cm)
Gift of the artists, 1924

In 1900 every lady in polite society carried a small bottle for scent and smelling salts on her person at all times. These little receptacles held the salts, bergamot vinegar, and balsamic eau de cologne intended to calm the nervous fits caused by the extreme sensitivity of their owners—who also wore their corsets far too tight.

The Vever brothers were scions of a family of jewelers and goldsmiths. The firm was established in Metz in 1821 by their grandfather Paul and was relocated in Paris by their father, Ernest, in 1871. Following the tradition of the trade, they apprenticed to their father and in 1881 took over the business. In 1897 they decided to follow the example of the innovative jeweler René Lalique, committing to a specialization in Art Nouveau jewelry. They were the first to introduce plique-à-jour to jewelry making. With this technique they captured the delicate colors of leaves and stalks, while using diamonds and other gemstones for buds and blossoming flowers.

Renowned for the extraordinary refinement of their works, the Vever brothers also made pieces of gold- and silverware such as table services, centerpieces, and sewing kits, as well as small convenience items much sought after by elegant ladies, such as boxes for pills or candy, jewelry cases, mirrors, and little bottles. Like Chinese opium holders, these bottles were often made of hard stone—jade, rock crystal, or agate—with an enameled gold mount forming the stopper.

Here, Vever gave the stopper the shape of a peacock's head and neck, its plumage spreading down over the shoulder of the bottle. The vessel itself is carved out of a quartz having inclusions of black tourmaline in slivers, known as "Cupid's arrows." By tradition, the peacock was associated with the goddess Juno, wife of Jupiter, regarded in antiquity as the patroness of married women and noted for her vanity. The peacock thereby became the symbol of vanity, luxury, and pride. —E.P.

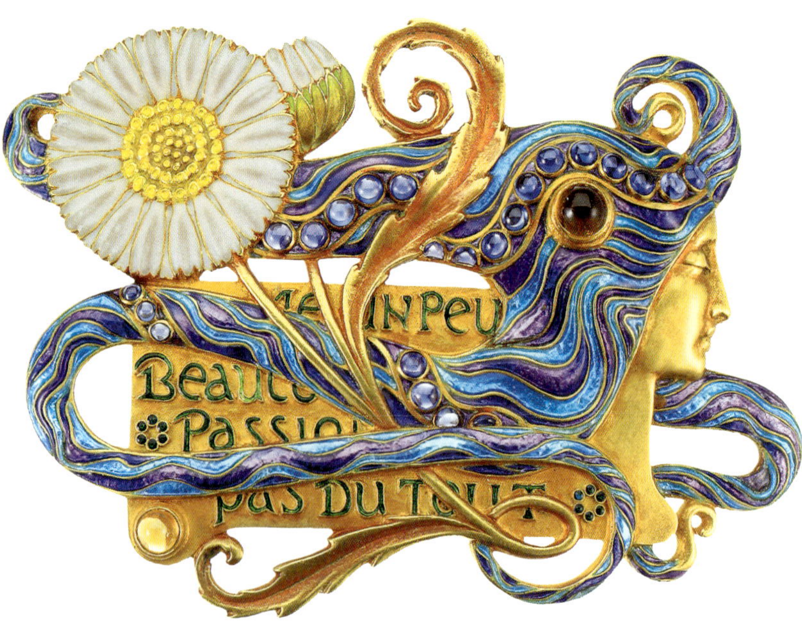

MARGUERITE BROOCH

FRENCH, 1900
PAUL VEVER (1851–1915) AND HENRI VEVER (1854–1942)
DESIGN: EUGÈNE GRASSET (1845–1917)
GOLD, ENAMEL, SAPPHIRES, TOPAZ.
H. 2½ IN. (6.5 CM), W. 3½ IN. (9 CM)
GIFT OF HENRI VEVER, 1924

The Marguerite, or Daisy, brooch has as its theme a popular French chant recited by lovers as they pluck the petals off a daisy: "Je t'aime un peu, beaucoup, passionément, pas du tout" (I love you a little, a lot, passionately, not at all)—a slightly more elaborate version of the English "She loves me, she loves me not." The game consists of seeing which degree of love tallies with the last petal plucked. The rectangular brooch depicts a woman's face in profile. Her long hair, embellished with a daisy, flows across the plaque, partly obscuring its text and making the well-known chant into something of a riddle. Turning away from Japanese influence, Grasset focused here on age-old French sources to derive a new, simple, and natural interpretation for this timeless incantation.

At the 1900 Paris World's Fair, the firm of Vever, along with René Lalique, carried off the top prizes in jewelry. In addition to producing a significant body of work to their own designs, the Vever brothers called on the talents of the Swiss painter and decorator Eugène Grasset. Grasset was a disciple of the architect Eugène Viollet-le-Duc and combined influences from Celtic and Irish art as well as his own study of Japanese art into a personal graphic style. He had illustrated an edition of the medieval epic *Les quatre fils Aymon* for H. Launette & Company, and in 1892 Vever asked him to design a deluxe binding for it. For the 1900 Paris World's Fair, Grasset designed some twenty pieces of jewelry for Vever: necklaces, brooches, and belt buckles, all in the same vein. In these pieces, often described as *barbares* (barbarian), Grasset depicted chimerical female figures, such as the one we see in this brooch. In realizing these designs in jewelry, Vever added to their primitive character by using opaque enamels in intense hues and studding the surface with colorful cabochon-cut gemstones. —E.P.

Owl comb

French, 1900
Paul Vever (1851–1915) and
Henri Vever (1854–1942)
Horn, translucent enamel, emeralds.
H. 6⅛ in. (15.5 cm)
Gift of Henri Vever, 1924

Since antiquity, the owl has symbolized night, while the rooster has represented day. This association of the nocturnal bird with night and dreams occurs in many cultures, including the two main sources of inspiration for Art Nouveau artists—the Japanese tradition and medieval art.

During most of the 19th century, tortoiseshell was the only material used for making accessories for the hair, like the combs used to keep fashionable hairstyles in place. At the turn of the century, thanks to the Japanese combs acquired by Parisian collectors, artists discovered the possibility of a broader range of materials—ivory, wood, lacquer, and horn, the latter having been used rarely in Europe up to this point. René Lalique was the first to be won over by this translucent material, which came from the most common of creatures but, when worked, could produce warm honey-colored hues with a lovely transparent quality or darker, more opaque shades. At that time there was no such thing as horn specially prepared for jewelers and sculptors, but they could buy it from Paris slaughterhouses. In 1897 Lalique exhibited a whole set of horn and ivory combs, which were tremendously popular, and his competitors followed suit. —E.P.

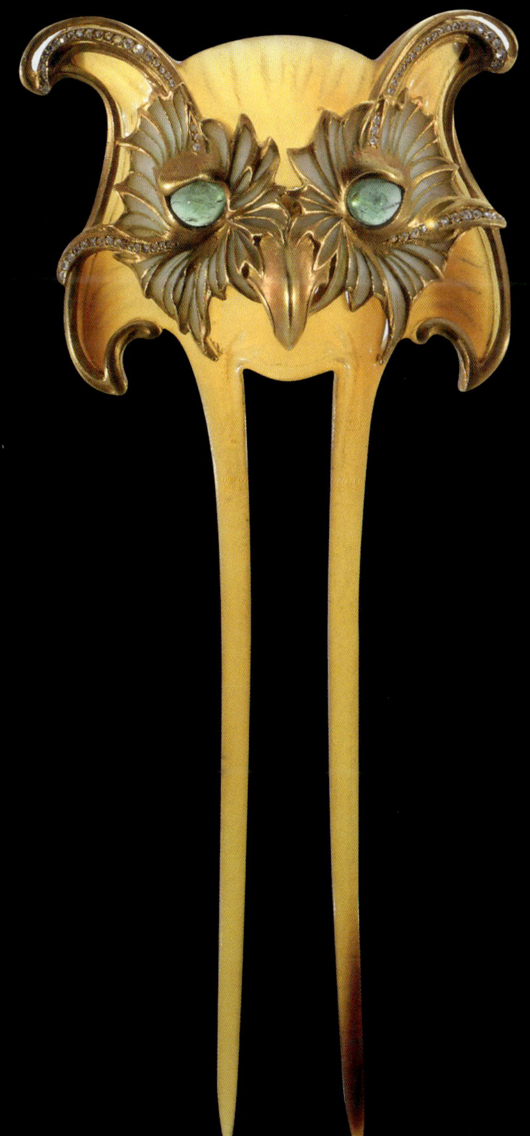

Daphnis and Chloe Comb

French, 1900
Paul Vever (1851–1915) and Henri Vever (1854–1942)
Ivory, pearls, gold. H. 7⅛ in. (18.2 cm)
Gift of Henri Vever, 1924

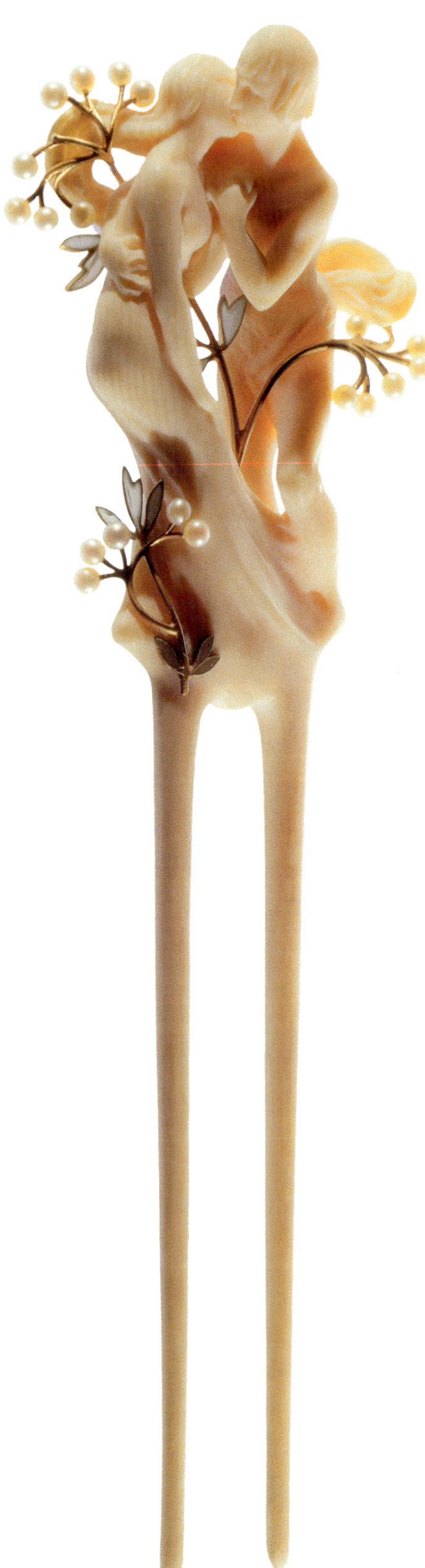

Henri Vever, a collector of ancient medals, drew inspiration for this piece from a pastoral novel by Longus (a Greek author of the early Christian period), which tells the tale of two children, Daphnis and Chloe, who were found and brought up by shepherds. As a teenager, Daphnis falls in love with Chloe. After many an adventure, the young pair are reunited with their respective parents and get married. This unusual theme was also used by Maurice Ravel for his symphony *Daphnis et Chloé,* which he composed between 1906 and 1911.

On this comb, the intertwined hero and heroine are carved in ivory, its whiteness set off by delicate gold leaves and sprays of pearls. When it came to rendering the subtle complexion of the human body, Art Nouveau jewelers favored working with carved ivory. To do so, they followed the example of René Lalique, who developed a new technique for working ivory in 1893. He adapted the scale lathe method used by medal engravers, having his plaster or wax models mathematically scaled down by the sculptor Janvier to the size needed for a piece of jewelry, while retaining all the preciseness of detail desired by the artist. In no time, the Janvier workshop was flooded with orders from jewelers, in particular the house of Vever, who used the scale lathe for both ivory and horn. —E.P.

The figure on this pendant is part woman, with head, arms, and bust carved out of translucent white carnelian and with a gown of yellow and black enamel. She is also part insect, with transparent wings of plique-à-jour (enamel with a metal frame and no backing, similar to stained glass).

Flora and fauna were favorite sources of inspiration for Art Nouveau. In the animal kingdom, insects such as dragonflies, butterflies, bees, bumblebees, wasps, and grasshoppers were especially popular. They were often depicted naturalistically in the manner of Japanese art, but they could also be associated with female representations in hybrid figures. The colorful wings of the butterfly and the diaphanous wings of the dragonfly were perfectly suited to the aesthetics and techniques used by Art Nouveau jewelers.

When the Sylvia pendant was exhibited at the 1900 Paris World's Fair, contemporary critics praised its technical virtuosity and imagination. The piece illustrates the Vever firm's comprehensive technical mastery of gold and enamelwork and their creative and sensitive use of gemstones. —E.P.

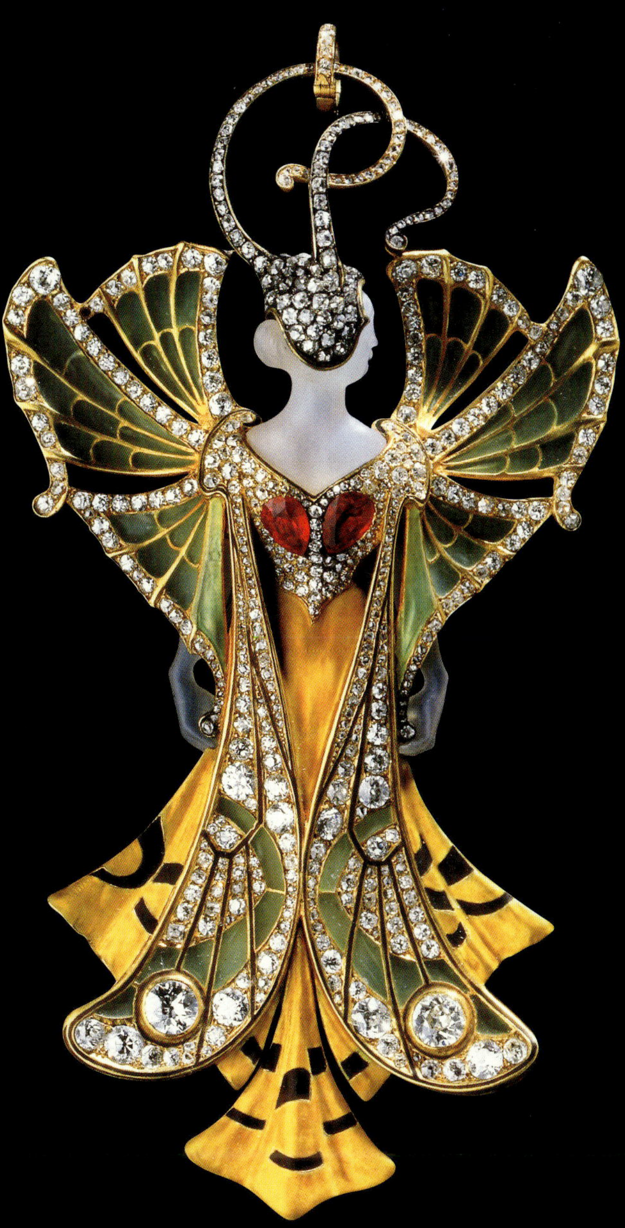

SYLVIA PENDANT

FRENCH, CIRCA 1900
PAUL VEVER (1851–1915) AND
HENRI VEVER (1854–1942)
GOLD, ENAMEL, CUT DIAMONDS, RUBIES, AGATES.
H. 4¾ IN. (12 CM)
GIFT OF J. PEYTEL, 1917

Cabbage Vase

French, 1901
Lucien Gaillard (1861–1942)
Patinated bronze. H. 8⅜ in. (21.2 cm)
Purchased from the artist, 1901

Cabbage leaves in low relief with delicately rendered veins decorate the long neck and round belly of this vase and form two handles. The decoration illustrates Lucien Gaillard's admiration for the naturalism of 18th-century French goldsmiths, who chased motifs of garden vegetables and flowers to a degree of realistic perfection approaching trompe l'oeil. The lifelike leaves on Gaillard's vase, however, may well have been produced by a natural imprint technique first borrowed from Japanese craftsmen in the 1880s by silversmiths of the Paris firm of Christofle.

Inspired by Japanese metalwork, Gaillard explored techniques for combining materials—alloys, gilding, patinas. He learned the makeup of the Oriental alloys, and he applied techniques that were still little used in France at the turn of the century. In a tricky, labor-intensive process, he developed original patinas to create variations of texture and color. His chemical treatments penetrate deeply into the material, producing rich colors, as in this bronze vase, whose patina has resulted in a palette of subtle modulated tones of reddish brown and black. —H.A.

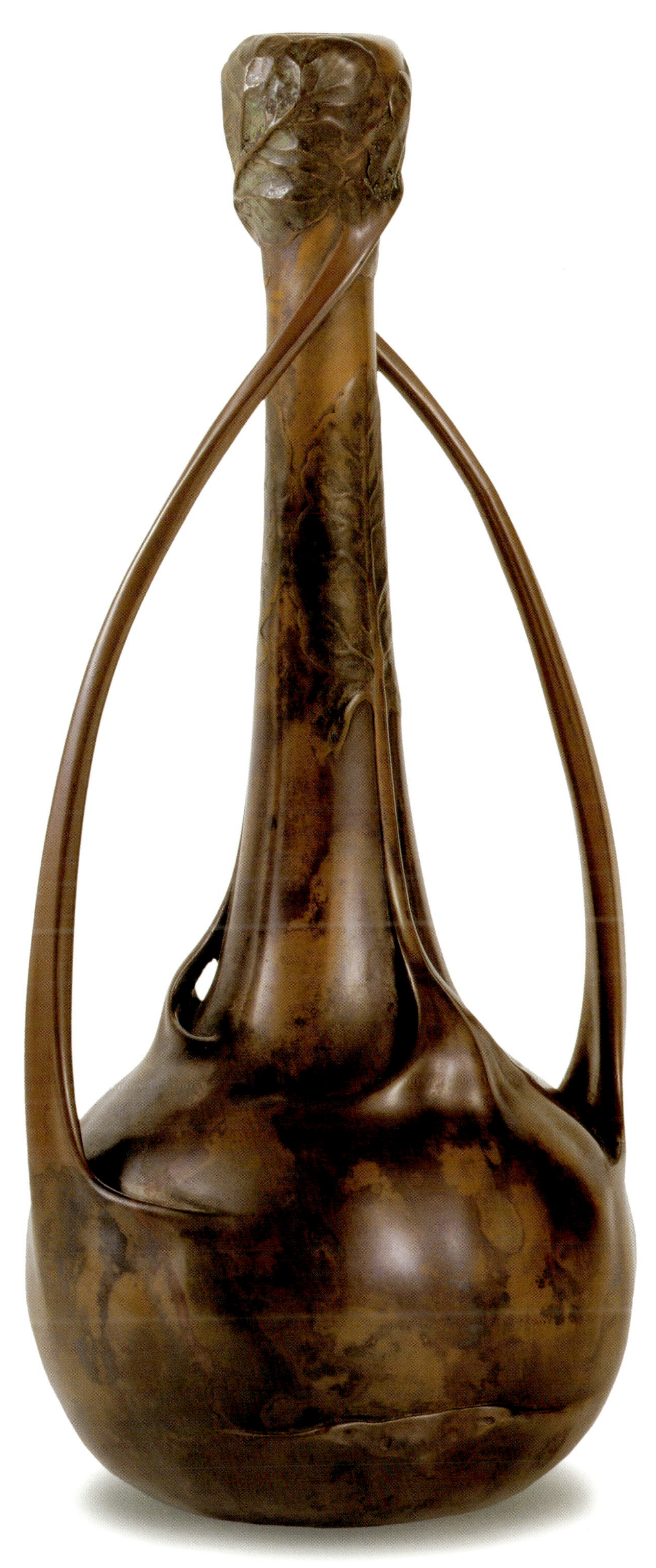

Bat Vase

French, 1900
Lucien Gaillard (1861–1942)
Cast iron, silver. H. 6⅜ in. (16.2 cm)
Purchased from the artist, 1900

Two bat's heads rise in low relief from this vase. Their wings fan out across the surface of the vase, overlaying a full moon rendered with thin silver inlay. The material discreetly conforms to the requirements of the theme and conveys the silent and precipitous flight of this nocturnal creature.

Lucien Gaillard, like his contemporaries, was intrigued by the works of Japanese craftsmen and borrowed considerably from their decorative repertoire and their animal themes. In Japanese culture the bat is a symbol of happiness and longevity and, as such, represents one of the vital ingredients in the preparation of aphrodisiacs. It was this mysterious vision of nocturnal life that inspired Gaillard.

The son and grandson of jewelers, Gaillard turned to Japanese craftsmen specializing in metal- and lacquerwork. For the compositions of old, traditional alloys such as *shakudō* (a Japanese alloy of copper and gold) and *shibuichi* (an alloy consisting of three parts of copper to one of silver), he came up with complex mixtures of cast iron and precious metals such as silver and copper. Color was usually introduced by means of inlays, like the silver moon here. The cast iron has probably been polished to achieve the soft texture that wonderfully conveys the bats' downiness and lilac-brown color, which suggest night and the reflection of the blue-gray moon. —H.A.

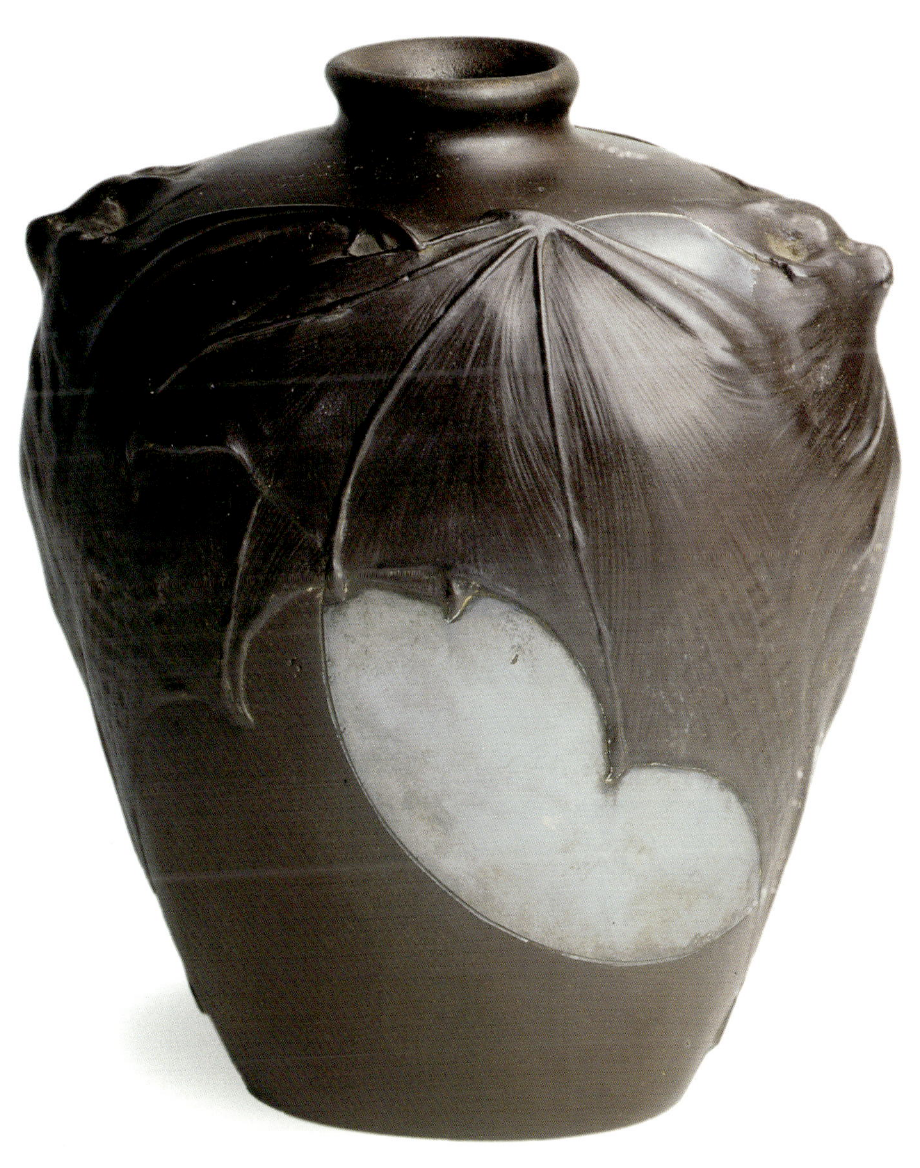

Opium poppy seedpod jar

French, 1898
Eugène Feuillâtre (1870–1916)
Translucent enamel on silver, gilt silver.
H. 2⅜ in. (6 cm), Diam. 2¾ in. (7 cm)
Purchased from the artist

Artichoke vase

French, circa 1903
Eugène Feuillâtre (1870–1916)
Translucent enamel on silver, gilt silver.
H. 3¼ in. (8.3 cm), Diam. 3½ in. (9 cm)
Gift of the artist, 1903

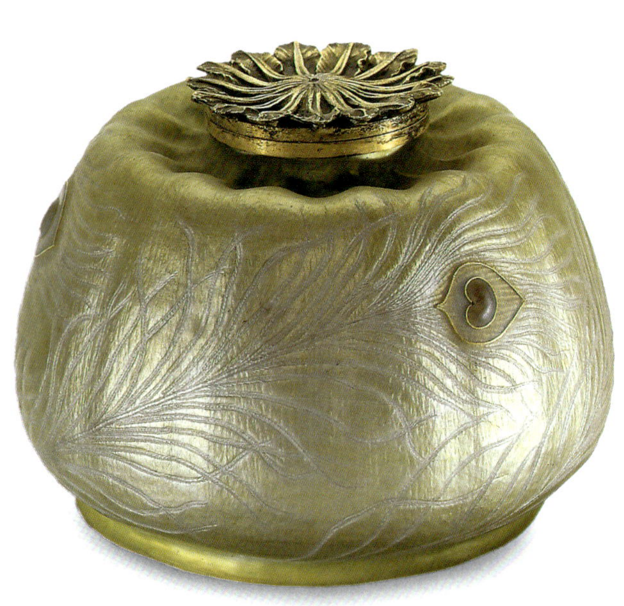

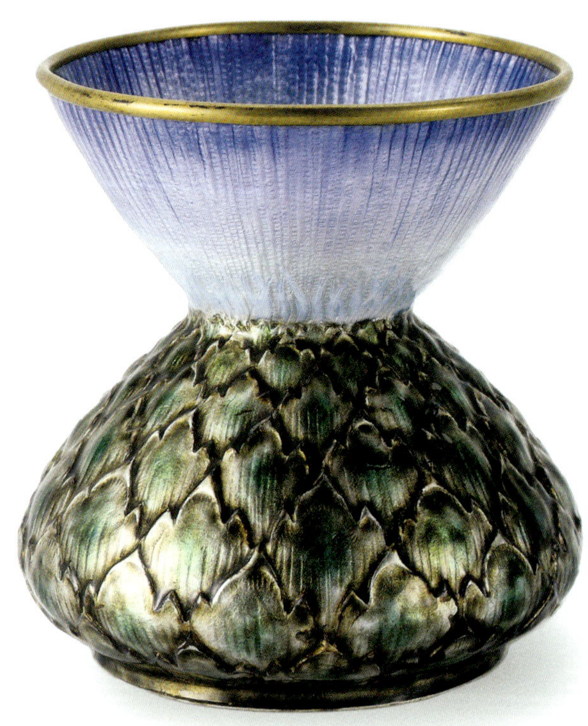

This enameled jar and vase derive their forms from the world of plants—the opium poppy and the artichoke. The vase accurately reproduces the form of the plant and realistically reflects its colors, but the bottle, while replicating the form of an opium poppy seedpod, has an unrelated surface decoration of peacock feathers.

The enameler and jeweler Eugène Feuillâtre embarked on his career in 1890 as foreman of René Lalique's enamel workshop. In 1897 he opened his own enterprise but went on working with his former employer and other jewelers. He exhibited his own pieces—jewelry and enameled objects—at the various Paris art fairs and at the Salons from 1898 to 1914.

Renowned as one of the best Art Nouveau enamelers, Feuillâtre was a specialist in enamel on silver. Enamel can be applied to any metal, but gold is the enameler's favorite ground. Silver and copper can oxidize, risking an alteration in the color of the enamel during firing. Enameling on silver is a very tricky technique, but when it is successful the enameler obtains very soft, pearly milk-white shades impossible to create with any other medium. These two pieces, with their delicately iridescent hues, illustrate the great refinement achieved by Feuillâtre in these purely decorative objects. —E.P.

Music stand

French, 1901
Alexandre Louis Marie Charpentier (1856–1909)
Waxed hornbeam. H. 48 in. (122 cm)
Purchased from the artist, 1906

The pedestal of this small piece of furniture unfurls gently upward from the base in a sweeping movement that tapers to create a feeling of maximum fragility at just the point where the two-sided music rest is affixed. The upper portion of the stand pivots, giving the piece a variable of four different geometric views. The stand is part of a set, composed of two identical double music stands and a cabinet for housing the instruments of a quartet, which was exhibited by the artist at the Salon of the Société Nationale des Beaux-Arts in 1901.

French Art Nouveau artists followed the example of the Belgian architect Victor Horta, taking the stems of plants rather than their flowers as a guiding principle for the lines and construction of their furniture. Alexandre Charpentier was a virtuoso with wood, bringing to the inert material both strength and tension while creating the impression that it is still alive and running with sap.

A sculptor and medalist, Charpentier became one of the leading exponents of Art Nouveau in Paris. Between 1890 and 1902 he was kept extremely busy in every area of decoration: decorative sculpture and carving, furniture, locks, and objects made of pewter, ceramics, and leather. He both created and contributed to a large number of interior furnishing projects, in particular the dining room of the Villa de Champrosay for Adrien Bénard (today on view at the Musée d'Orsay). A patron of Art Nouveau artists, Bénard was the chairman of the Paris mass transit system and commissioned the famed Métro entrances from architect Hector Guimard. —E.P.

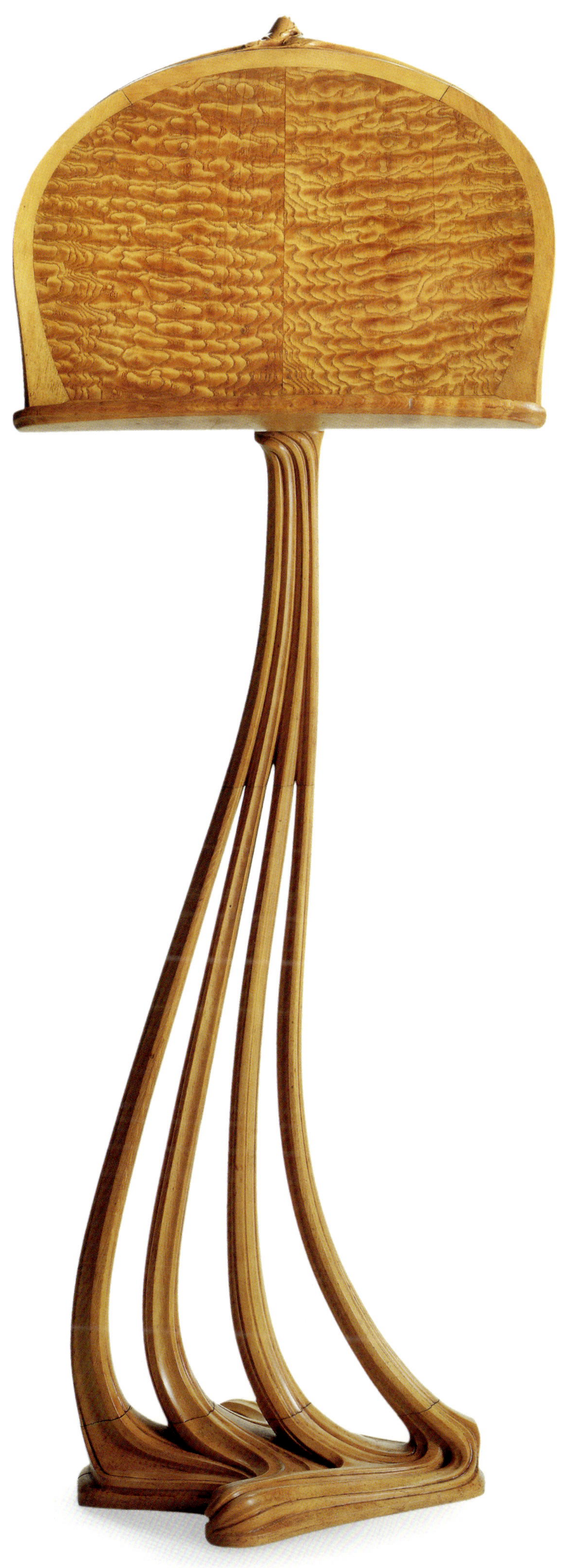

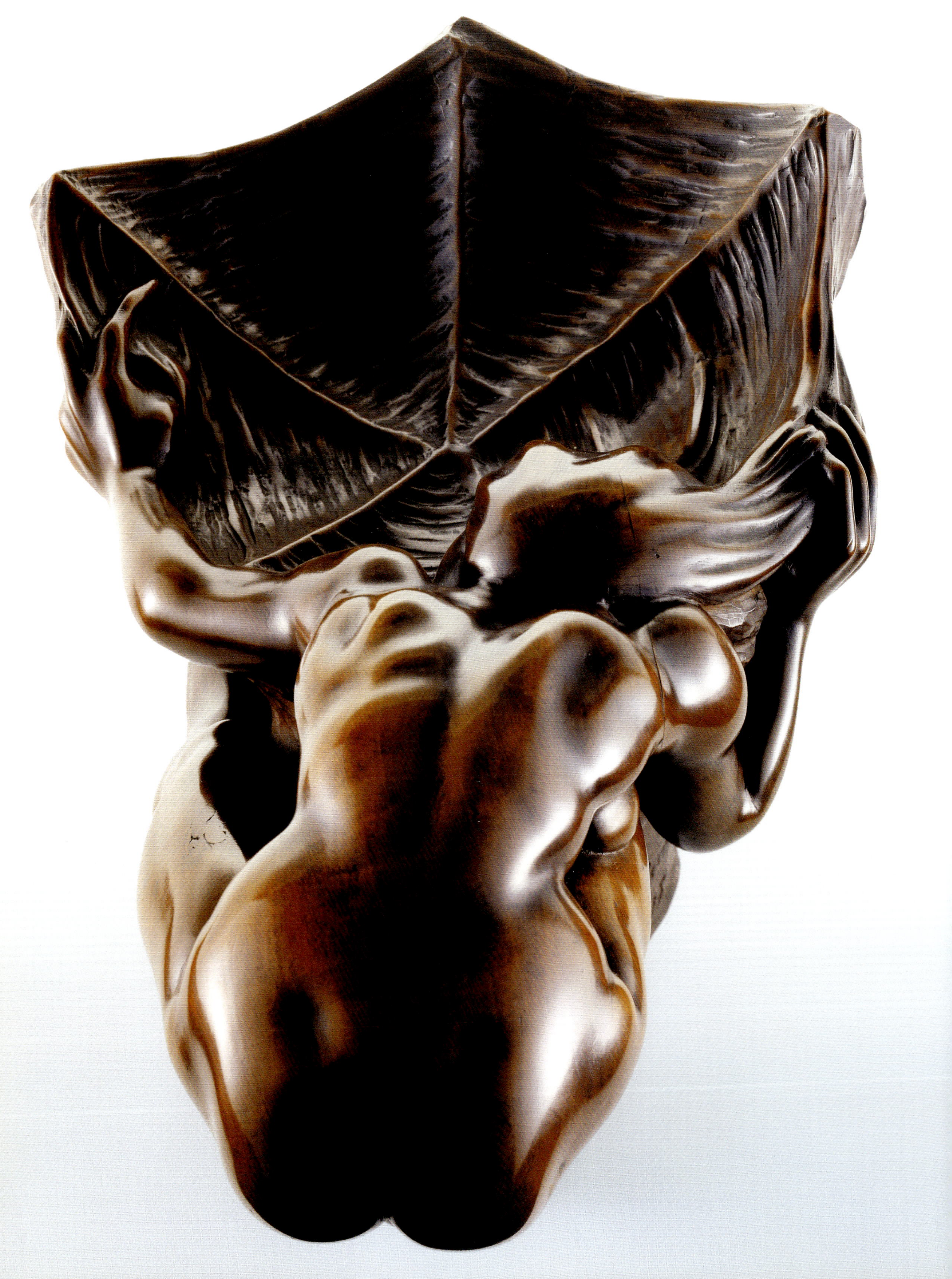

SPIDER PIN TRAY

FRENCH, 1908
FRANÇOIS-RUPERT CARABIN (1862–1932)
PEAR WOOD. H. 7⅞ IN. (20 CM), L. 15 IN. (38 CM)
PURCHASED FROM THE ARTIST, 1909

François-Rupert Carabin made six different models of spider-women. In this pin tray, a woman bends forward, holding a spiderweb formed from the tresses of her own long hair. She is balanced on the stump of a tree against which she rests her body. The shiny, oiled treatment of the surface gives this female body, with its massive forms, a very primal sensual impact.

Primarily a sculptor, Carabin worked in wood, making furniture and objets d'art, for which the naked, muscular female body, with its powerful anatomy, formed the theme and sometimes the very structure of the works. His women are often associated with an animal, such as the cat, but may also be represented as hybrids: peacock-tailed women, mermaids, frog-women, and spider-women. The latter is the symbolic representation of all-consuming motherhood, or the mother castratrix —a latent fear of the sexual power of women haunted the imaginations of late-19th-century artists.

In Carabin's furniture pieces, usually designed for spaces inhabited by men, the woman's body is subjugated and dominated. To the sculptor, Woman—by her primal and passive character—is close to Nature itself, instinctive, subconscious, and sensual. —E.P.

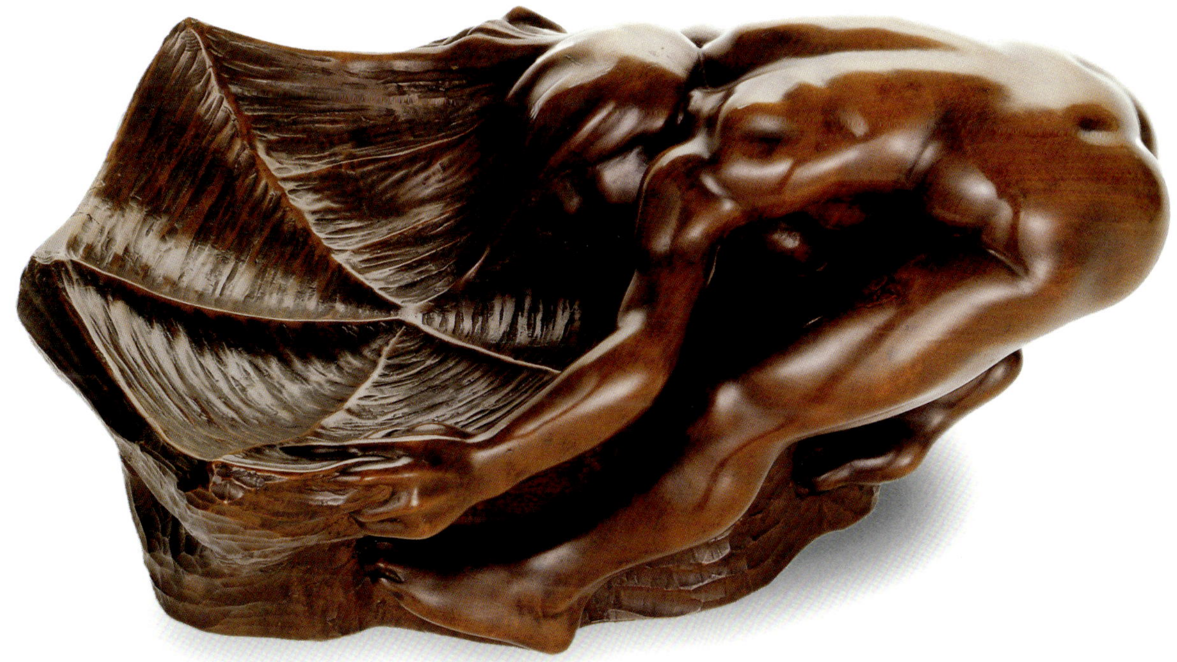

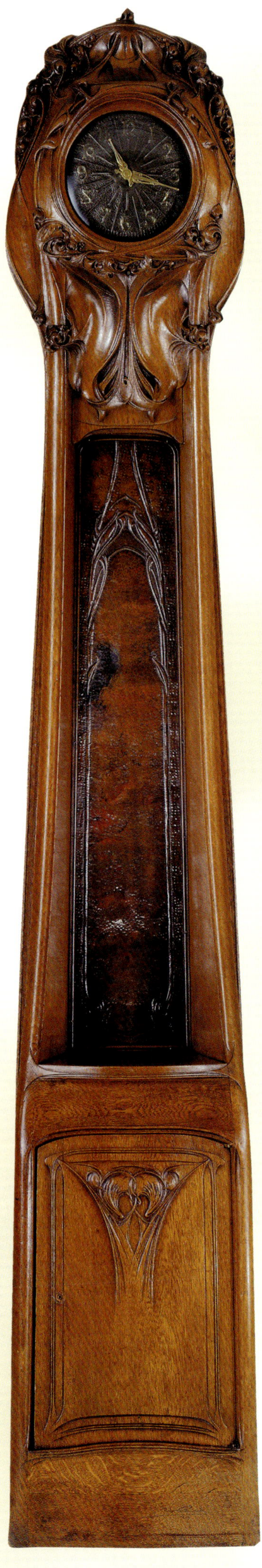

Long-case clock

French, circa 1910
Hector Guimard (1867–1942)
Oak, copper. H. 94½ in. (240 cm)
Gift of Madame Adeline Oppenheim-Guimard, 1948

The long-case clock, a timepiece conceived as a major independent piece of furniture, has a history covering the 17th through 19th centuries. Hector Guimard's model was one of the last expressions of this great furniture tradition.

The clock here was donated to the Musée des Arts Décoratifs in 1948 by Madame Adeline Oppenheim-Guimard, widow of the architect. It came from their house, which was built and furnished between 1910 and 1912 at 122 avenue Mozart in Paris. Guimard designed every aspect of the home and its interior furnishings. The couple's private apartments were on the second and third floors, while the fourth floor housed a painter's studio for Madame Guimard.

Old photographs of the residence, in the collection of the Cooper-Hewitt Museum in New York, suggest that it contained two examples of this clock. One stood in the hallway on the ground floor, the other in the third-floor anteroom. One (possibly this one, which has no clockworks) was shown at the Société des Artistes Décorateurs exhibition of 1910, while the other, which bears the date 1910, is in a private collection.

The clock is designed with deliberate simplicity. It was intended not as a showpiece for the living room but as a functional element for secondary spaces. The wood is oak, instead of the more luxurious fruitwood Guimard favored, and the ornament is discreet. This restraint stands in sharp contrast to his other furniture.

Guimard had all the furniture he designed made in his own Ateliers d'Art et de Fabrication. From 1904 on, these workshops were located in the mansion built by Guimard for his client and patron, Léon Nozal, on avenue Perrichont-Prolongée (no longer extant). When Nozal died in 1914, Guimard was forced to close his manufacturing workshops, which put an end to his furniture making. The pieces he produced from 1897 to 1914 demonstrate exceptional formal and technical quality, and it is a great pity indeed that the names of his craftsmen—be they sculptors or carpenters—have not come down to us. —E.P.

Side table

French, circa 1903
Hector Guimard (1867–1942)
Pear wood. H. 30⅛ in. (76.5 cm),
W. 18⅛ in. (46 cm), D. 20⅞ in. (53 cm)
Gift of Mrs. Albert Pézieux, on behalf
of Mrs. Léon Nozal, 1937

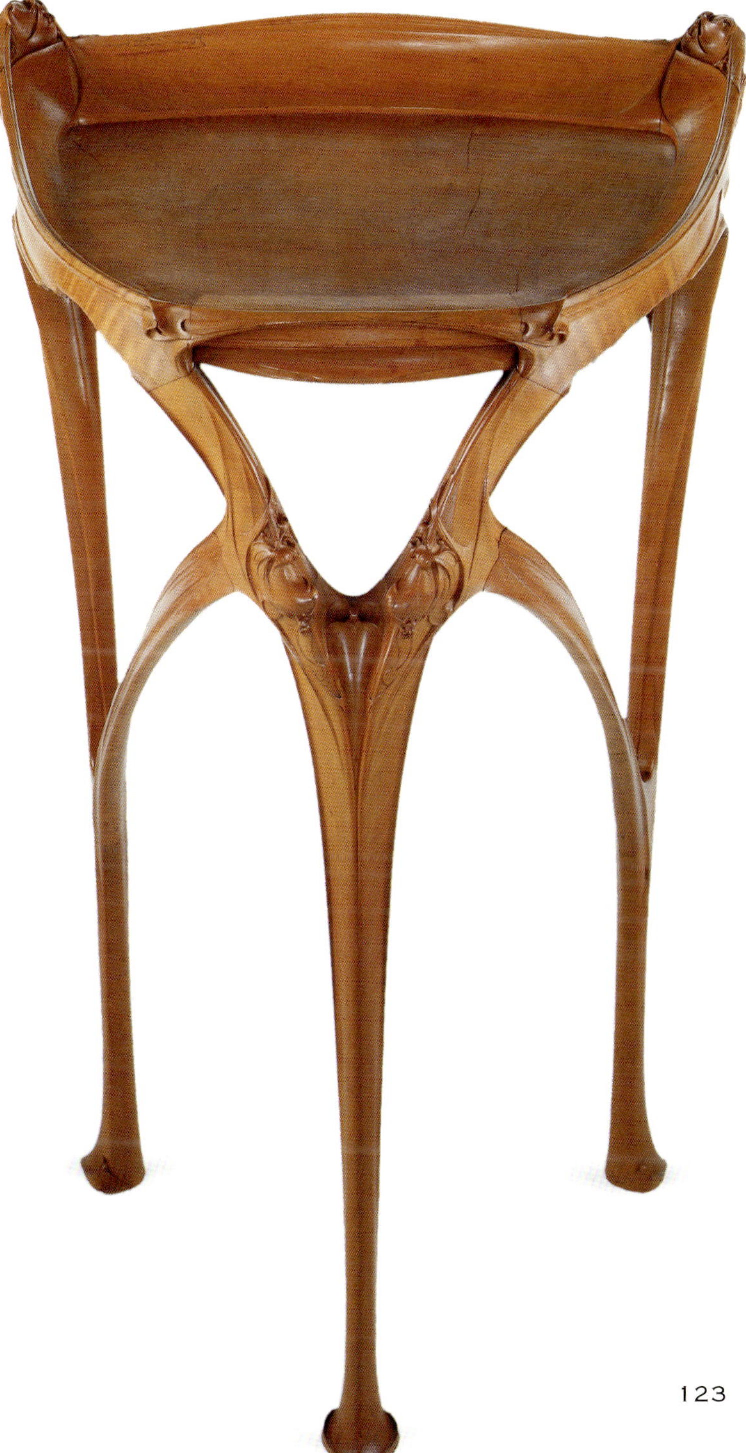

This table was part of the furnishings of the residence of the Léon Nozal family at 52 rue de Ranelagh. Located in the 16th arrondissement, the most fashionable neighborhood of Paris, the house was one of two built for Nozal by Hector Guimard between 1904 and 1906. Although it was destroyed in 1957, it ranks among the high points of Guimard's work, along with Castel Béranger and the great architect's own residence. Guimard conceived of such residential projects as an architectural totality in which he determined every detail, but in this case his control of the interior decoration was limited. Still, he was responsible for the library woodwork and a few pieces of furniture, including the bedroom suite, created to mark the marriage of Nozal's daughter Caroline to Albert Pézieux. The most important elements (the bed, wardrobe, two glass-fronted corner cupboards, chairs, and this table) were donated by the family to the Musée des Arts Décoratifs.

This small piece of furniture, with its elegant, sinewy forms, was carved of pear wood, a very hard fruitwood. Triangular in shape, the raised lip on one side indicates that it was designed to be set against a wall. The three legs are joined by two cross-struts to give better stability when the sliding writing tablet at the front is extended. The almost abstract decoration consists of grooving on the legs and carved seeds, knots, and leaves where the legs intersect. These motifs recur on the angles of the tabletop.

The pure lines, warm hue of the wood, and refined decoration make this small table one of Guimard's loveliest pieces of furniture. —E.P.

Chandelier

French, circa 1904
Emile Gallé (1846–1904)
Wrought iron, cameo glass.
H. 52¾ in. (134 cm), Diam. 41 in. (104 cm)
Gift of Denyse Chardin, 1968

With the switch from candles to gas and later to paraffin, lighting went through many spectacular changes during the 19th century. Then the arrival of the electric lightbulb made it possible for the first time in the history of lighting to actually direct the beam of light and, in particular, to focus it downward. At the 1900 Paris World's Fair, from which the "Electricity Fairy" emerged triumphant, new forms of lights appeared, one such being this chandelier by Emile Gallé.

Large clusters of umbel flowers tumble down from the central shaft of the chandelier. Light is transmitted upward through the pink-and-white or yellow-and-white globes. Toward the bottom, a crown of nine umbels in varying states of bloom diffuses the downward light.

This chandelier is part of the interior commissioned by Edouard Hannon, a Belgian engineer who worked with Ernest Solvay on his Brussels residence. For this piece, as with the other furniture, Gallé produced naturalistic forms. The iron structure, made in the small forge that Gallé had set up in his workshops, is actually a very large spray of umbels, with cascading flowers. This chandelier belongs to the last period of Gallé's career, when he was interested in the association of metal and glass.

Gallé was one of the leaders of the Ecole de Nancy, a group of Art Nouveau artists located in the eastern French town of Nancy. He was renowned for his innovations in ceramics, glass, and furniture. Here he shows his interest in lighting, a field in which he made pieces of great formal originality and technical mastery. —H.A.

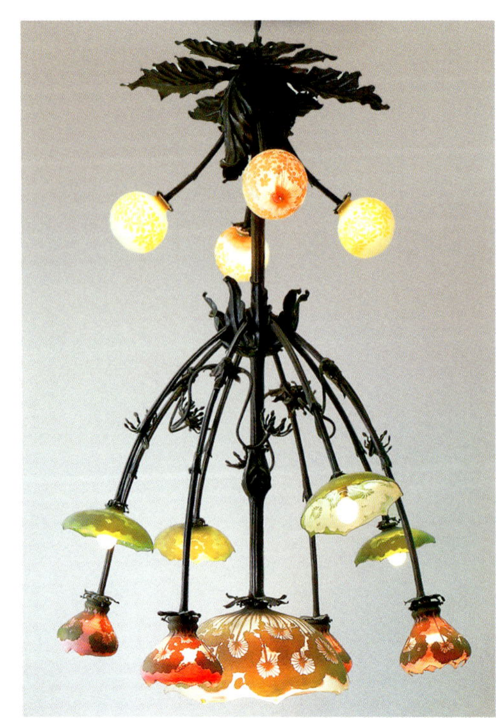

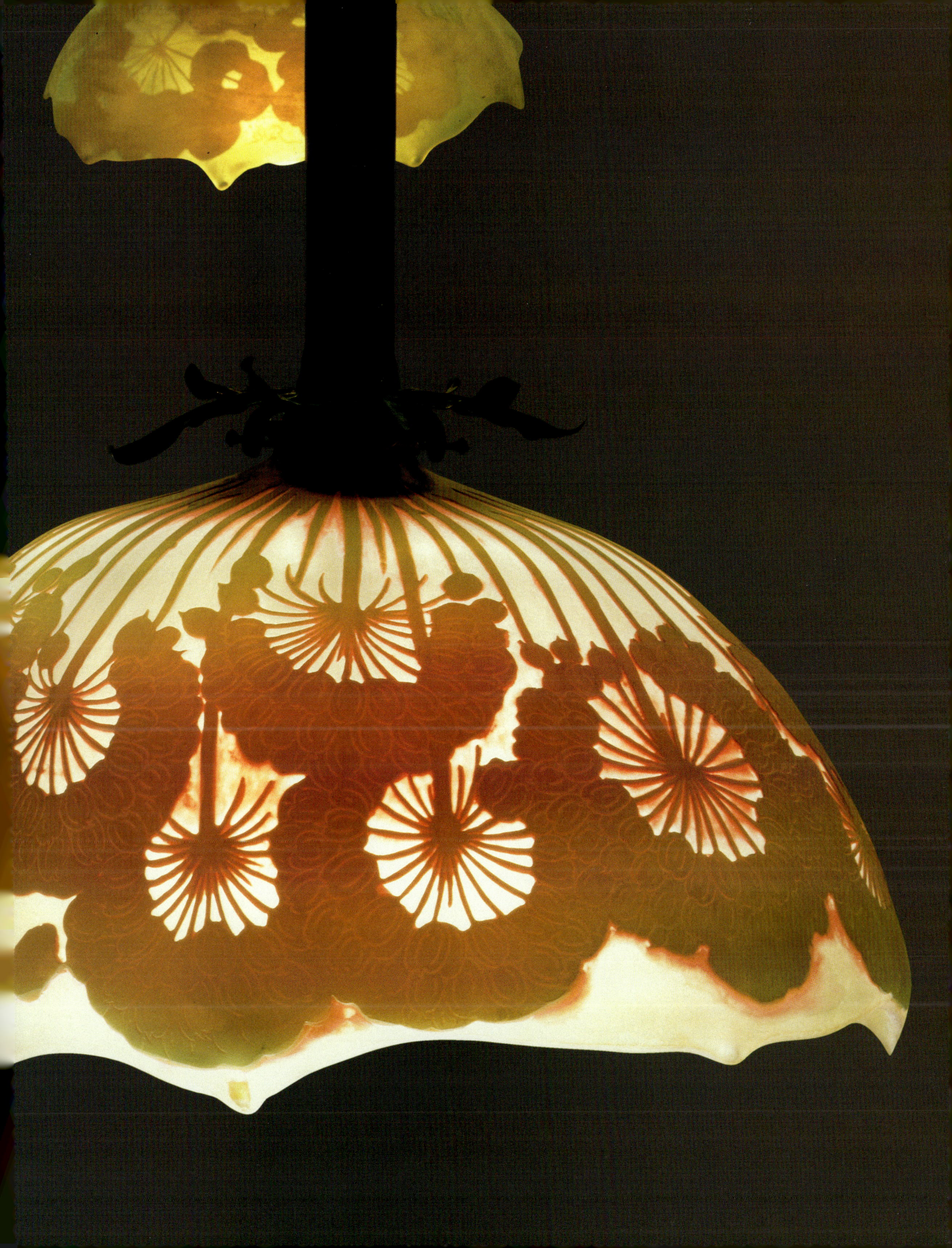

Hippocamp vase

French, 1901
Emile Gallé (1846–1904)
Inscribed on foot: *Joseph Reinach Emile Gallé 1901;*
on back: *Vitam impendere vero* (Devoting one's life to truth)
Glass. H. 7½ in. (19 cm)
Joseph Reinach bequest, 1925

After mastering the technique of glass marquetry, the glaziers working with Emile Gallé embarked on an actual sculpture in hot-worked glass. With this small object, which fits in the palm of the hand and has a powerful tactile presence, the process was so successful that very few interventions after cooling—the engraver's touches—were required to complete the work.

The range and originality of materials imitated by glass show the extent of the chemist's work with color. The coils of coral and the curves of the sea horses, applied with heat, reflect the shape of the piece, which vaguely resembles a ewer or jug. Its contours are animated by the living shapes of the animals: the spout is echoed in the sea horse's snout, and the curve of the "handle" merges with the coiled shape of its prehensile tail. These formal similarities resonate like the echoes of poetic rhymes.

Gallé found inspiration mainly in the insect kingdom, but here he presents one of his most moving visions of the animal world, in which two human-like sea creatures evoke a fragile bond of affection. Did Gallé decide to offer this work to Joseph Reinach in 1901 because he associated this fragility with justice, truth, and liberty, or did this physical and mysterious humanization of the animal kingdom simply seem a fitting tribute? Reinach was the author of a history of the Dreyfus affair, which in 1901 was still dividing France into two camps. Like Gallé, Reinach was sure that Alfred Dreyfus, a Jewish army captain accused of spying for Germany, was innocent. Many of Gallé's works would be associated with his ideas about Dreyfus, but it was not until 1906 that the clearance of Dreyfus's name would signal the victory of those advocating justice and truth over those backing a military order and an authoritarian state playing on the anti-Semitic myth of the traitor.

This work is an aesthetic and technical masterpiece as well as an historical object. It is one of the most entrancing of those resulting from Gallé's fascination with the depths of the sea, persuaded as he was by reading Darwin that therein lay the origin of life. —J-L.O.

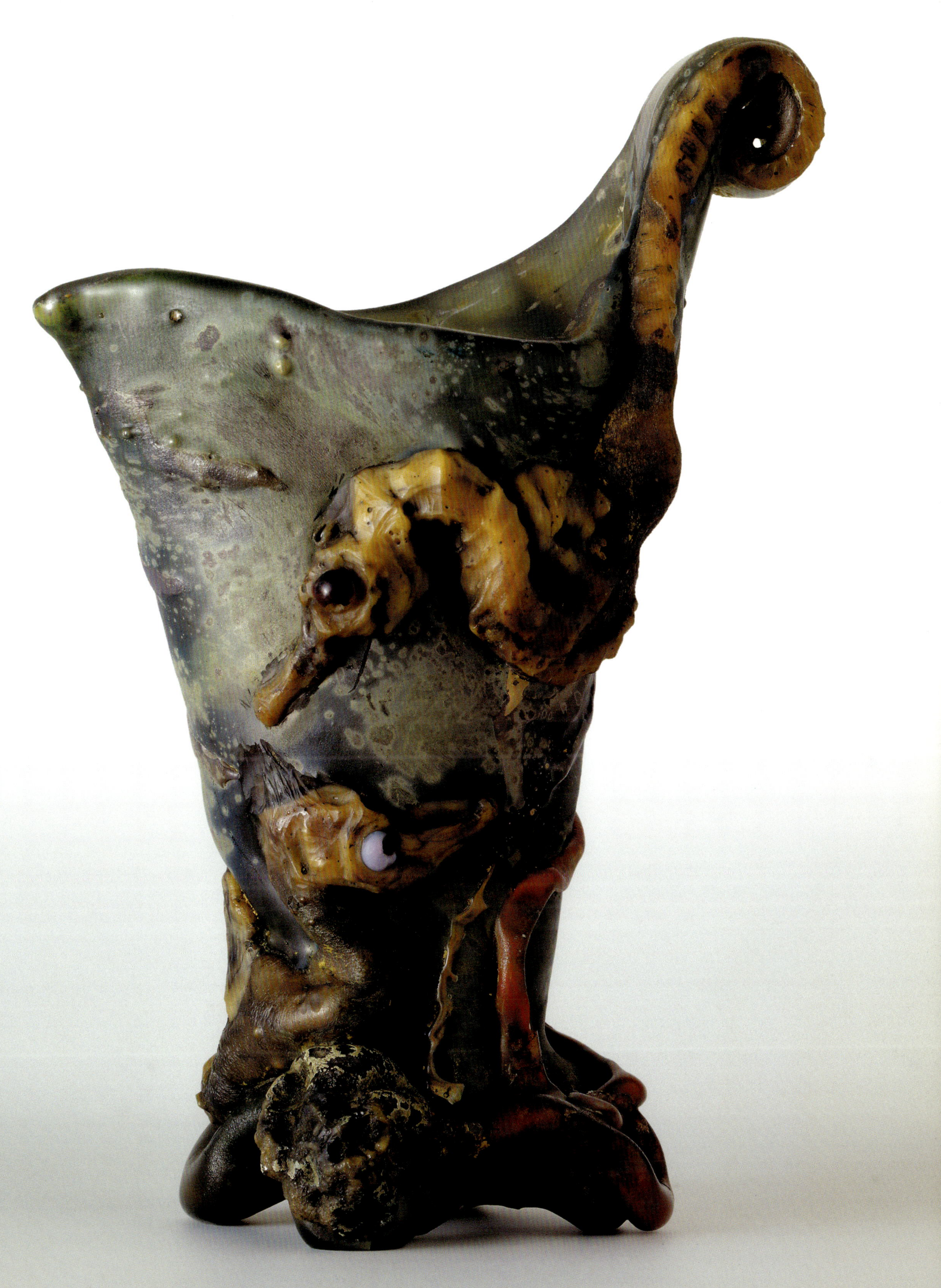

Thistle Vase

French, 1900
Emile Gallé (1846–1904)
Glass. H. 17½ in. (44.5 cm)
Purchased from the artist, 1900

The world's fairs held in Paris in 1878, 1889, and 1900, in which Emile Gallé took part, marked the different stages in his career and the mounting international renown for his work in three fields: ceramics, cabinetmaking, and glass. It was above all in glass that his genius was most acclaimed and where his influence was most felt. From 1878 until 1903, the Musée des Arts Décoratifs regularly acquired Gallé glass masterpieces, not only at world's fairs but also from professional shows and annual exhibitions, which opened their doors to objets d'art beginning in 1891. However, this monumental vase was the museum's sole acquisition from Gallé's outstanding exhibits in 1900.

The imposing mass of glass that forms this vase was built up in many gathers and manipulated hot. Its wealth of colors conjures up the depth of an almost abstract landscape, brought to life by a swirling dynamic. In the foreground, a single thistle flower stands out clearly. The vase was produced through the so-called glass marquetry technique invented by Gallé, which consists of applying fragments of colored glass to the body of the gather while it is still hot. This embedded decoration is then followed by blowing the glass gather in a two-part mold, which gives the vase its overall form of a thistle bud.

This thematic synthesis between the form of an object and its decoration was characteristic of Gallé's work in 1900, along with the acceptance of certain manufacturing flaws, which he regarded as part and parcel of the aesthetics of the arts involving fire. The imperfection here is the very visible seam of the mold. Gallé's drawing for the piece is preserved in the Musée d'Orsay, and two other examples of the model are known. Both are more refined but less forceful in their expression of Nature as something powerful and unpredictable.

The monumentality of the Thistle vase was shared by other works Gallé exhibited at the 1900 Paris World's Fair, including *La Grand Communion de la Nature,* a bowl in which he achieved a fully realized landscape encompassing the entire surface of the vessel and even penetrated the material with his marquetry. Gallé's combination of freedom and outstanding know-how reached its height between 1894, the year he established his own glass factory in Nancy, and 1904, the year of his death. —J-L.O.

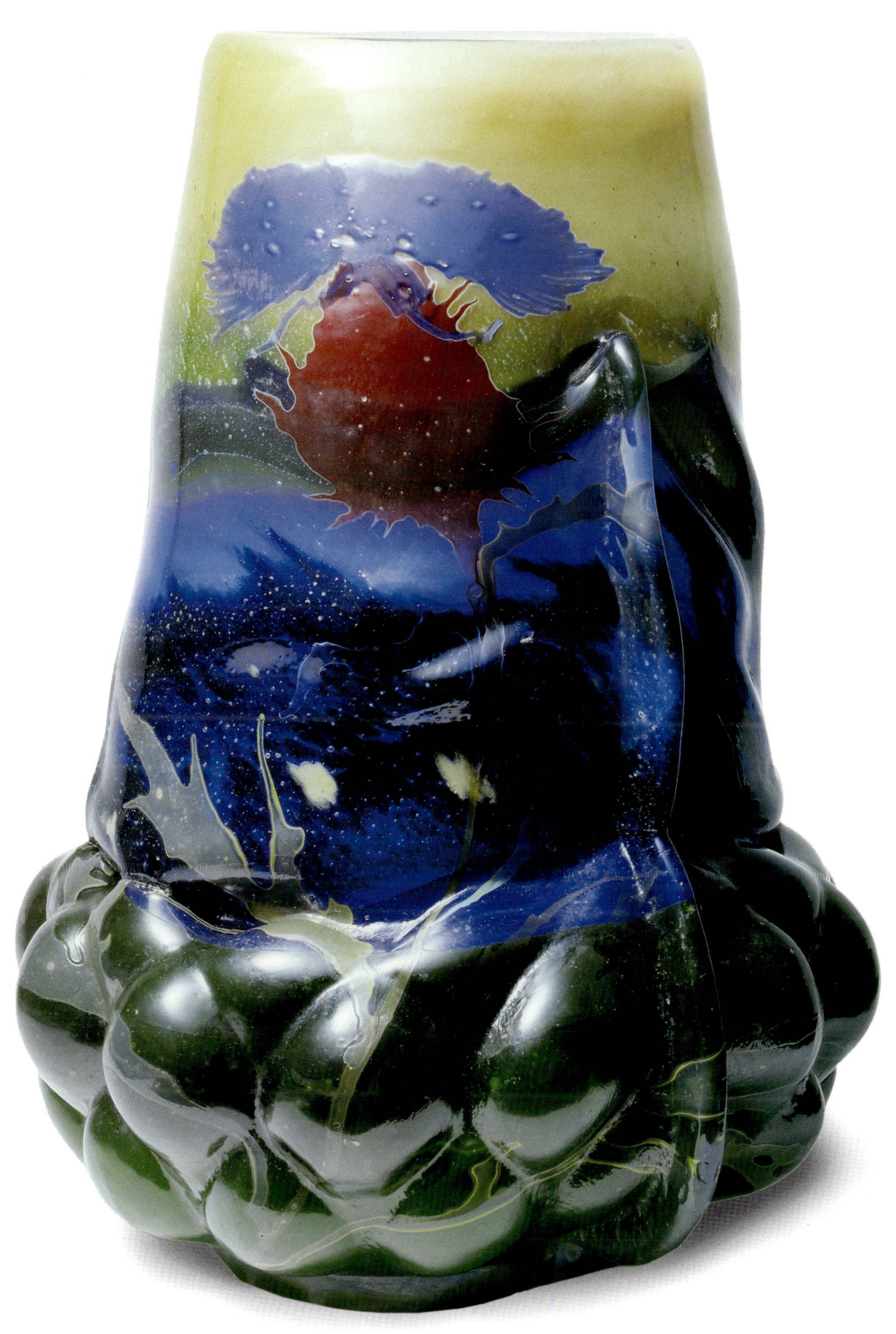

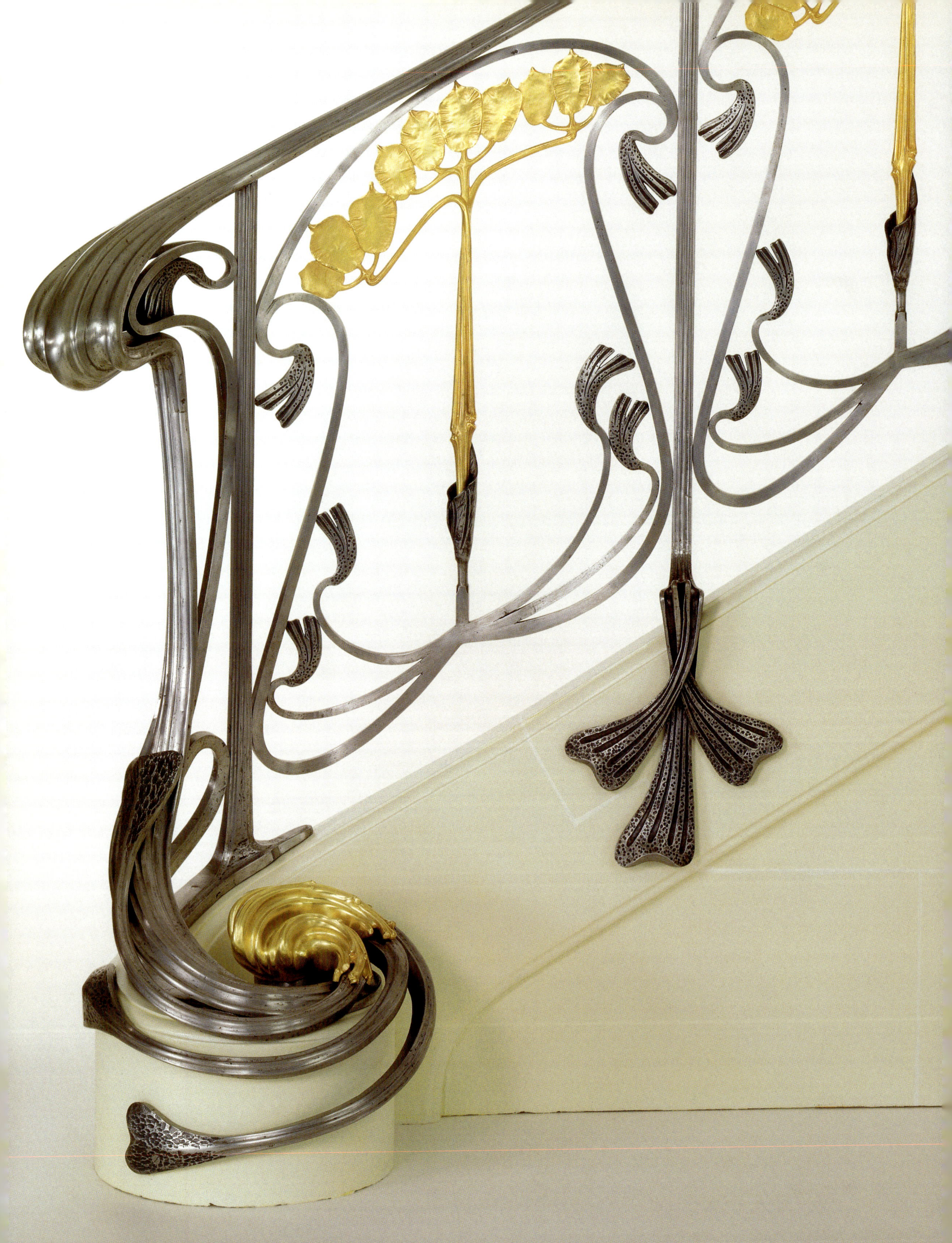

Banister

French, 1903
Louis Majorelle (1859–1926)
Polished cast iron, gilt bronze, brass.
H. 33½ in. (85 cm), W. 82⅝ in. (210 cm)
Purchased from the Majorelle brothers, 1904

The base of this banister is a coiled thrust of supple lines, a bit like roots and buds, surmounted by a motif in brass. Within each of three polished wrought-iron panels, framed in twisting "whiplash" lines, the stem, branch, and seedpods of the honesty plant are rendered in nitrate-gilded bronze. Louis Majorelle did not hesitate to combine the ironsmith's craft with the bronzecaster's to give realistic expression to the natural, many-colored aspects of the plant.

A branch of the honesty plant is a frequent motif in Art Nouveau. It was used, in particular, to embellish the stained-glass windows of the Villa Majorelle in Nancy, built by the architect Henri Sauvage. Botanists describe the plant *(Lunaria)* as "lunar" because of the milky coloring of its seedpods. It was given the common name "money plant" in the mid-19th century. Artists, especially glaziers, have always appreciated its translucent whiteness.

After two years at the Ecole des Beaux-Arts in Paris, in 1879, after the death of his father Auguste, Louis Majorelle took over the family cabinetmaking and ceramics establishment in Nancy. He soon abandoned ceramics and focused on the manufacture of Louis XV–style and chinoiserie lacquer furniture, for which his father's firm was known. Beginning in 1889, under the influence of Emile Gallé, he adopted a more personal style inspired by Art Nouveau, and in 1897 he embarked on industrial production.

To ensure control over every element of his firm's products, Majorelle added the bronzesmith's and ironsmith's crafts to his cabinetmaking and joinery workshops. In the summer of 1903, Jean Keppel, foreman of the ironworks, produced the model of the money plant banister and showed it at the Musée des Arts Décoratifs as part of the *Ecole de Nancy* exhibition. It is probably the same piece that was exhibited the following year at the Société Nationale des Beaux-Arts exhibition and acquired by the Musée des Arts Décoratifs. Another banister with one or two slightly different features still graces the Bergeret house in Nancy. —E.P.

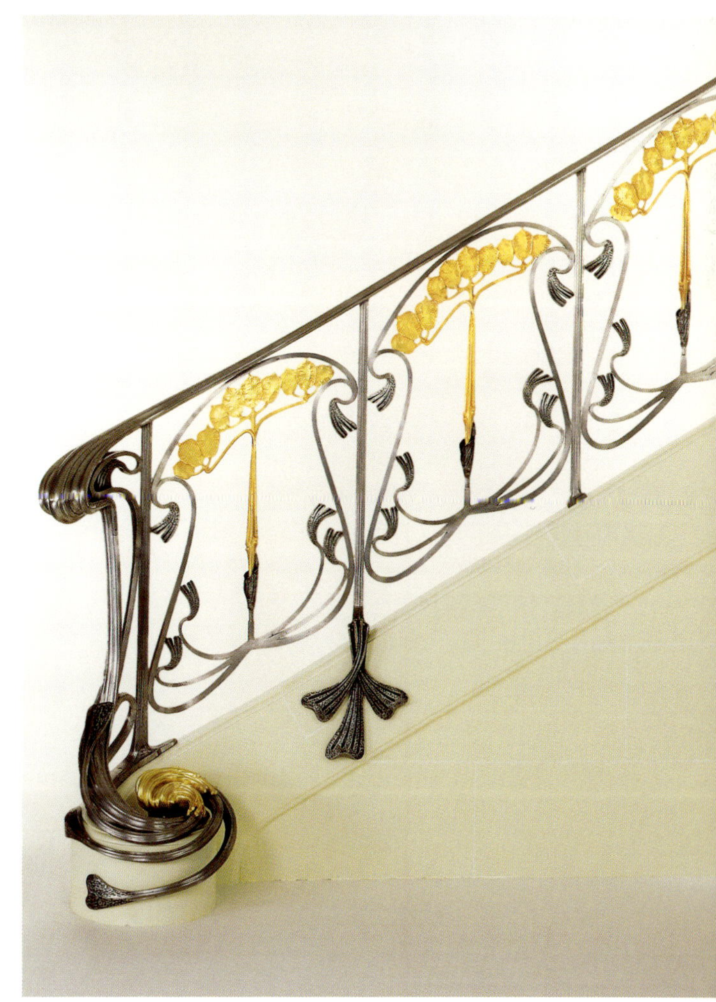

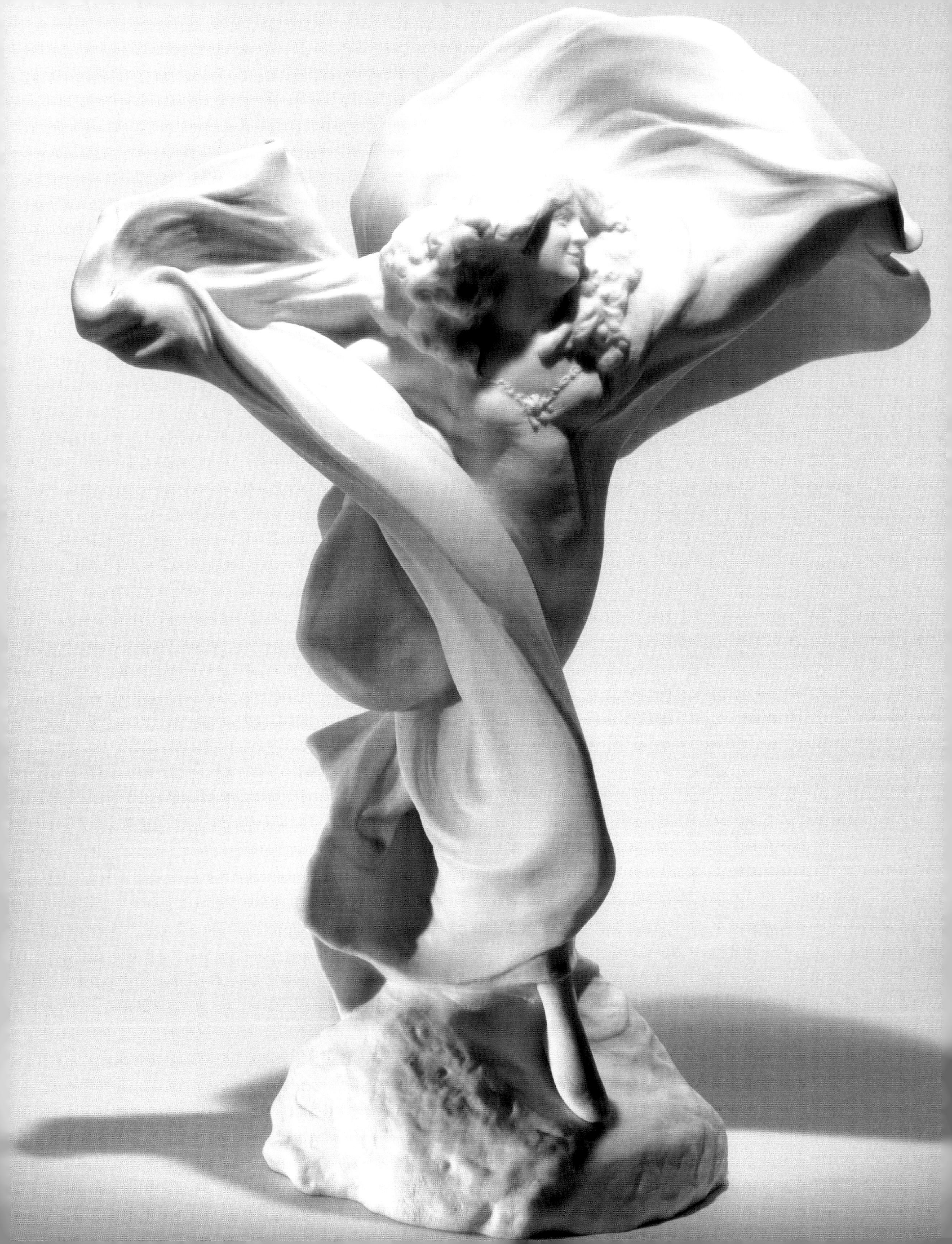

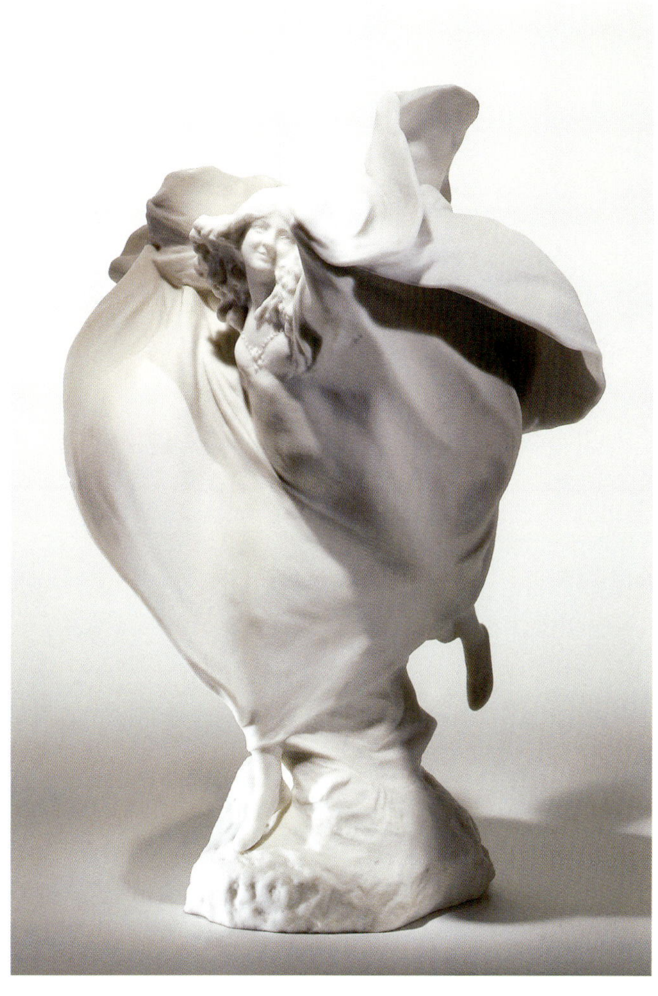

Loïe Fuller dancing

French, Sèvres factory, 1917 version of 1903 model
Louis-Auguste-Théodore Rivière (1857–1912)
Biscuit porcelain. H. 9½ in. (24 cm), W. 7½ in. (19 cm)
Loan from the Manufacture Nationale de Sèvres, 1925

The American dancer Loïe Fuller enjoyed international acclaim between 1890 and 1920 for her unique performances featuring her fascinating manipulation of veils, enhanced by sophisticated theatrical staging and colored lights. Her theater, built by the architect Henri Sauvage, was one of the main attractions at the 1900 Paris World's Fair. Transforming herself into a flower, a tree in the wind, or a butterfly, with sinuous elegance and amazingly flowing gestures, she personified the flower-woman who dominated the imaginations of the exponents of Art Nouveau. She was immortalized in the art of contemporaries such as Raoul Larche, Koloman Moser, Pierre Roche, and Henri Toulouse-Lautrec.

A sculptor fascinated by legends, Théodore Rivière followed his dreams to such far-off countries as Cambodia, India, and Japan. He was a great admirer of mysterious female figures from the past, such as Gustave Flaubert's heroine Salammbô and her contemporaries.

Rivière's Loïe Fuller sculpture exists in marble and bronze versions as well as in the biscuit produced by the former royal porcelain factory of Sèvres around 1910. Biscuit—porcelain left in the white state and deliberately not glazed—had been developed as a sculpture medium in the 18th century to imitate the effect of marble. This work reflects the Sèvres factory's quest for modernity in the choice of a contemporary subject and style, as the movement subsuming the figure makes it a quintessential statement of Art Nouveau. —H.A.

Chaise longue

French, circa 1912
Paul Follot (1877–1941)
Gilt beech. H. 31⅛ in. (79 cm), W. 23⅝ in. (60 cm),
L. 62½ in. (159 cm)
Acquired after Le Siège Français du Moyen Age à nos Jours
(The 1947 Exhibition on Seating)

The chaise longue, or daybed, has traditionally been an aristocratic piece of furniture used for resting and receiving close friends. Conceived as a seat that would allow the user to stretch out, it may have just a single armrest (as in this example). The form originated in classical antiquity and was revived in the 18th century. It has often been the vehicle for rarefied form executed in rich materials.

Paul Follot began his career in 1901 as a designer of decorative objects for Julius Meier-Graefe's La Maison Moderne gallery in Paris. Although he started out working in the Art Nouveau style, he very soon became one of those decorators who advocated a return to tradition and focused on the elegant forms of furniture developed in the 18th century. For this chaise longue, Follot borrowed from historic furniture in his use of gilt wood and saber-shaped legs. On the other hand, the rose motif, carved on the seat rail, is not rendered with traditional naturalism. Its geometric, almost Cubist treatment makes it emblematic of the nascent Art Deco style. —H.A.

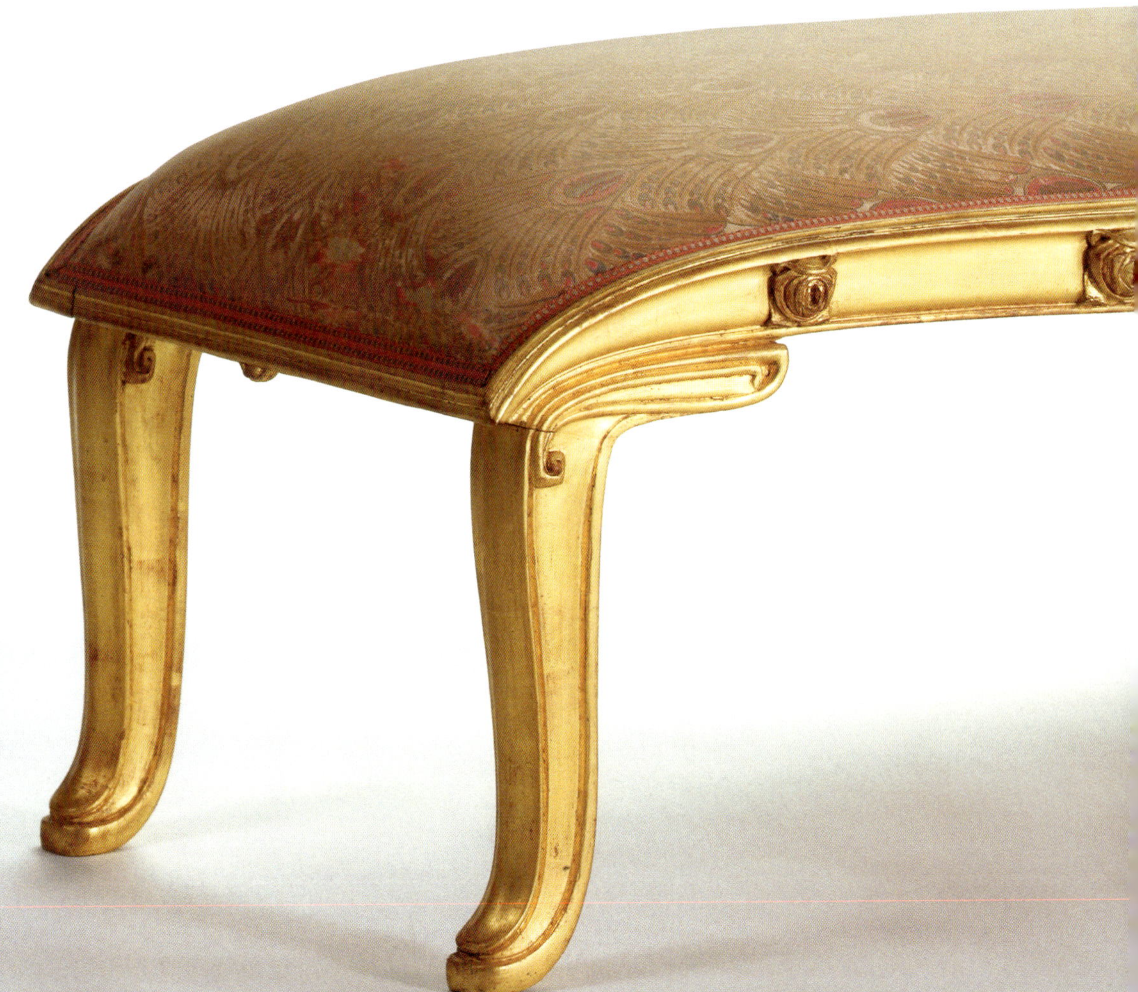

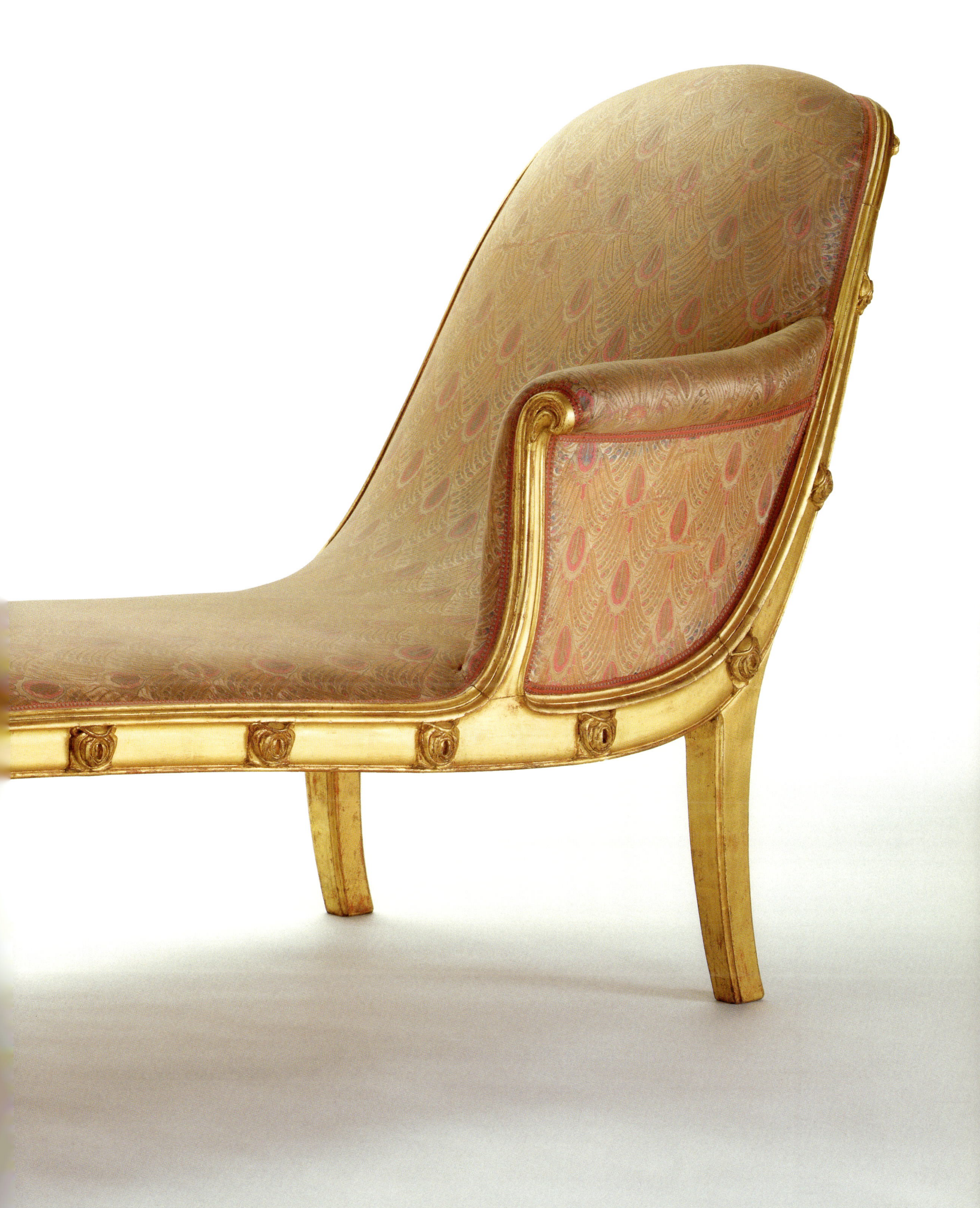

Bathroom

French, circa 1920–1922
Armand-Albert Rateau (1882–1938)
Marble, bronze, glass
Gift of Prince Louis de Polignac, 1965

In 1920 Armand-Albert Rateau was entrusted with refurbishing the mansion belonging to the famous couturier Jeanne Lanvin, at 16 rue Barbet-de-Jouy in Paris. The trends of the 1920s were irrelevant to Rateau, who relied on his own cultural knowledge and imagination, incorporating classical antiquity, the Orient, and animal and plant motifs into a highly personal decorative world. He shared Lanvin's taste for quality and rare materials, which is why she asked him to run her Faubourg Saint-Honoré interior design agency at the same time that he was remodeling her private home. When the mansion was demolished in 1965, Prince Louis de Polignac offered the complete contents to the Musée des Arts Décoratifs in memory of Lanvin's daughter, Countess Jean de Polignac. This gift included the furniture as well as private apartments with a bedroom, boudoir, and bathroom.

For Lanvin's bathroom, Rateau used marble, stucco, and bronze treated with the green patination of Roman antiquities. For the fittings, washbasin, bidets, and two built-in glass-fronted cupboards, he used beige Hauteville marble. He stuccoed the walls and decorated the alcove housing the bathtub with a bas-relief depicting a stag and a doe in woodlands. He had the floor laid with marble in two panels of geometric motifs in beige, black, and white on either side of a strip of black marble running from the washbasin to the bathtub. He designed wall lights and plumbing fixtures reproducing pheasants, daisies, and pinecones, as well as furniture made of patinated bronze like the fixtures and including a dressing table, tall lamps, and a table in the form of an ancient urn.

Rateau's art reflects a deep affinity for antiquity and the arts of the Middle East, particularly those of Persia. The unbelievable luxury of this bathroom calls to mind the marble-clad baths of the classical Romans and Turkish *hammams.* Body care was one of Lanvin's major concerns, and in tandem with her activities as a fashion designer, she created cosmetic and perfume lines, including the famous scent Arpège, which was launched in 1927. —E.P.

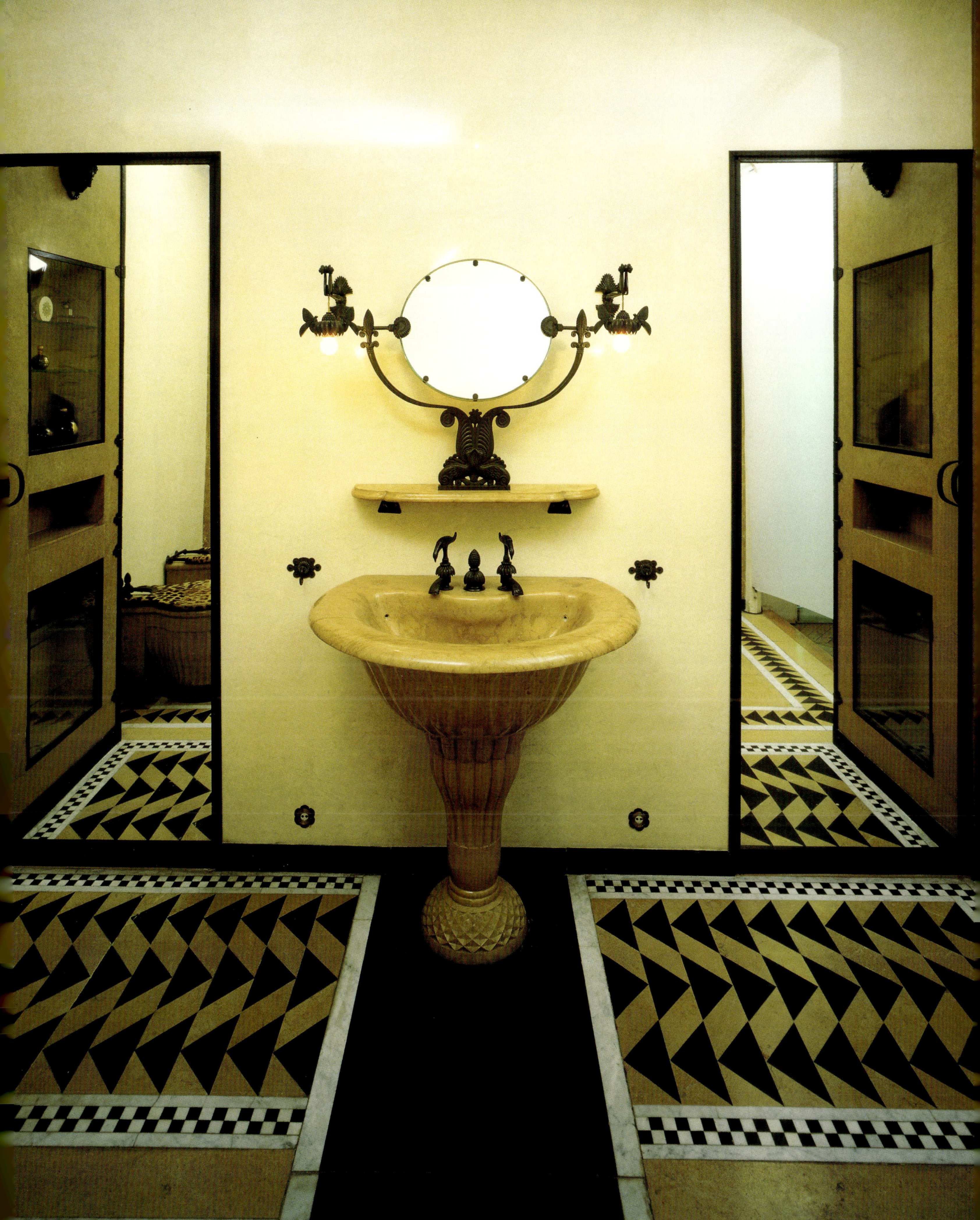

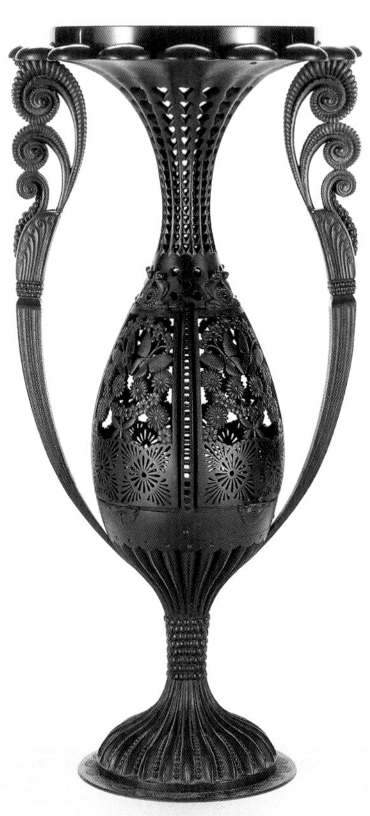

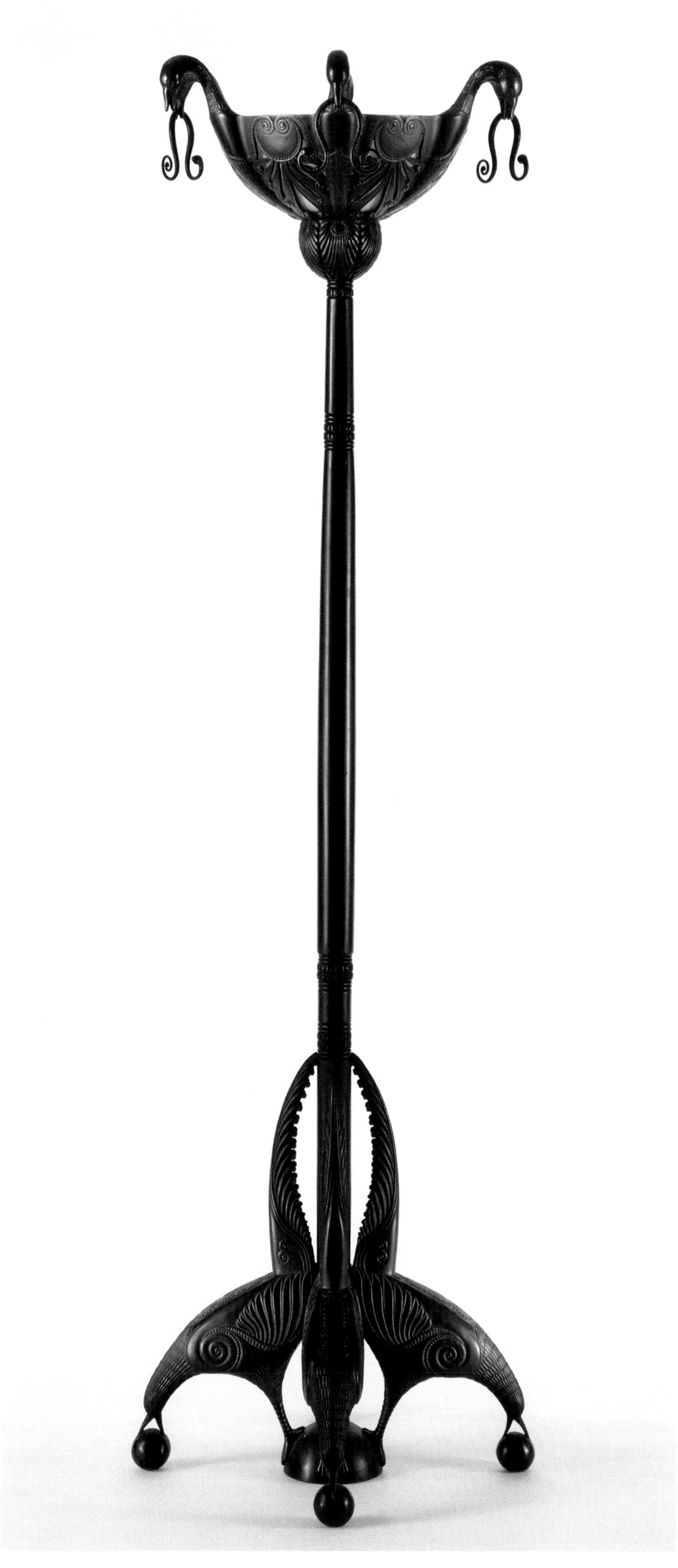

Round table, floor lamp, and dressing table from the bathroom of Jeanne Lanvin, by Armand-Albert Rateau, circa 1920–1922

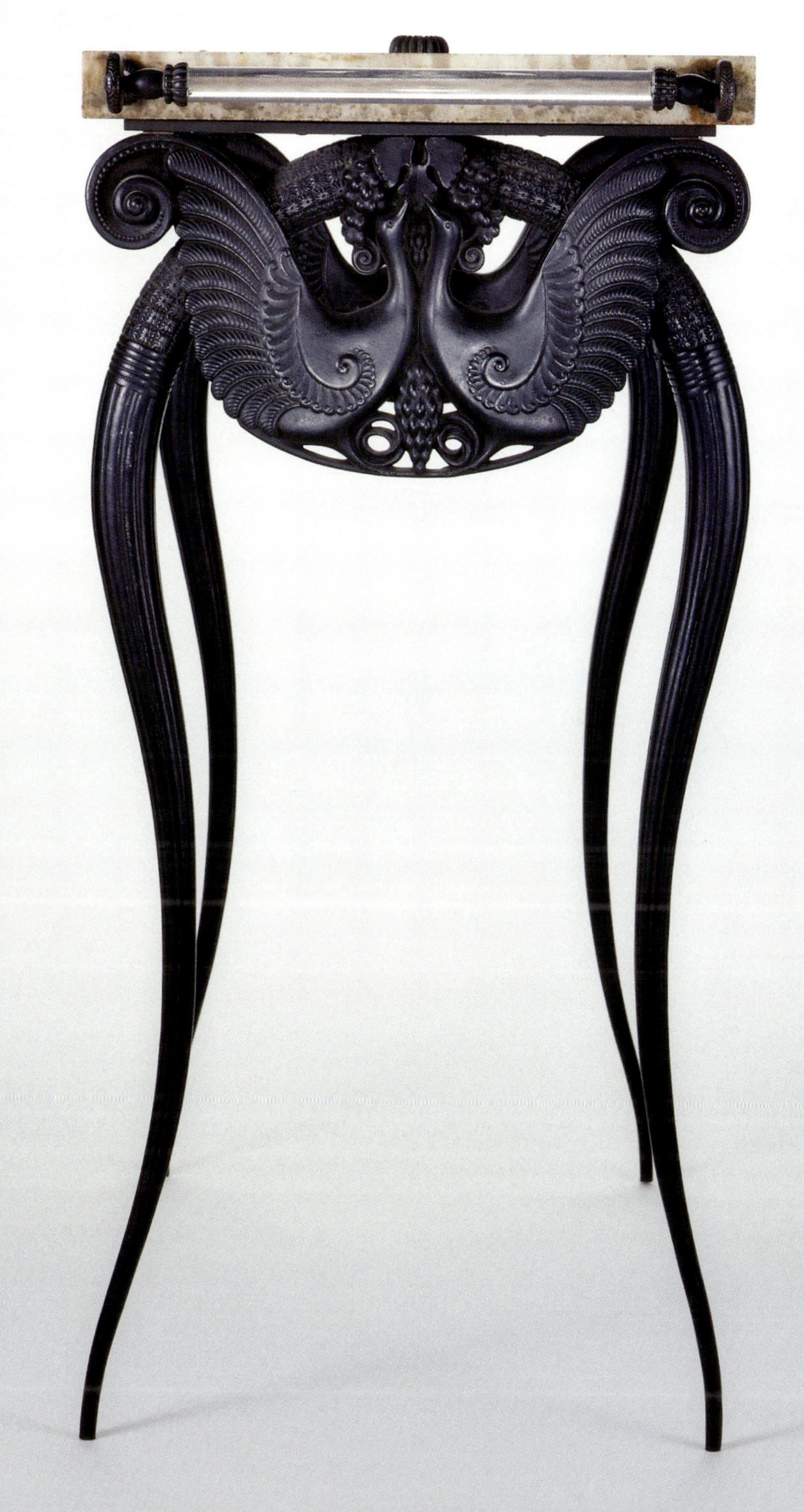

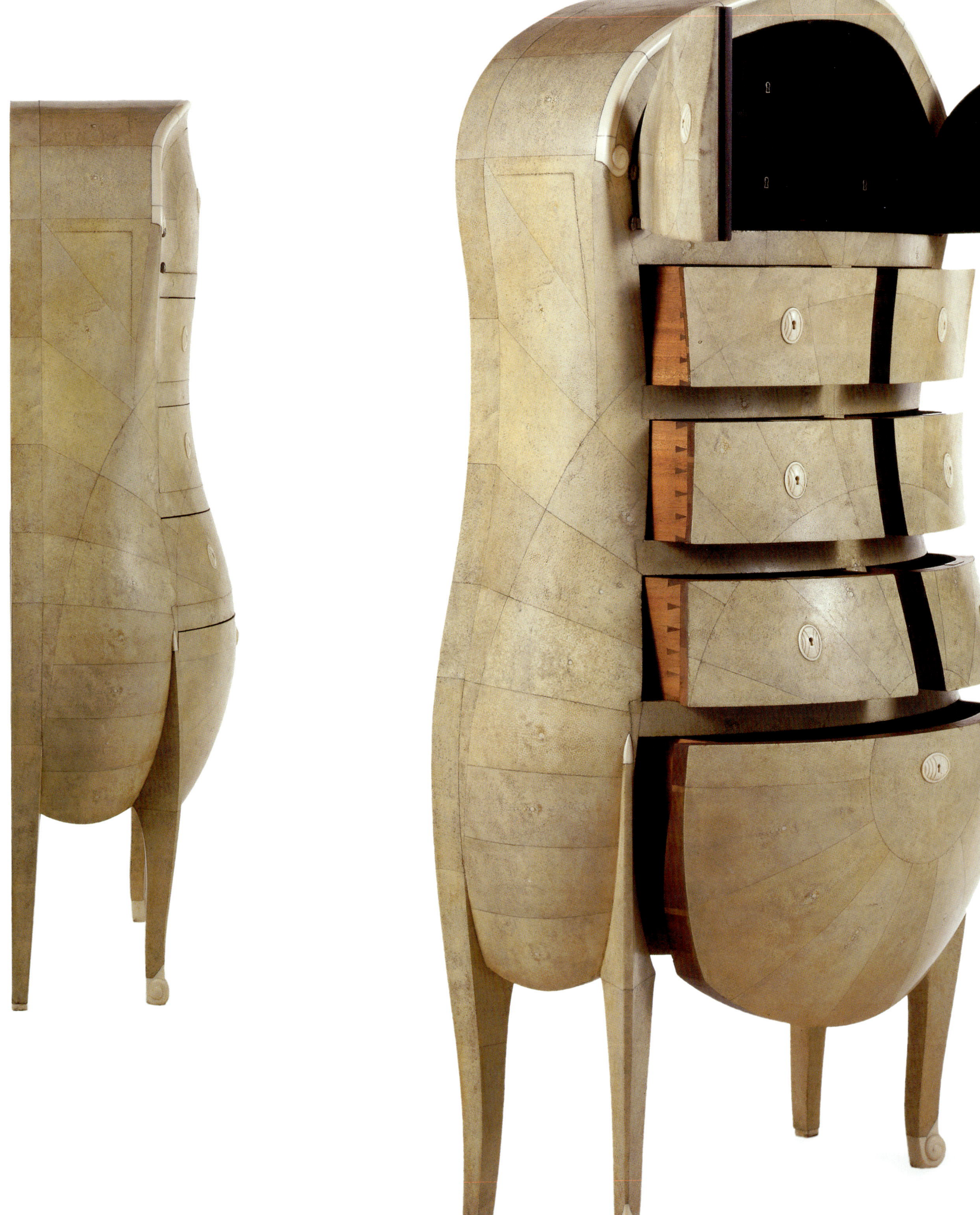

CHIFFONNIER

FRENCH, 1925
ANDRÉ GROULT (1884–1967)
SHARKSKIN, BEECH, MAHOGANY, IVORY.
H. 59 IN. (150 CM), W. 30⅜ IN. (77 CM),
D. 12⅝ IN. (32 CM)
PURCHASE, 1998

The chiffonnier, a tall chest of drawers, originated in the 18th century and was used by ladies for their "chiffon," sewing, jewelry, or even letters. André Groult revisited this traditional form to create a piece that is all emphatic curves and countercurves. The suggestively anthropomorphic shape is strengthened by the sharkskin veneer. The numerous skins are laid on in radial patterns centered at the positions of breasts and abdomen. The similarity between this chiffonnier and the female body cannot be dismissed, as the designer himself explained that he wanted to make a piece that was "curvaceous to the point of indecency."

Groult started his career in the 1910s and, like Paul Follot and Paul Iribe, reacted against Art Nouveau. They advocated a return to tradition and turned their attention to Restoration and Louis-Philippe (1810–1848) furniture, which they regarded as the last genuinely French styles. Groult always remained faithful to the enveloping and rounded shapes typical of the Restoration style. In the early days of his career, he used bright colors; later, in the 1920s, he covered his furniture with more precious materials in subtle hues—sharkskin, lacquer, and straw.

At the 1925 Paris World's Fair, which launched the style now known as Art Deco, Groult participated in one of the most important pavilions, an exhibit of the Société des Artistes Décorateurs titled *The French Embassy.* Here, Groult was entrusted with the decoration of the Chambre de Madame (Milady's bedroom). The concept was a harmony of grays and pinks with a wall covering of silk brocaded with a fan motif, which served as a foil for the sharkskin-veneered furniture. The furniture included a rounded bed set on a platform and surmounted by a canopy, enveloping upholstered armchairs, side chairs, a chest of drawers, a glass-fronted secretary, and, above all, this extraordinary chiffonnier. —E.P.

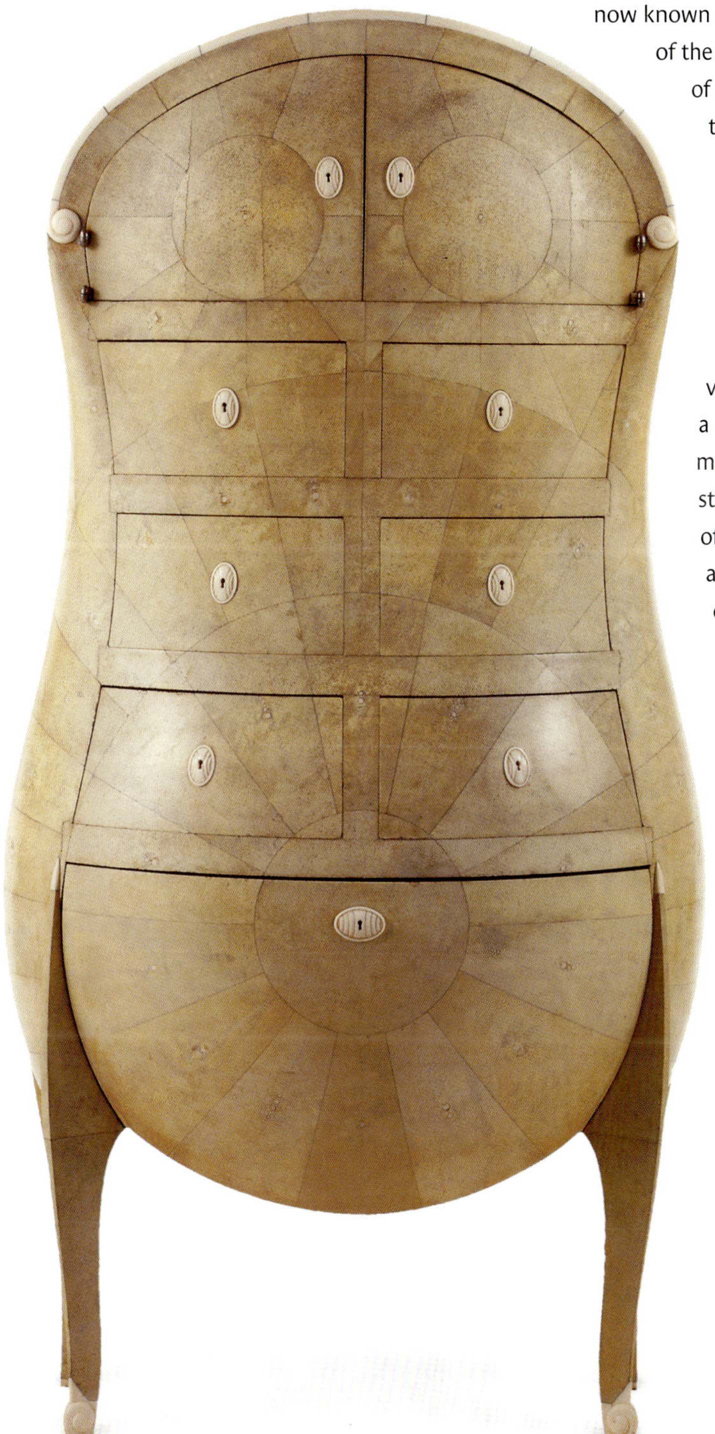

Reading Chair

French, 1925–1928

Pierre Legrain (1889–1929)

Mahogany veneer, silver-plated metal, leather.

H. 45¼ in. (115 cm), W. 17¾ in. (45 cm), D. 23¼ in. (59 cm)

Gift of Jean Edouard Dubrujeaud, nephew of Jacques Doucet, 1958

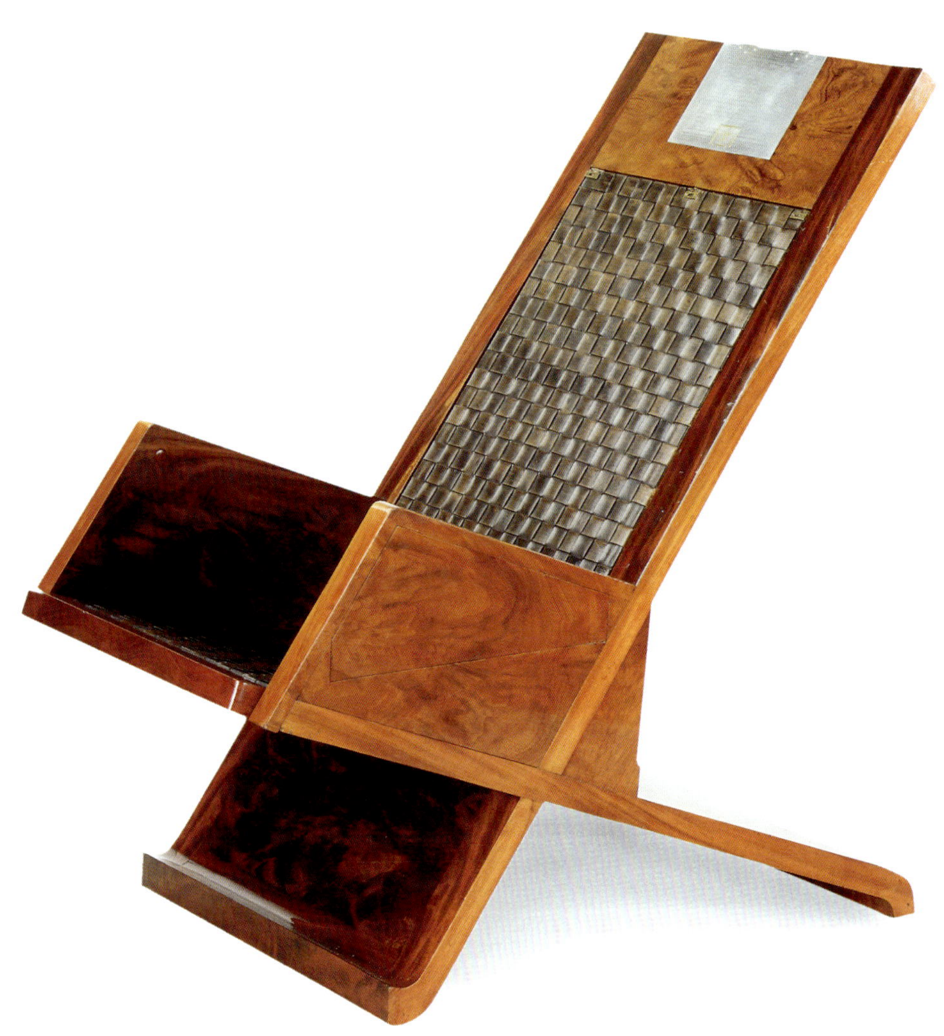

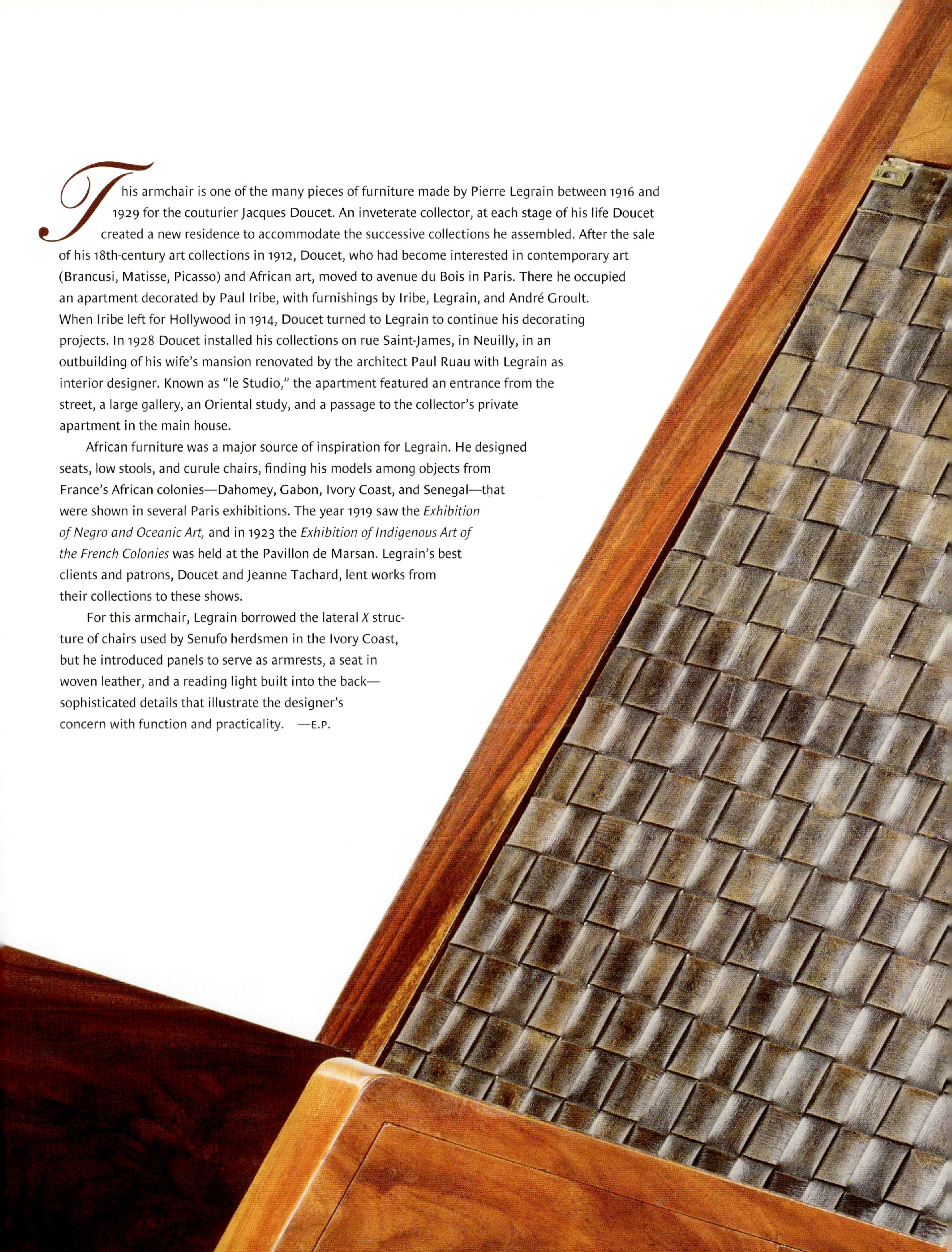

This armchair is one of the many pieces of furniture made by Pierre Legrain between 1916 and 1929 for the couturier Jacques Doucet. An inveterate collector, at each stage of his life Doucet created a new residence to accommodate the successive collections he assembled. After the sale of his 18th-century art collections in 1912, Doucet, who had become interested in contemporary art (Brancusi, Matisse, Picasso) and African art, moved to avenue du Bois in Paris. There he occupied an apartment decorated by Paul Iribe, with furnishings by Iribe, Legrain, and André Groult. When Iribe left for Hollywood in 1914, Doucet turned to Legrain to continue his decorating projects. In 1928 Doucet installed his collections on rue Saint-James, in Neuilly, in an outbuilding of his wife's mansion renovated by the architect Paul Ruau with Legrain as interior designer. Known as "le Studio," the apartment featured an entrance from the street, a large gallery, an Oriental study, and a passage to the collector's private apartment in the main house.

African furniture was a major source of inspiration for Legrain. He designed seats, low stools, and curule chairs, finding his models among objects from France's African colonies—Dahomey, Gabon, Ivory Coast, and Senegal—that were shown in several Paris exhibitions. The year 1919 saw the *Exhibition of Negro and Oceanic Art,* and in 1923 the *Exhibition of Indigenous Art of the French Colonies* was held at the Pavillon de Marsan. Legrain's best clients and patrons, Doucet and Jeanne Tachard, lent works from their collections to these shows.

For this armchair, Legrain borrowed the lateral *X* structure of chairs used by Senufo herdsmen in the Ivory Coast, but he introduced panels to serve as armrests, a seat in woven leather, and a reading light built into the back—sophisticated details that illustrate the designer's concern with function and practicality. —E.P.

Cigarette cases

French, 1928–1930
Raymond Templier (1891–1968)
Silver, lacquer. Below: H. 3⅞ in. (10 cm); Right, each: H. 5 in. (12.8 cm)
Gift of Raymond Templier, 1966

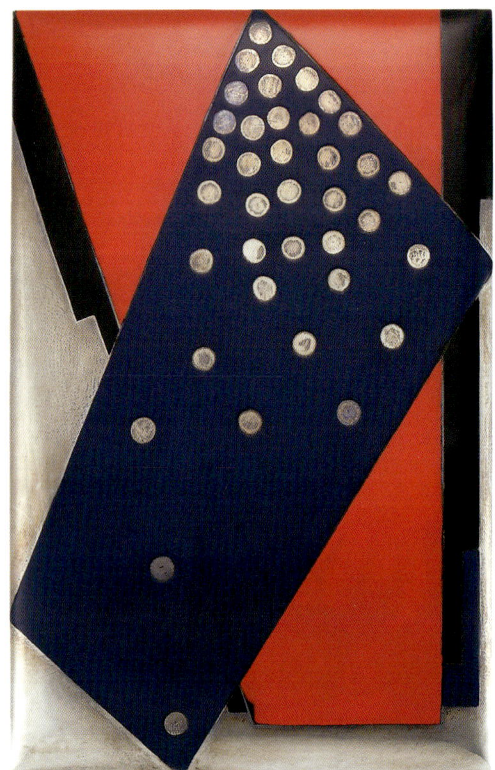

The cigarette case first made its appearance in the 19th century, and its use became widespread in the 1920s. During that period, when women became determinedly emancipated and gradually asserted their right to adopt the clothing and attitudes that were previously the exclusive realm of men, they claimed the right, in particular, to smoke in public. From that time on, goldsmiths made delicate and luxurious cases—veritable symbols of modernity—that women could slip into their evening bags.

These three cigarette cases illustrate the influence of early abstract art on designers in the 1930s. Geometric shapes of red, black, and bright blue enamels contrasting with the gray shades of silver are arranged as if on the flat surface of an abstract painting. Raymond Templier made his love of the modern cityscape and the tools of contemporary life evident in his designs. In the composition on one of the cases, paired engraved curved lines juxtaposed with the color blocks suggest tracks as seen in an aerial view of a railway station.

A member of a famous family of Parisian jewelers, Templier attended the Ecole Nationale des Arts Décoratifs from 1909 to 1912 and was one of the founding members of the Union des Artistes Modernes in 1929. This important association brought together designers who were keen to incorporate in their work new shapes and materials from the world of industry, such as man-made fibers, metal pipes, aluminum, and steel. —H.A.

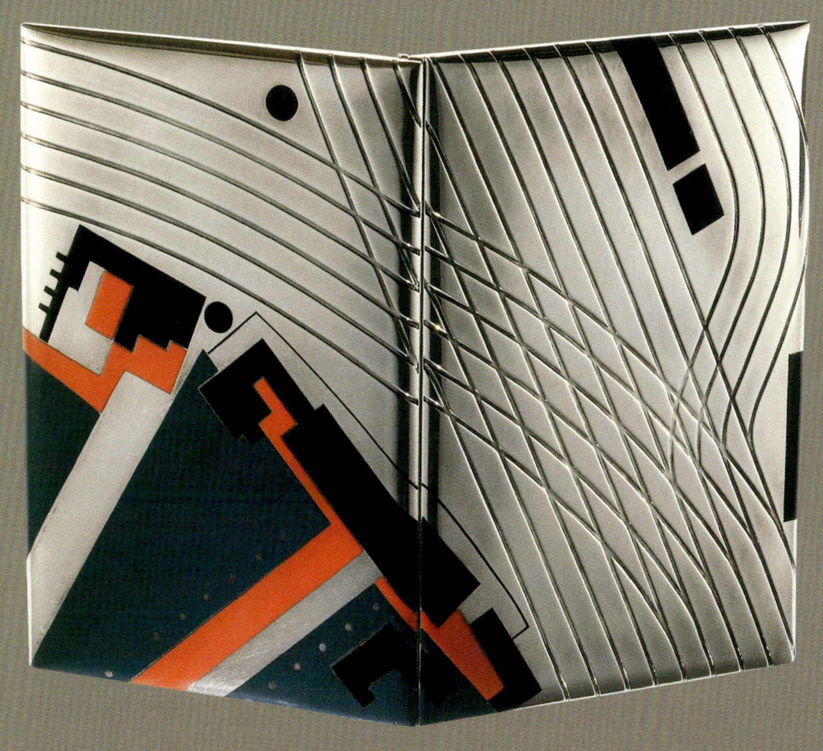

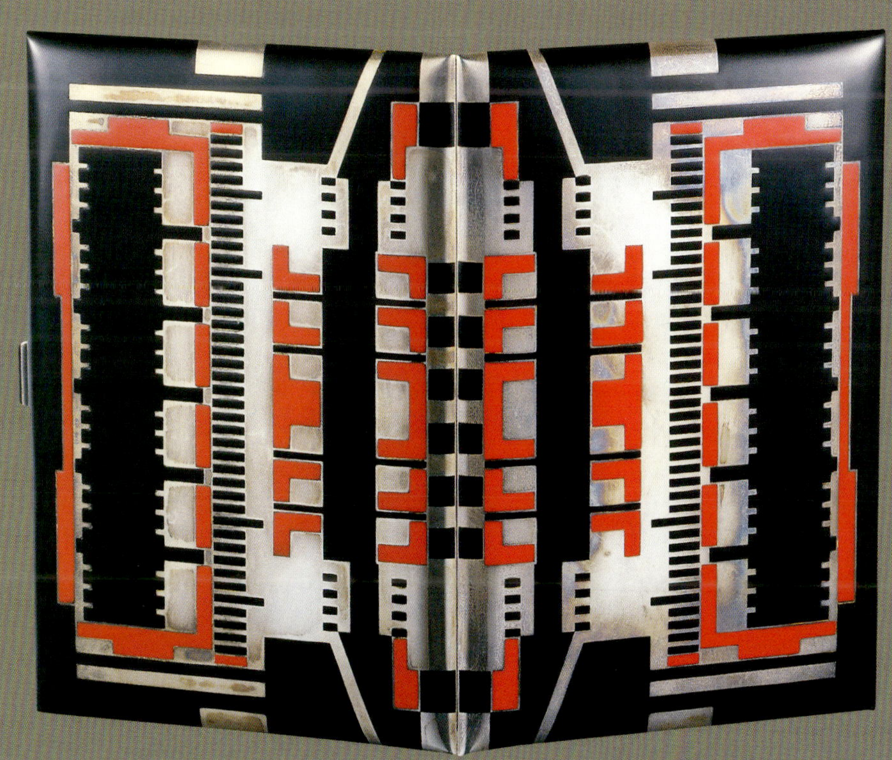

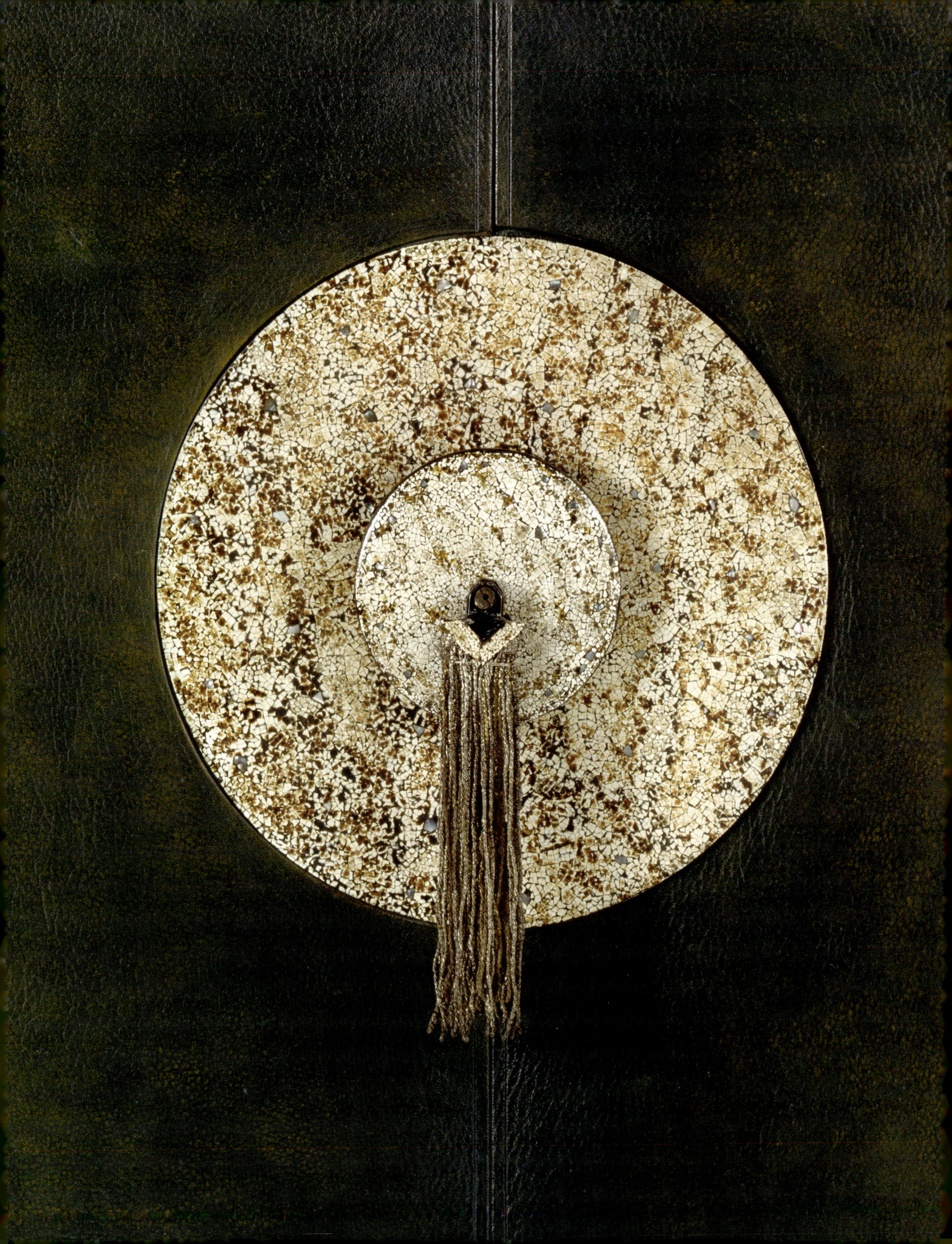

Cabinet for Manuscripts

French, circa 1928
Paul-Louis Mergier (1891–1986)
Cape Morocco leather, parchment, ivory, mother-of-pearl, eggshell lacquer. H. 40½ in. (103 cm), L. 51⅛ in. (130 cm), D. 15⅜ in. (39 cm)
Gift of Jean Edouard Dubrujeaud, 1958

This luxury piece was commissioned by the couturier, collector, and patron Jacques Doucet to house his collection of manuscripts of modern authors. It stood in Doucet's Neuilly "Studio," in the same room with such outstanding paintings as Pablo Picasso's *Les Demoiselles d'Avignon* and Le Douanier Rousseau's *La Charmeuse de Serpent.*

The cabinet's simple lines were inspired by Korean marriage chests, but the highly refined materials represent a novelty. The exterior is sheathed in green Cape Morocco leather, while the inside is completely lined with parchment. The lock and hinges are in the form of lacquer medallions inlaid with mother-of-pearl and eggshell; the tips of the legs are surrounded by small ivory-colored plastic strips.

Paul-Louis Mergier was an aeronautical engineer who pursued a parallel career as a painter, brassworker, and furniture designer. From 1925 on, he exhibited furniture, made by cabinetmakers to his designs, at the Salon des Artistes Décorateurs, where the technical perfection and innovative selection of materials that typified his work caught the attention of Doucet. —H.A.

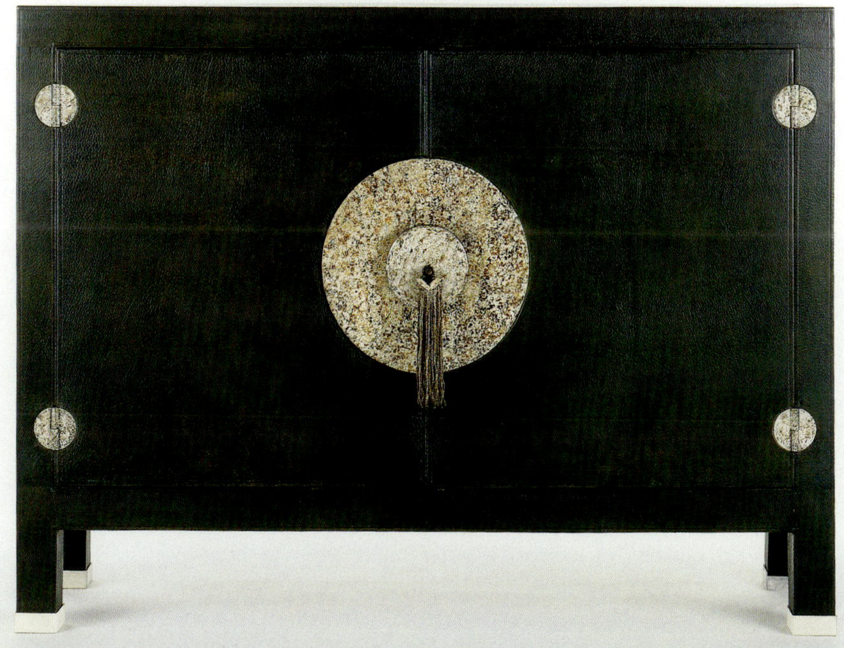

Vases

French, circa 1924
Jean Dunand (1877–1942)
Metal, lacquer, eggshell. Left: H. 4⅜ in. (11 cm);
Right: H. 9⅞ in. (25 cm)
Purchased from the artist, 1924. On loan from the Musée National d'Art Moderne

True lacquer is an extract of the sap of *Rhus succedanea* and *R. vernicifera,* trees that grow only in the Far East. It was first developed as a medium for artistic decoration in China around 200 B.C. and introduced into Japan in about the 7th century A.D. Not until the 17th century did European craftsmen master an imitation of the technique, known as "japanning."

The Swiss-born decorative sculptor Jean Dunand became a specialist in hammered metalwork in the European tradition of *dinanderie* (brassware). An admirer of lacquered Oriental wares, he first investigated the technique when asked for restoration assistance by Seizo Sugawara, the Japanese master craftsman dispatched by Emperor Mutsu-Hito to represent his country at the 1900 Paris World's Fair. Dunand learned the secrets of the arduous Japanese process from Sugawara and incorporated the techniques in his own original work from 1912 on.

These two vases by Dunand present an almost perfect purity of form, one a sphere, the other a cocoon. The natural lacquer colors are hemmed in red and black at the collar of each vase. The surface pattern was created by the addition of the broken shells of chicken eggs (preferred to other kinds of shell because of their even thickness). The bits of shell were set with tweezers on a coat of fresh lacquer, then sealed with subsequent coats. The network of fine cracks between the eggshell fragments creates the effect of a precious mosaic. —H.A.

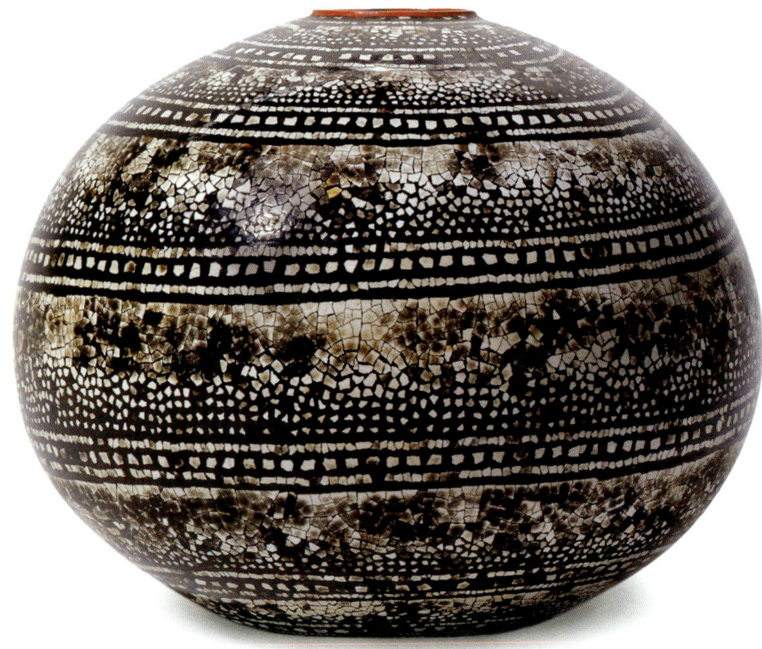

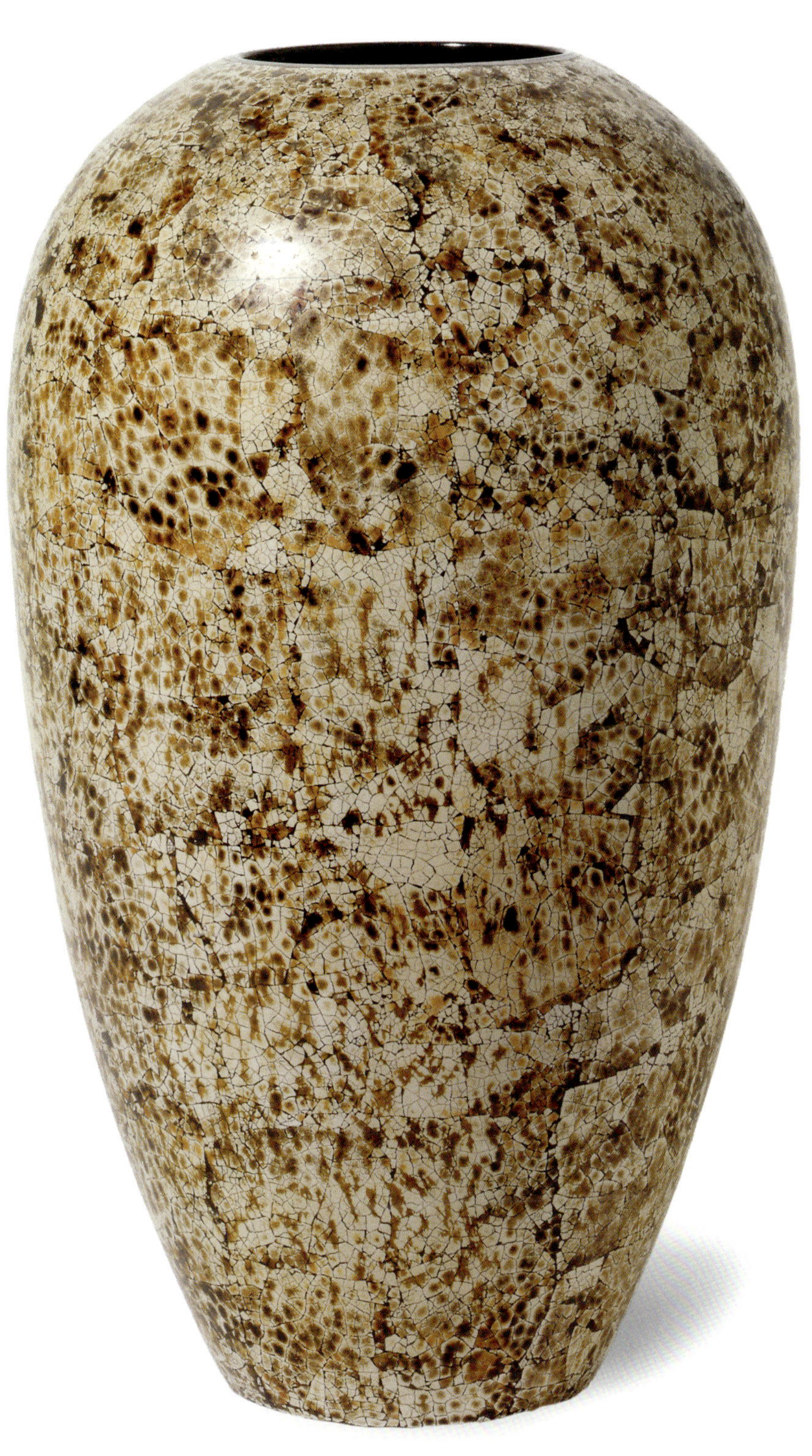

Golden Parrot bottle

French, 1928
Maurice Marinot (1882–1960)
Glass. H. 6⅛ in. (15.5 cm)
Louis Barthou bequest, 1934

"I protest against the words 'decorator' and 'decorative art.' My trade as a glazier is a game that's every bit as gratifying as painting and sculpture." With these key words, Maurice Marinot, initially a painter and later the creator of one-of-a-kind blown-glass pieces, summed up his most essential intellectual and artistic conviction.

Marinot began experimenting with enameled glass techniques and acid etching in 1911. He continued his investigation of glass for two decades, gradually building his skill at hot-working, and from 1922 on, he exhibited glass he had blown himself. His understanding of the "private meaning" of the material, compared in its molten phase to a living organism, led him to develop a new aesthetic of glass, one that was thick, smooth, and fleshy.

The Golden Parrot bottle is one of the masterpieces of the artist's mature years. The ample, powerful body and stopper are alive with a ferment of bubbles and colored patches of oxides. Because the bottle seems to restitute and give substance to the idea of the breath that created it, it is one of the artist's most telling archetypes. The effects of colors and oxide inclusions give depth to the thickness of the material and contribute to the illusion that a split second in the existence of molten glass has been frozen within the bright, smooth walls of this piece. —V.A.

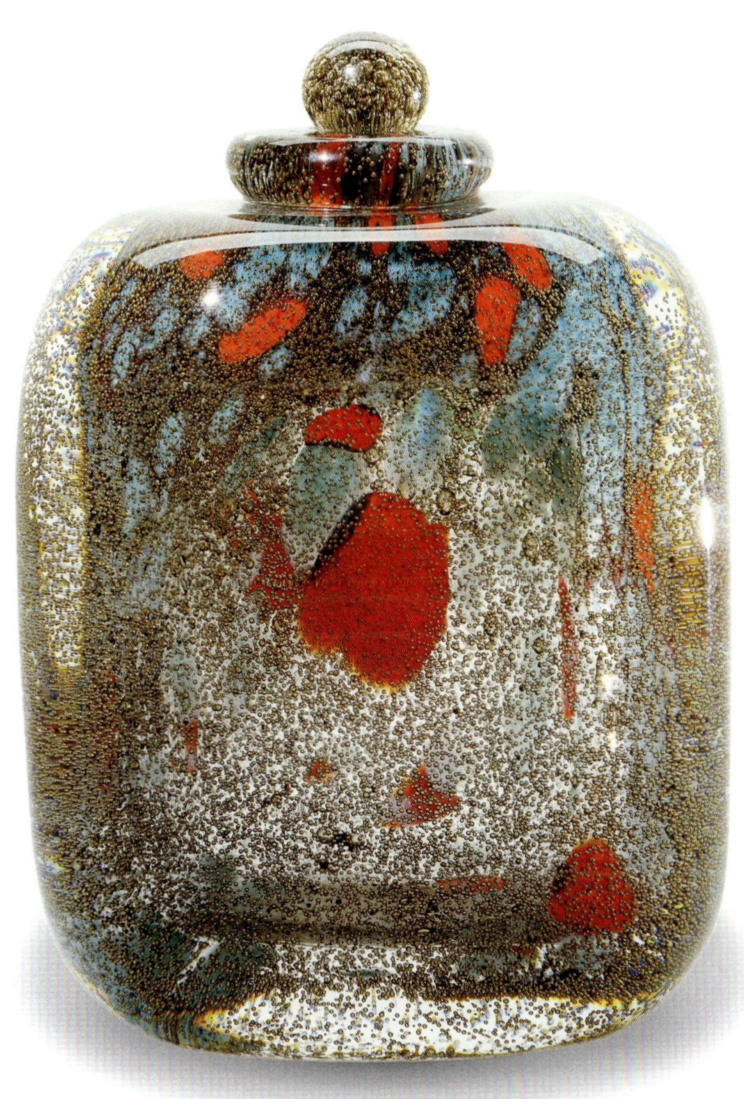

Chaise longue

French, 1931
René Herbst (1891–1982)
Metal tubing, springs. H. 31⅞ in. (81 cm),
L. 68⅛ in. (173 cm), W. 22½ in. (57 cm)
Purchase, 1995

In 1931 this seat by René Herbst read as a symbol of modernity. Its frame is made of metal tubing, an industrial material adopted by avant-garde furniture designers between 1925 and 1930. Despite the formality of the design, the chaise longue takes into account the needs of the human body in terms of comfort and relaxation, in tune with current concerns about health.

Springs stretched between the metal tubes make the seat flexible. The backrest is adjustable. A telescopic tube controlled by a handle links the bottom bar of the tilting backrest to the crossbar connecting the rear legs. The adjustment device

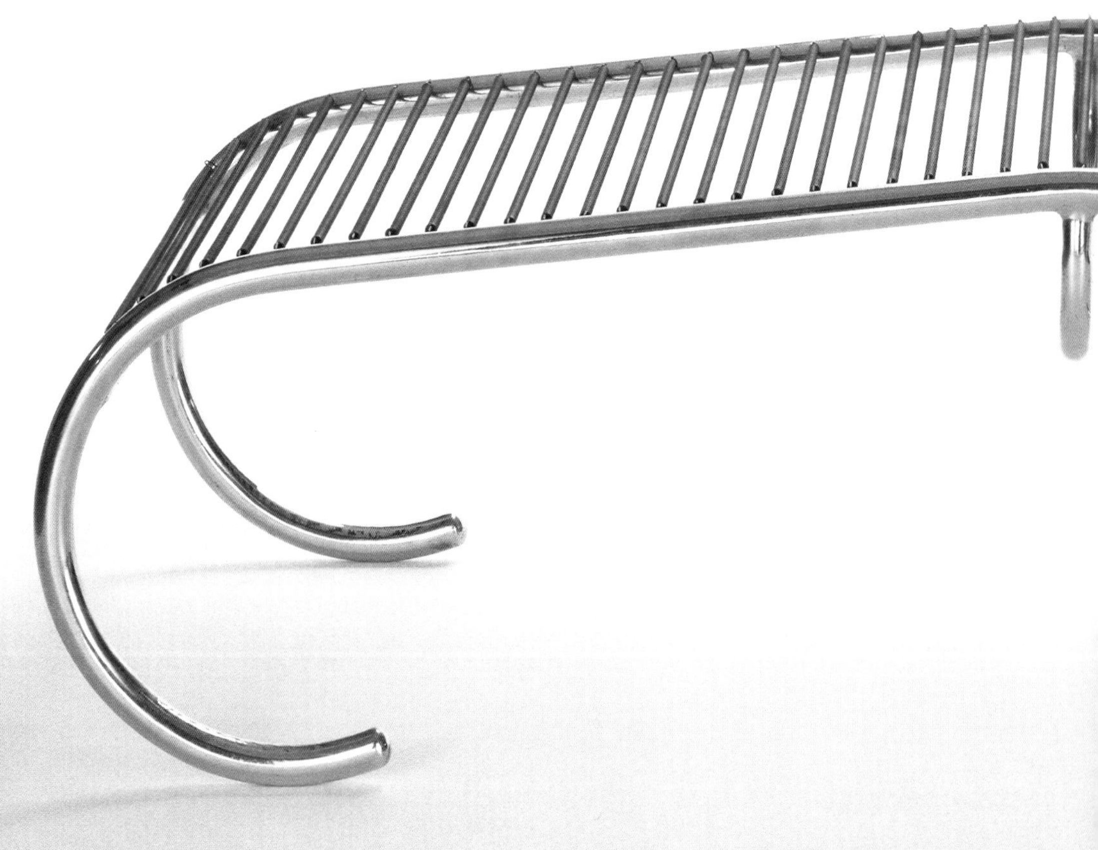

shows a delight in mechanisms and technical solutions drawn from new industries, such as the automobile industry. Herbst shares this approach with the artists belonging to the Union des Artistes Modernes, of which he was one of the founders.

We know from Herbst's archives that this chaise longue could be made in a variety of forms: with fixed as well as adjustable back, with fabric stretched over the structure, or with a mattress covering the springs. The version here no longer has its original mattress. Another example of the adjustable chaise longue was made for Manik Bagh, the palace of the maharaja of Indore in India, which was furnished by the German architect E. Muthesius. —C.R.

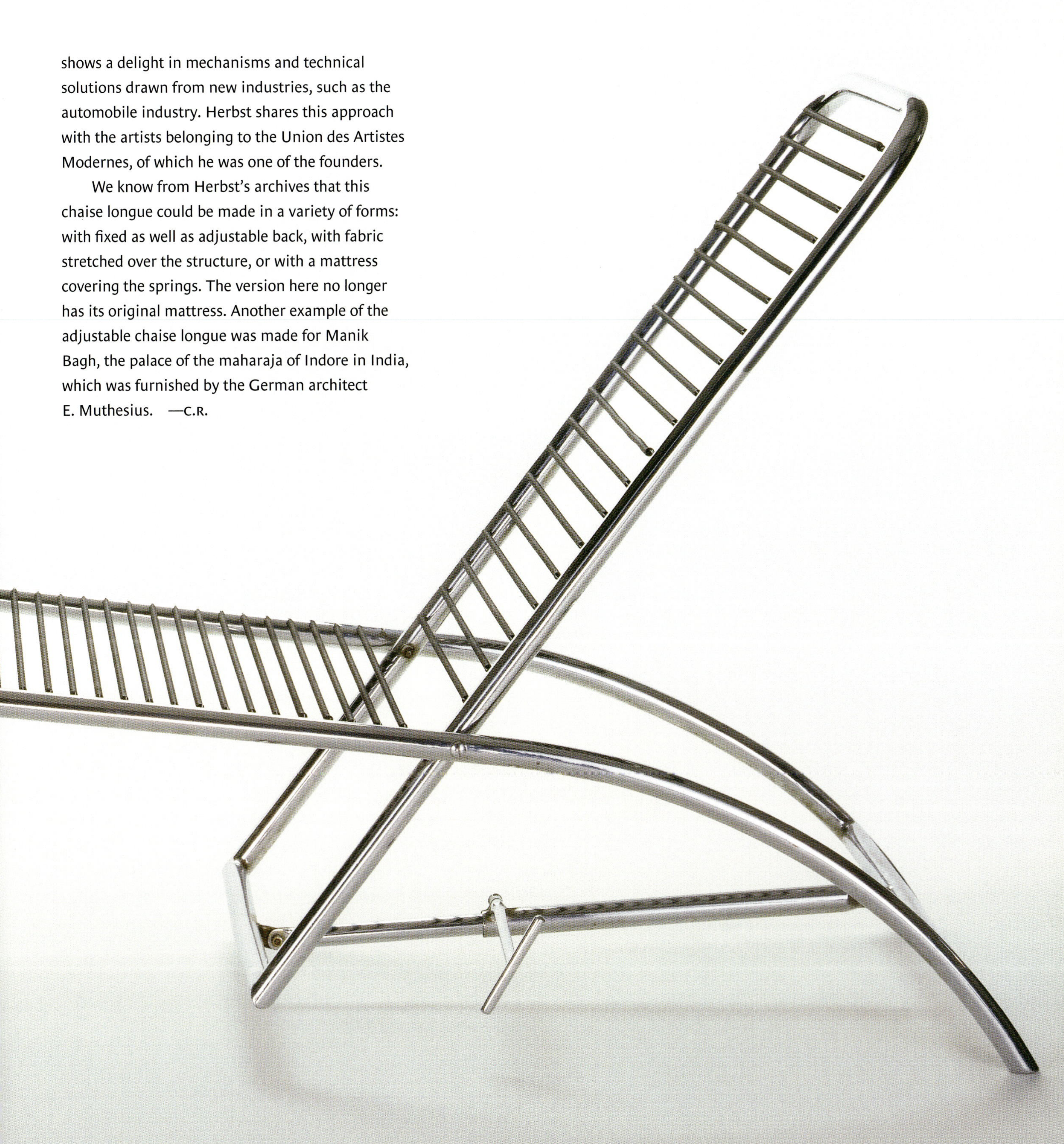

Brooch

French, 1933–1934
Raymond Templier (1891–1968)
Onyx, cut diamonds, frosted glass, platinum.
H. 1¾ in. (4.5 cm)
On loan from the Musée National d'Art Moderne

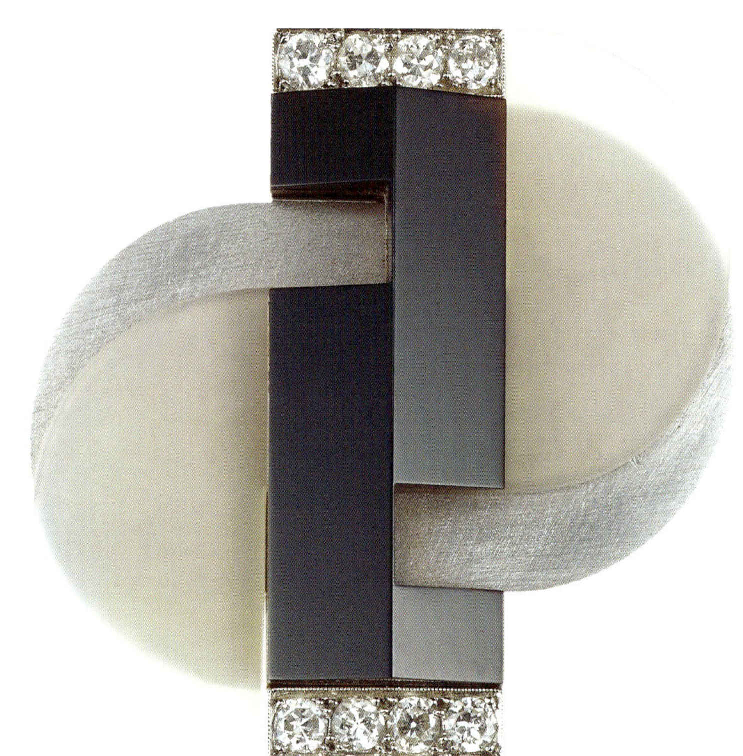

The design of this brooch involves an interaction of materials and overlaid layers, attracting a play of light. Curved and parallel lines and countercurves all blend harmoniously to make a perfect whole. In Raymond Templier's own words, "The composition of a jewel must be at once free, salient and condensed, and enclosed." In his treatment of color for this piece, he restricts himself to gray, black, and white. Contrary to convention in setting gemstones, the diamonds are not the essence of the piece, but rather a small part of the ensemble.

From 1990 on, the art of jewelry evolved rapidly in France. Templier played an important part in the Paris World's Fairs of 1925 and 1937, exhibiting work that overturned the rules of traditional gemwork. He sought innovation in unprecedented combinations of materials and the use of hitherto disparaged metals like steel, platinum, and aluminum. Templier was quick to realize that if his jewelry was to be accepted, it would have to align with fashion trends, following the dictates of Coco Chanel and Jean Patou: freedom, flexibility, and sober restraint. His jewels are suitably devoid of ornamental excess, with an aesthetic that reflected the current enthusiasm for sport and the admiration for the machine.

The emphatic composition and order that characterize Templier's art devolve from his design drawings, of which the Musée des Art Décoratifs has a significant representation. They demonstrate a clarity akin to projects of interior decoration being undertaken in France during those same years by Pierre Chareau, Jean-Michel Franck, Pierre Legrain, and Mallet-Stevens. With good reason the press of the day proclaimed Templier an "architect of the jewel." —F.B.

Clip

French, 1936–1937
Georges Fouquet (1862–1953)
Design: Jean Lambert-Rucki (1888–1967)
Gold. W. 1¾ in. (4.5 cm), L. 2½ in. (6.5 cm)
Purchased from the artist, 1952

Georges Fouquet belonged to one of the great families of jewelers working in Paris in the 19th century. While subscribing to the tradition of gemwork, he was eager to find new sources of inspiration, which he did by calling on artists who were not part of his professional world. These artists often steered his work toward greater simplicity. For the Exposition Internationale des Arts Décoratifs in 1925, he enlisted the architect Eric Bagge, the poster artist Cassandre, and the painter André Leveillé. His joint projects with the sculptor Jean Lambert-Rucki date from 1936, when they started preparing for the 1937 Paris World's Fair. For this project, Lambert-Rucki designed rings, clips, and bracelets, inspired in part by the vocabulary of Cubism and in part by his own highly personal imagery.

This totally geometric clip belongs to the era's modernist movement in jewelry, also expressed in the work of Jean Després, Gérard Sandoz, and Raymond Templier. While the house of Fouquet was known above all for its gemwork, Lambert-Rucki has here done away with precious stones and focused on a single material—gold—punctuated by forms in prominent relief: small rods on the sides and a half-sphere on the front. In its sobriety, the clip represents Lambert-Rucki's work at its purest extreme.

As a sculptor and member of the Union des Artistes Modernes, Lambert-Rucki was involved in many areas: religious art, designs for Jean Dunand, and sculptures in a wide range of materials (e.g., plaster, wood, copper, sheet metal). His foray into the world of jewelry was brief. His work with Fouquet occurred just when the jeweler, for financial reasons, had ceased all production except for the 1937 fair. The pieces of jewelry resulting from this collaboration were actually executed by independent craftsmen. —D.F.

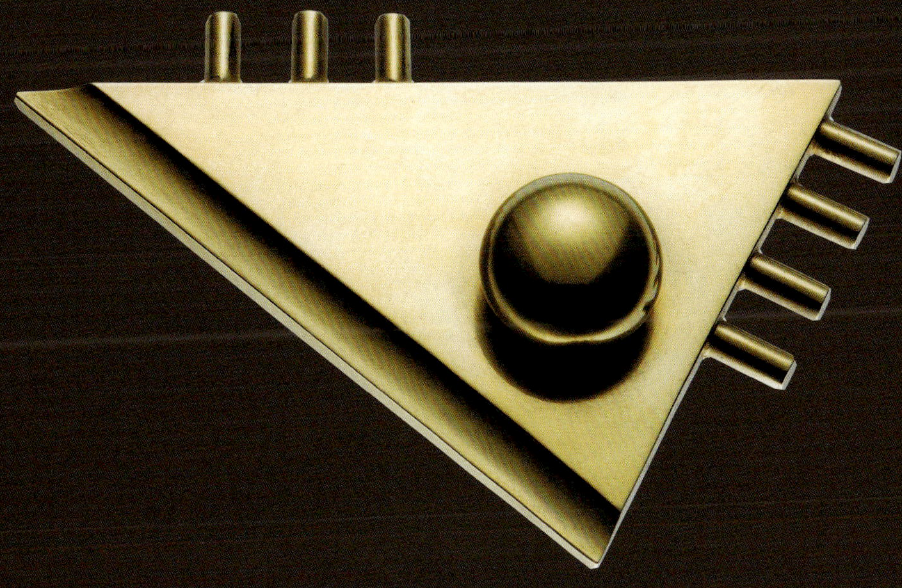

Tureen

French, after 1937
Jean Puiforcat (1897–1945)
Silver, silver gilt. H. 9⅞ in. (25 cm)
On loan from the Musée National d'Art Moderne, 1981

A model of this tureen in silver and silver gilt was featured at the 1937 Paris World's Fair, where Jean Puiforcat had his own pavilion. In his work, Puiforcat explored the possibilities of color in contrast with silver, here using gilding discreetly on the foot and finial of the tureen. In other examples in the Metropolitan Museum of Art in New York and the Museum of Decorative Arts in Montreal, gilding is applied to different areas, altering the accent. This tureen is typical of a general stylistic evolution that was treated analytically by Puiforcat, as the curve, technically more complex to make, took the place of the straight line.

Puiforcat was the most famous French silversmith of the first half of the 20th century, and a worthy heir to his family profession. He exhibited in 1921 at the Salon des Artistes Décorateurs, and by the time he took part in the 1925 Paris World's Fair, his reputation was assured. He quickly moved from the slightly Art Nouveau feel of pieces produced in the early 1920s to an architecture in silver based on geometric figures derived from the golden section. With his perfect technical mastery, the purity of his simple but harmonically calculated forms, and his introduction of new materials such as glass and rare woods, he was responsible for a renaissance in French silver. In 1930 he became a member of the Union des Artistes Modernes, thus joining the avant-garde of contemporary architects and decorators. —D.F.

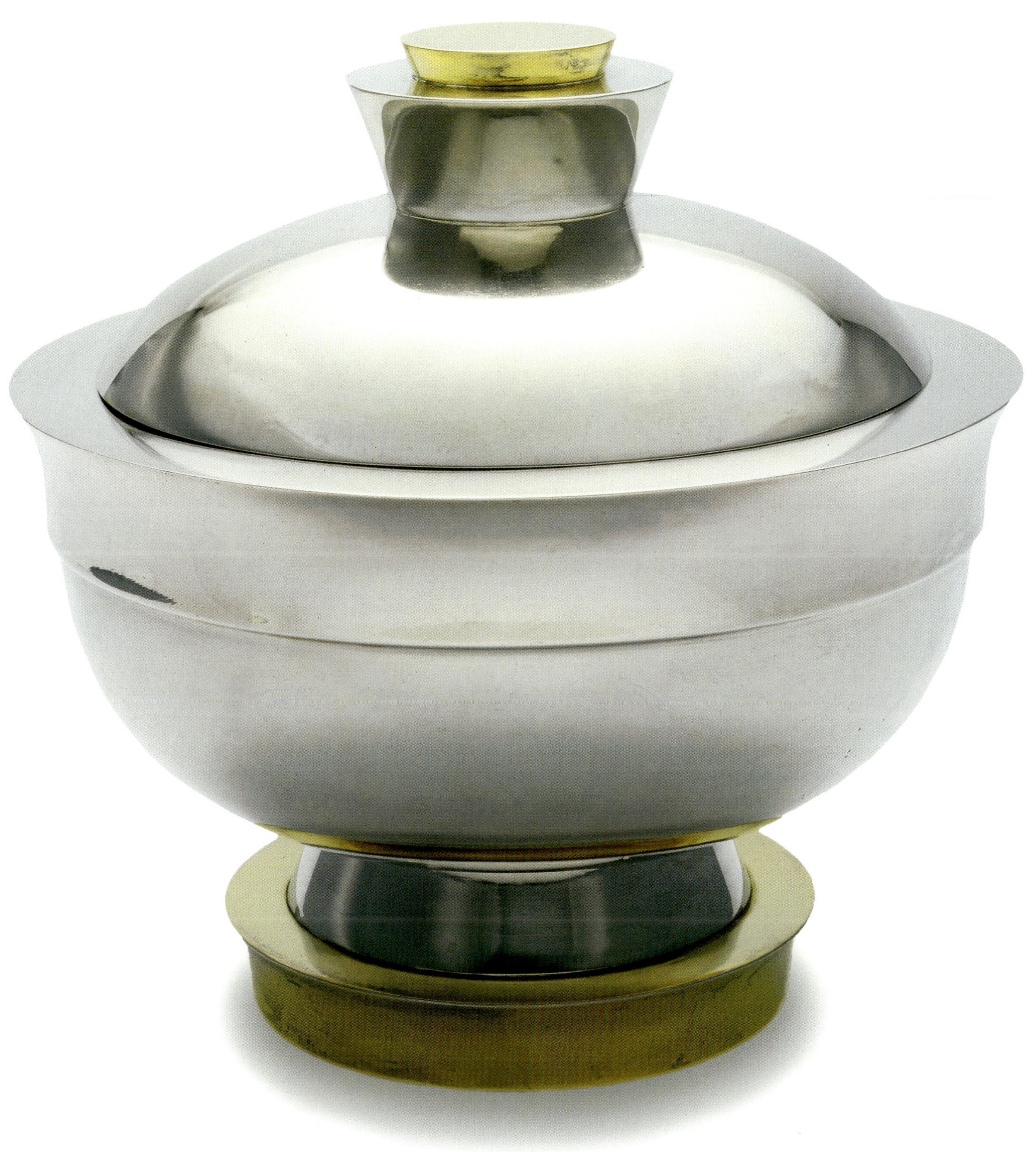

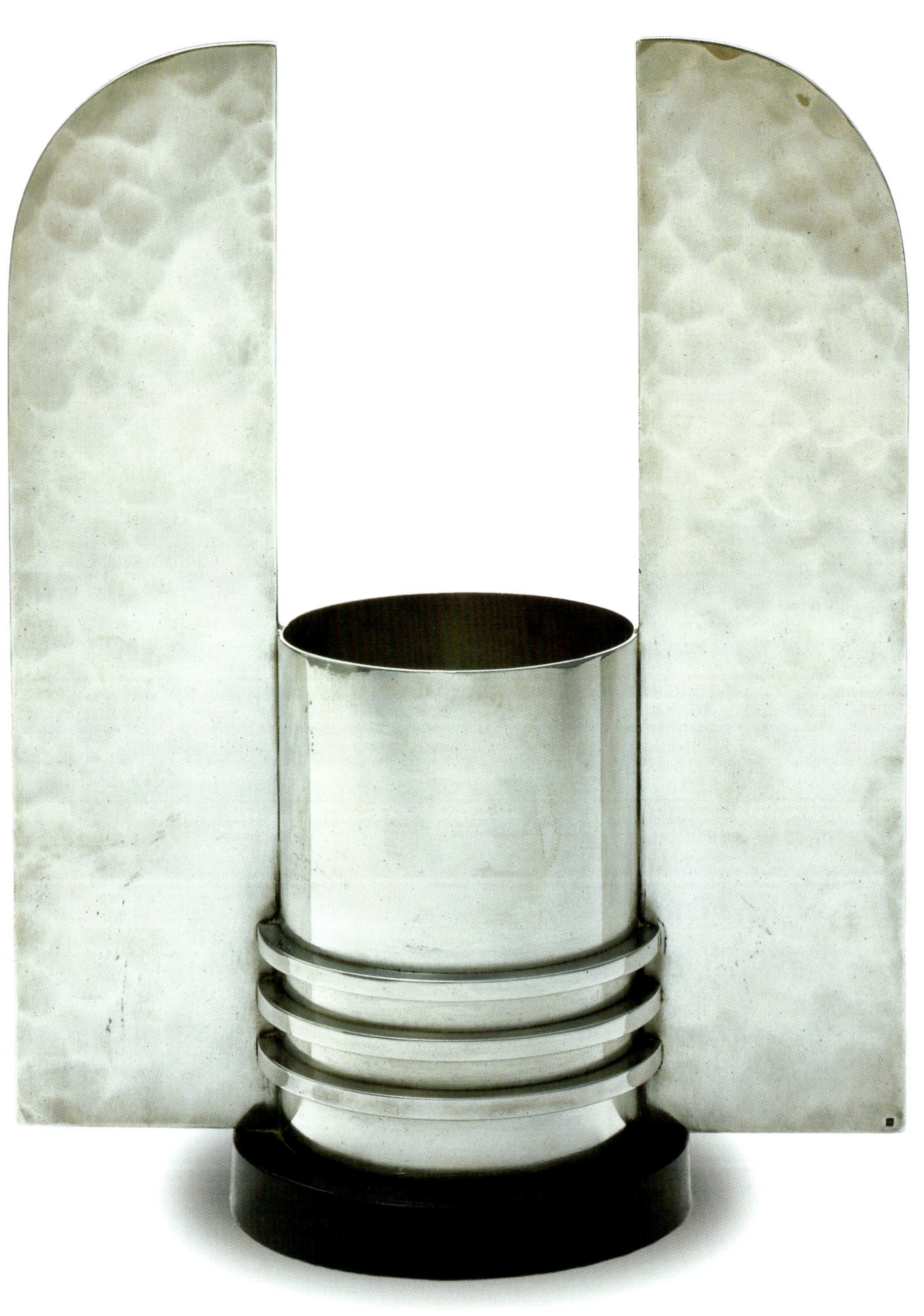

Maquette for an Aviation Cup

French, 1934
Jean Després (1889–1980)
Silver-plated metal, rosewood. H. 8⅝ in. (22 cm)
Gift of Jean Després, 1977

This silver-plated cup is a model for a larger trophy executed in pewter, now in the museum at Avallon, where Jean Després was born. Conceived as a cylinder encircled by a set of rings, the cup is typical of Després's constructionist impulse. He applied the rings, a signature device in his work, to the teapots, vases, and even pieces of jewelry he crafted. While silversmiths usually smooth and polish away any evidence of the hammering by which a shape is formed from a sheet of metal, Després, quite to the contrary, left the signs of handwork clearly visible. This forceful way of working metal is combined with a robust construction in original forms—e.g., the two large handles of this trophy thrusting skyward suggest two unfolding wings.

Després's artistic activities covered jewelry, silversmithing, and pewter work. For his jewelry he collaborated with Etienne Cournault when he wanted to incorporate glass, and with Jean Mayodon for ceramics. He showed regularly at decorative arts exhibitions from 1925 on, and his career took off in the 1930s, lasting well into the 1960s. In both silverwork and jewelry, Després's creations are a powerful expression of the machine aesthetic.

Besides the traditional items of vases, tureens, boxes, and place settings, Després's repertoire included liturgical silver and numerous sports trophies. Most silversmithing establishments, such as Christofle, also made sports trophies, but Després received particular acclaim for this specialty during his lifetime. In 1934 his trophies were exhibited in his gallery L'Art et La Mode, and in 1936 they earned him a gold medal from the Aéro Club de France. —D.F.

Vase

French, 1938
Raoul Dufy (1877–1953)
Faience. H. 9½ in. (24 cm)
On loan from the Musée National
d'Art Moderne, 1981

More than any other painter, Raoul Dufy was interested in the applied arts. His fabrics for the silk manufacturer Bianchini-Férier and his tapestries for the Beauvais factory are among his most successful works. His ceramics, which number slightly more than two hundred pieces, are also important. Most were produced in Paris in the studio of José Llorens Artigas from 1923 until World War II, with a few pieces made in Perpignan with Jean-Jacques Prolongeau from 1943 on.

Paul Gauguin, who worked with the ceramicist Ernest Chaplet, was the first painter of the late 19th century to be interested in making ceramics. In the first half of the 20th century, a growing number of painters would develop a similar interest—from the Fauve painters who worked in André Metthey's studio around 1907, to Pablo Picasso, who made ceramics at Madoura beginning in the 1940s. Dufy's ceramic work falls between these two key periods.

The Spanish potter Llorens Artigas was well known for his own production as well as his collaboration with painters including Dufy, Albert Marquet, and Joan Miró. While Miró took on ceramics as a sculpture medium, this was certainly not the case with Dufy, whose main interest lay in the painted decoration of vases and tiles.

Dufy's work with Llorens Artigas came to a halt in 1930 but started up again in 1937. This 1938 vase was potted by Llorens Artigas and painted by Dufy with one of his favorite themes. Marine subjects, coming straight from his canvases, are the most frequent in his ceramic work: the volume of a pot lent itself to conveying the movements of his nude bathers and nymphs. —D.F.

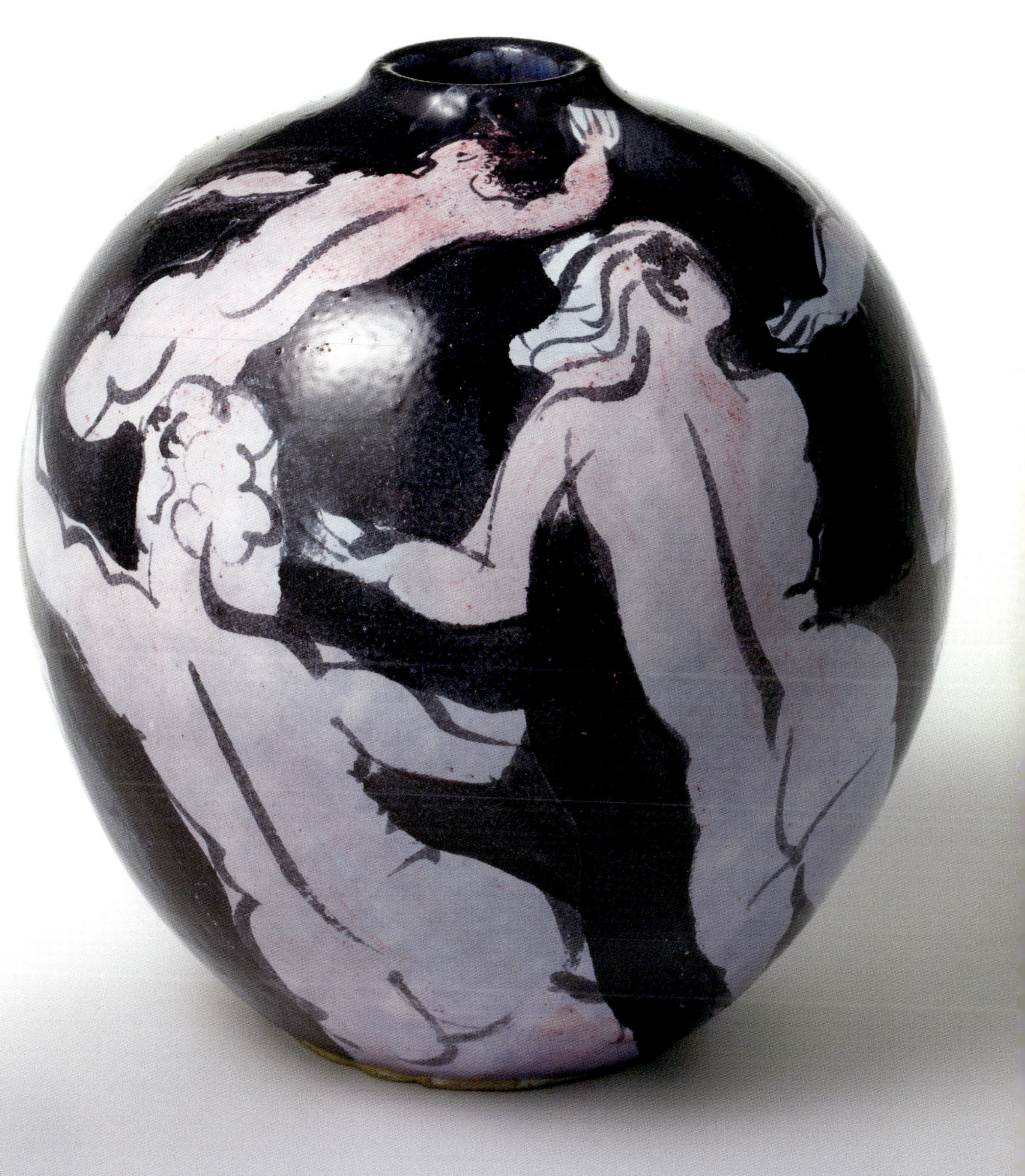

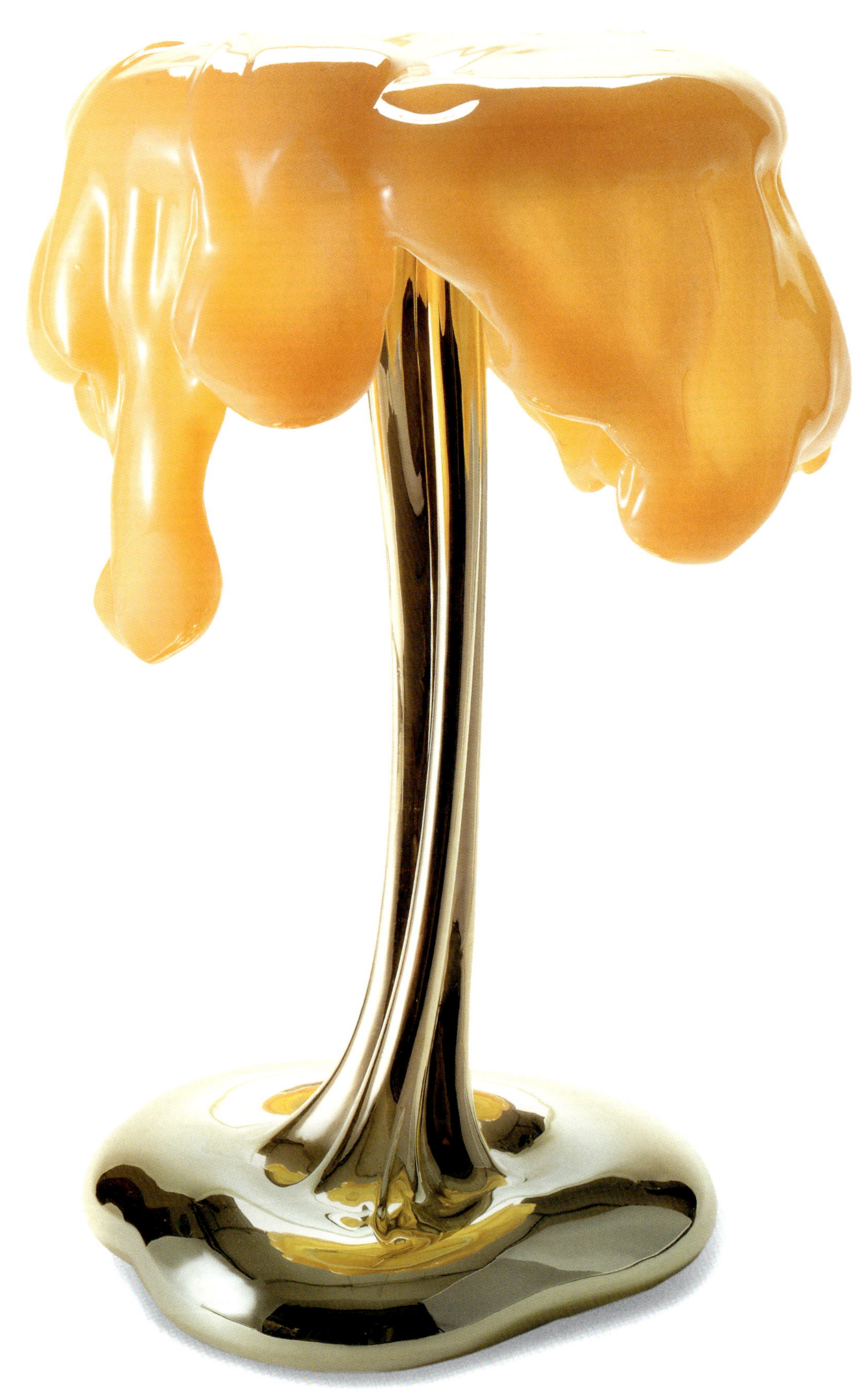

Expansion lamp

French, 1975
César (César Baldaccini) (1921–1998)
Bronze, polyester resin. H. 30¼ in. (77 cm)
Gift of César, 1996

In 1965 the sculptor César stopped producing his "metal compressions," which were made using mechanical industrial methods, and started experimenting with the expressive possibilities of plastics. The synthetic resins he used expanded when exposed to air and solidified almost instantly. César introduced a purely chemical and random language, similar to the processes involved in his compressions. The shade for his Expansion lamp was formed organically without the use of a mold, as the synthetic resin determined its own shape. The only principle guiding the way it evolved was internal expansion.

With resin, César managed to produce the visual equivalent of a lampshade. The model of the base was made in plastic by the same process of expansion, but it was then cast in bronze. The combination of plastic and bronze is particularly bold. "All materials are precious when I talk to them: tires, gold, sheet metal, crystal, and even plastic." The sculptor extended the formal vocabulary that he developed with resins into very diverse materials (bronze in collaboration with the founder Blanchet, glass with Daum, etc.).

The involvement of painters and sculptors in creating furniture and functional objects was encouraged by the *Objet* exhibition organized by the Musée des Arts Décoratifs in 1962. From 1968 on, César produced single pieces or very limited editions with utilitarian purposes. This Expansion lamp, which was made in 1975 and donated to the museum by the sculptor in 1995, is one of the two artist's prototypes for the edition. César's functional creations are inseparable from his overall artistic oeuvre. —F.B.

L'Homme chair

French, 1970; second edition, 1986
Ruth Francken (born 1924)
White polyester. H. 40⅛ in. (102 cm),
W. 22 in. (56 cm), D. 26⅜ in. (67 cm)
FNAC fund

This anthropomorphic seat consists of an anonymous figure whose body ends abruptly at shoulder height. The body is treated in a realistic way, with all the physical details—muscles, joints, and even wrinkles in the skin—incorporated in the plaster cast made from a live model, but it is nevertheless faceless. The coldness of the white polyester and the shininess of the surface further this impersonal effect. The idea of sitting on a naked body may be somewhat disconcerting, but the impression was taken from the back. The front, which is the actual seat, is completely smooth. This body, which has no sexual parts, is not provocative. It visually echoes the body of anyone sitting in the seat, creating an ambiguity between the image of the person sitting and that of the cast form.

Ruth Francken is an independent artist who does not limit herself to one particular discipline. This chair, together with a table of which only five examples were made, are her only forays into furniture making. With the L'Homme chair, Francken alludes to the sit-in demonstrations of the 1960s, in which the protestors' physical presence was a show of defiance. —C.R.

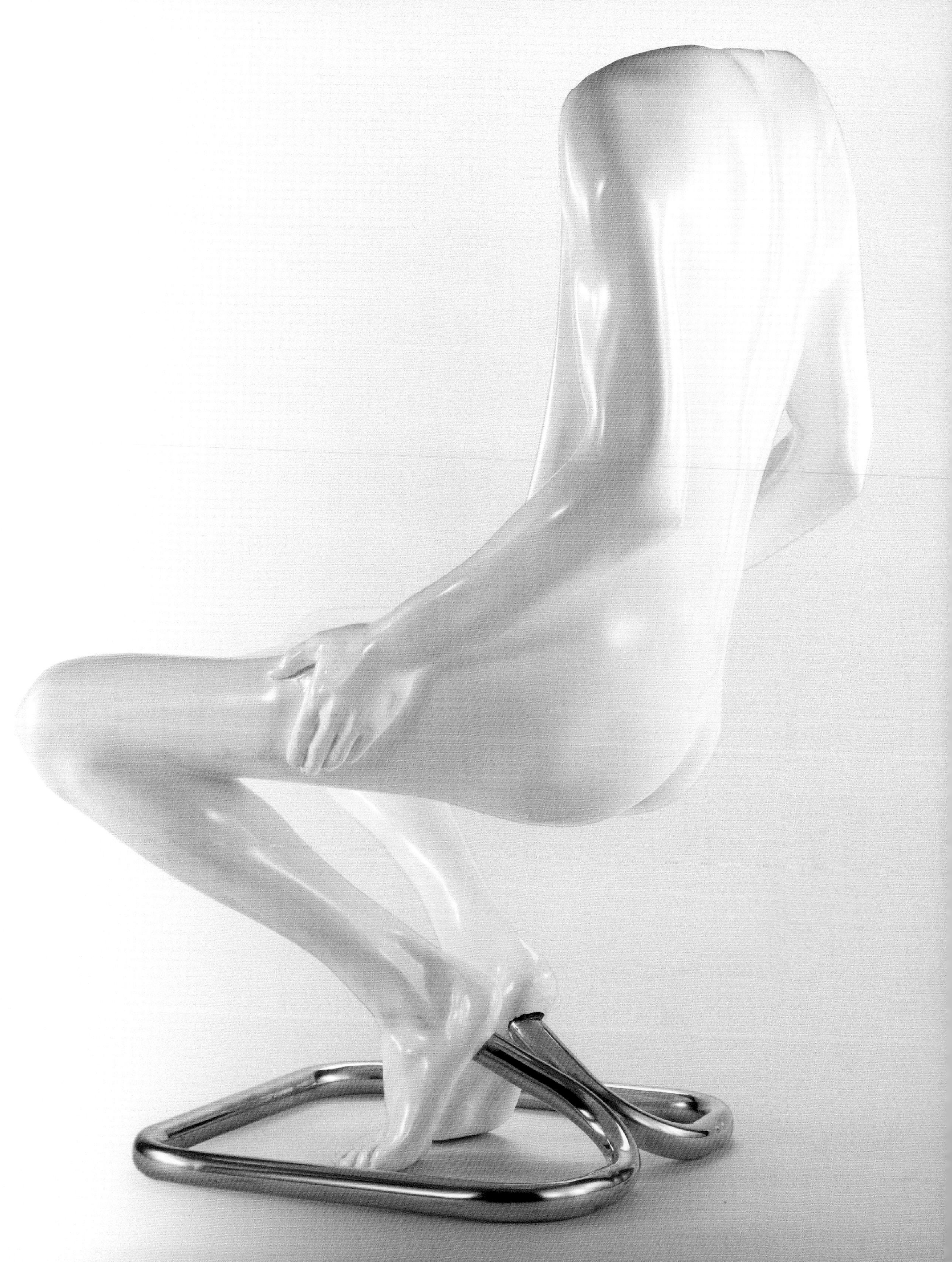

Enfer (Inferno) Cabinet

French, 1998
Mattia Bonetti (born 1952) and Elisabeth Garouste (born 1949)
Wrought iron, enameled terra-cotta, sheet glass.
H. 40½ in. (103 cm), W. 53⅛ in. (135 cm), D. 18⅞ in. (48 cm)
FNAC Fund

Working together since the 1980s, the creative duo of Mattia Bonetti and Elisabeth Garouste has taken the lead in a neo-Baroque trend not seen in France since the great decorators of the 1940s. Their work is laden with literary and visual references, and they define it in terms of linking images or making a puzzle, as they seek furniture that tells a story. The free spirit of their concepts is given concrete expression by the many skilled craftsmen working on the production, in particular the Atelier Jakubec (ceramics) and the Coligny foundry.

Here, Bonetti and Garouste play with the idea of the collector's cabinet, a piece of furniture intended to protect precious objects from prying eyes. This contemporary version, which was produced in 1998 by the Neotu Gallery in an edition of eight, breaks with any idea we might have of a secure storage unit like a safe. It is ornamental, consisting of open tracery work, and gives the impression of having been fashioned directly in the raw materials of which it is made—iron and clay. Interstices between the ceramic panels and their iron frames add to the oddity and mystery of the piece. The bold colors and the unexpected relationships between the different materials give the cabinet the theatrical look of a stage prop.

Enfer is made up of twenty-eight sheets of enameled terra-cotta that are nailed to a painted wrought-iron structure resembling reddish spines and brambles. The bright red and the "imprisoning" expressiveness of the wrought iron prompted the two designers to call this piece "Inferno." The idea of the metal cage is not new in Bonetti and Garouste's work; they had already used wrought-iron rhizomes on the wooden body of a chest of drawers produced in 1990. The mosaic idea of free shapes and the juxtaposition of the panels are a continuation of a theme presented in earlier projects, such as the 1989 furniture collection called "Patchwork." —F.B.

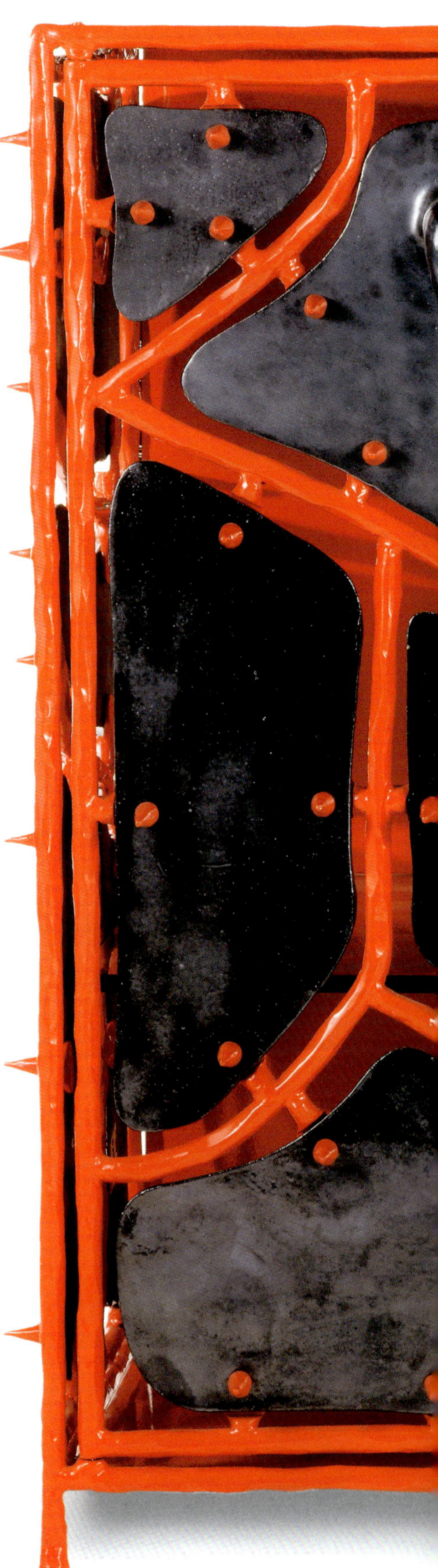

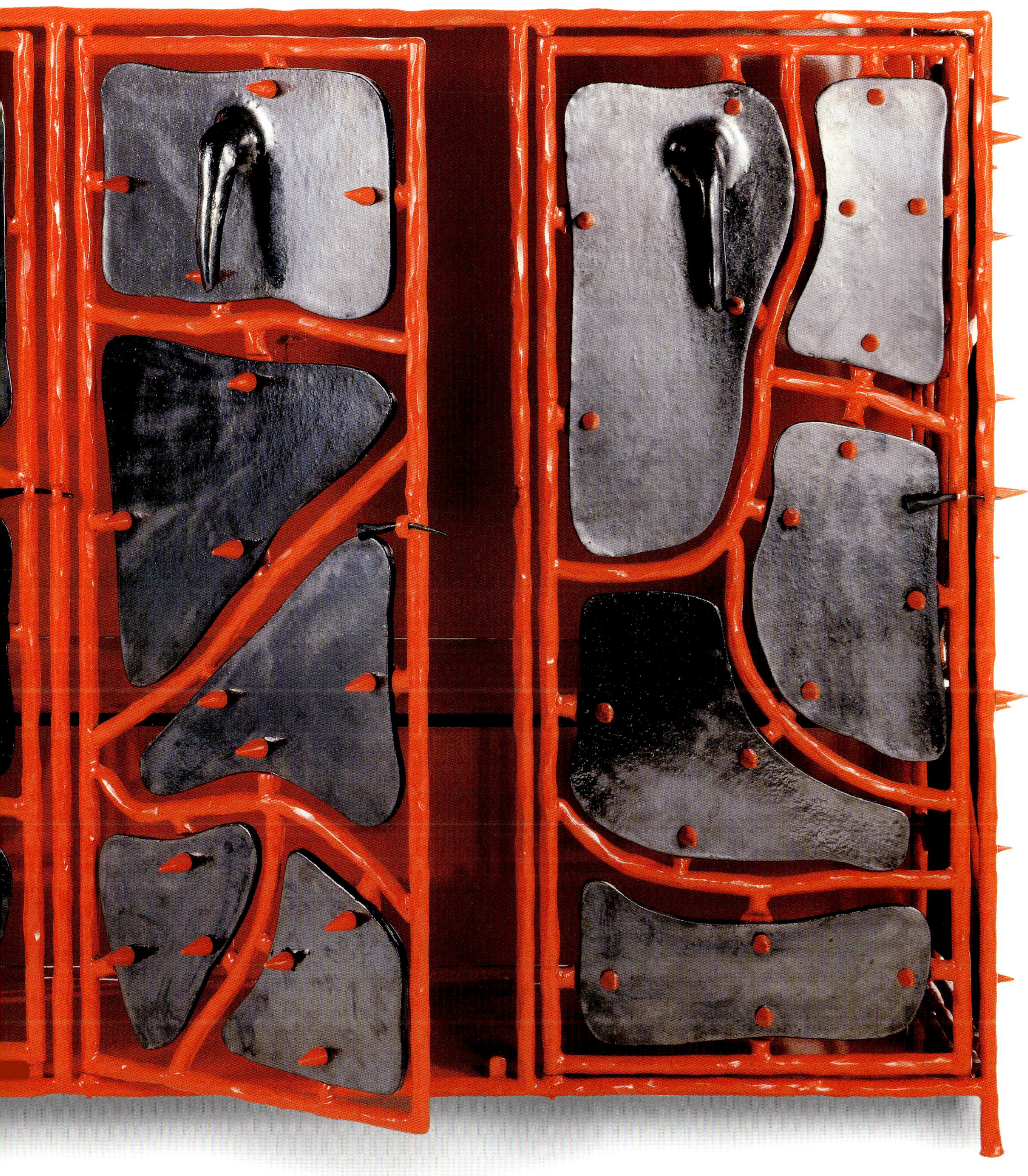

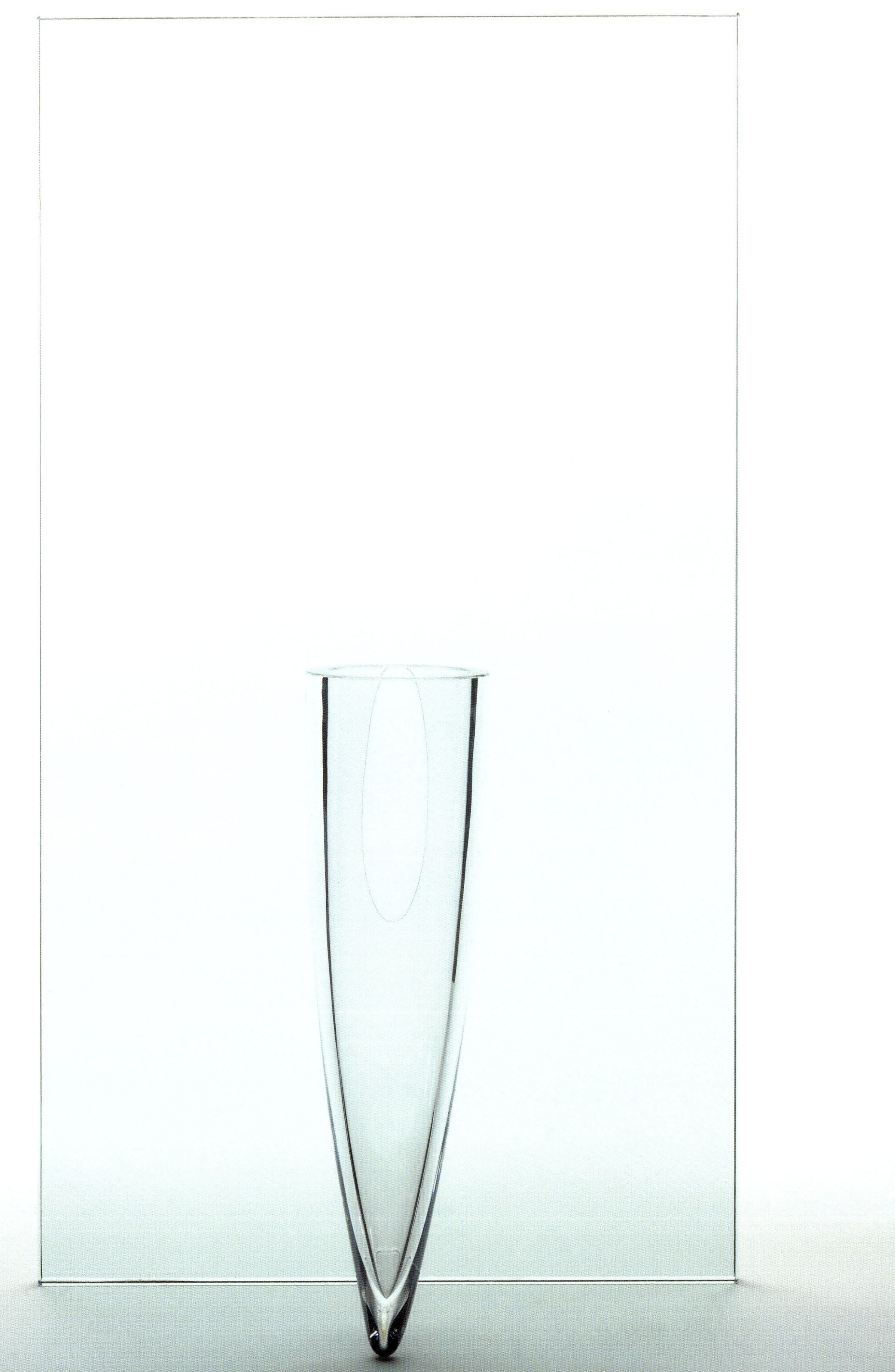

Une étrangeté contre un mur (Something strange against a wall)

French, Daum factory, 1988
Philippe Starck (born 1949)
Glass. H. 27½ in. (70 cm)
FNAC fund

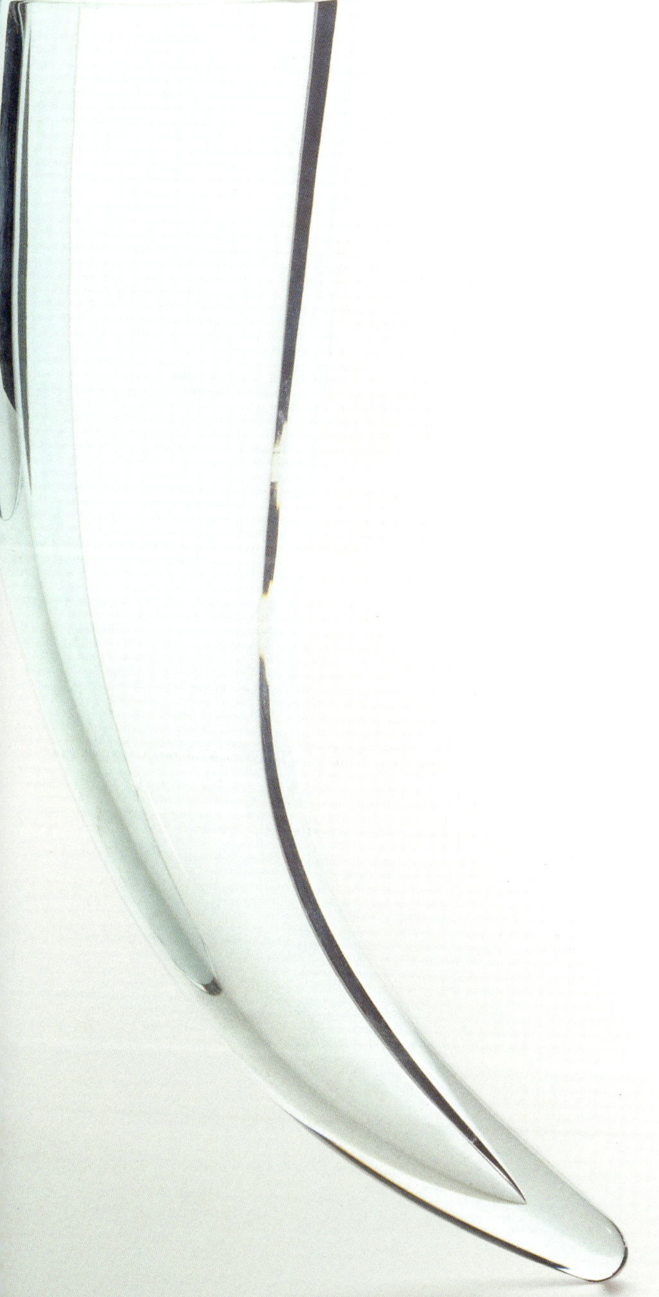

The Daum factory in Nancy started producing decorative glass in 1891. It is the only enterprise from the late-19th-century Art Nouveau activity of the Ecole de Nancy to remain prominent through the 20th century. Its longevity was made possible by the outstanding artistic direction of members of the Daum family, who regularly called on outside artists and designers and adapted production to the taste of the day.

After a difficult period, the 1980s saw a new wave of joint projects with collaborators chosen from among the leading lights of new European design. It was in this context that the collaboration between Daum and Philippe Starck came about, and it culminated in a powerful advertising slogan: "This Starck is a Daum—this Daum is a Starck."

The vase titled *Une étrangeté contre un mur* (Something strange against a wall) is part of a line of products made by Starck, who called a horn-shaped blown piece "something strange" and the associated flat surface a "wall." The number of horns and the size and position of the wall led to the production of a series of six vases in several colors.

This strange horn is not so much a functional receptacle—it is very awkward to clean—as it is a Starck leitmotif, verging on a signature. There is also the suggestion of a cornucopia, which highlights the symbolic value of the piece rather than its use.

The "something strange" could also refer to the combination of the artisan's blown glass and industrial plate glass. This combination violated the taboos of traditional fine glassmaking, as it required the use of glue for the attachment. The fact that the designer demanded this spurred the company to develop new techniques involving contemporary glues, which are no longer barred from prestigious products. —J-L.O.

Paysage Métaphysique 2 (Metaphysical Landscape 2)

French, 1983–1984
Jutta Cuny (1948–1983)
Glass, biscuit porcelain. H. 8⅝ in. (22 cm), L. 25⅝ in. (65 cm), W. 9⅞ in. (25 cm)
Gift of Ruth Maria Frantz, 1985

Three extremely busy years between 1981 and 1983, abruptly brought to an end by her accidental death, enabled the Austrian-born artist Jutta Cuny to leave her decisive stamp on the revival and internationalization of the contemporary glass scene in France, which she represented, for example, at the meeting of the Glass Art Society in New York in 1982.

Cuny set up her studio in the Vosges mountains, working regularly with the sculptor Francesco Somaini in Italy, and embarked on her sculptural experiments with sandblasted glass in 1976. In December 1981, a few months before the exhibition at the Musée des Arts Décoratifs that introduced her work to Paris,

she contacted the national porcelain factory at Sèvres, eager to experiment with a novel combination of materials: molded porcelain biscuit and sand-carved optical glass. Between 1982 and 1983, several projects were undertaken but only two were completed, both after the artist's death.

Between the vision of geologic erosion and the evocation of organic process, an allusion to Baroque draperies like those of Bernini's Saint Theresa is encompassed in the metaphysical sensibility of this woman sculptor. From the immaculate white of the fragile porcelain to the transparency of the solid block of glass, Cuny blazes an enigmatic trail toward the immaterial. —J-L.O.

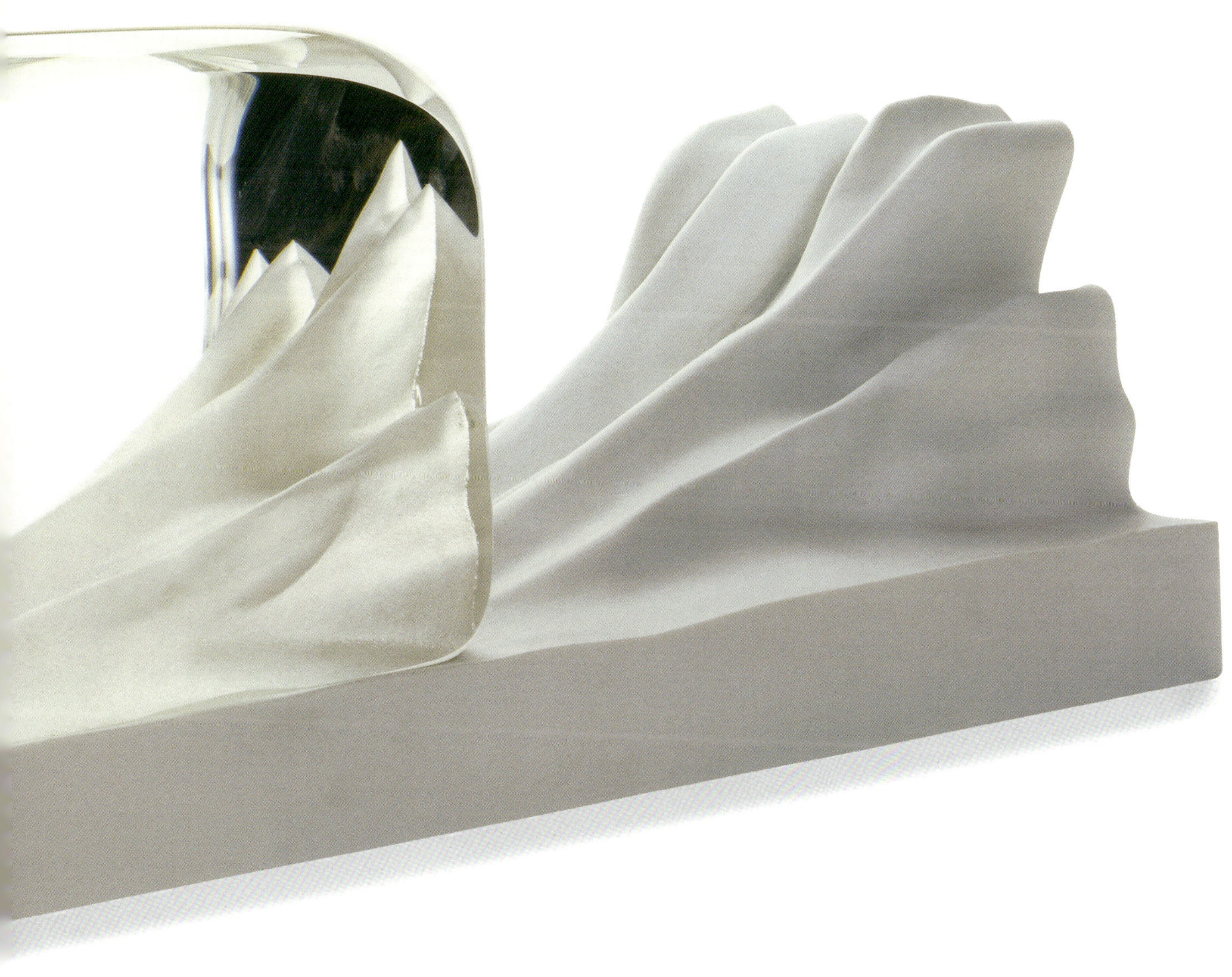

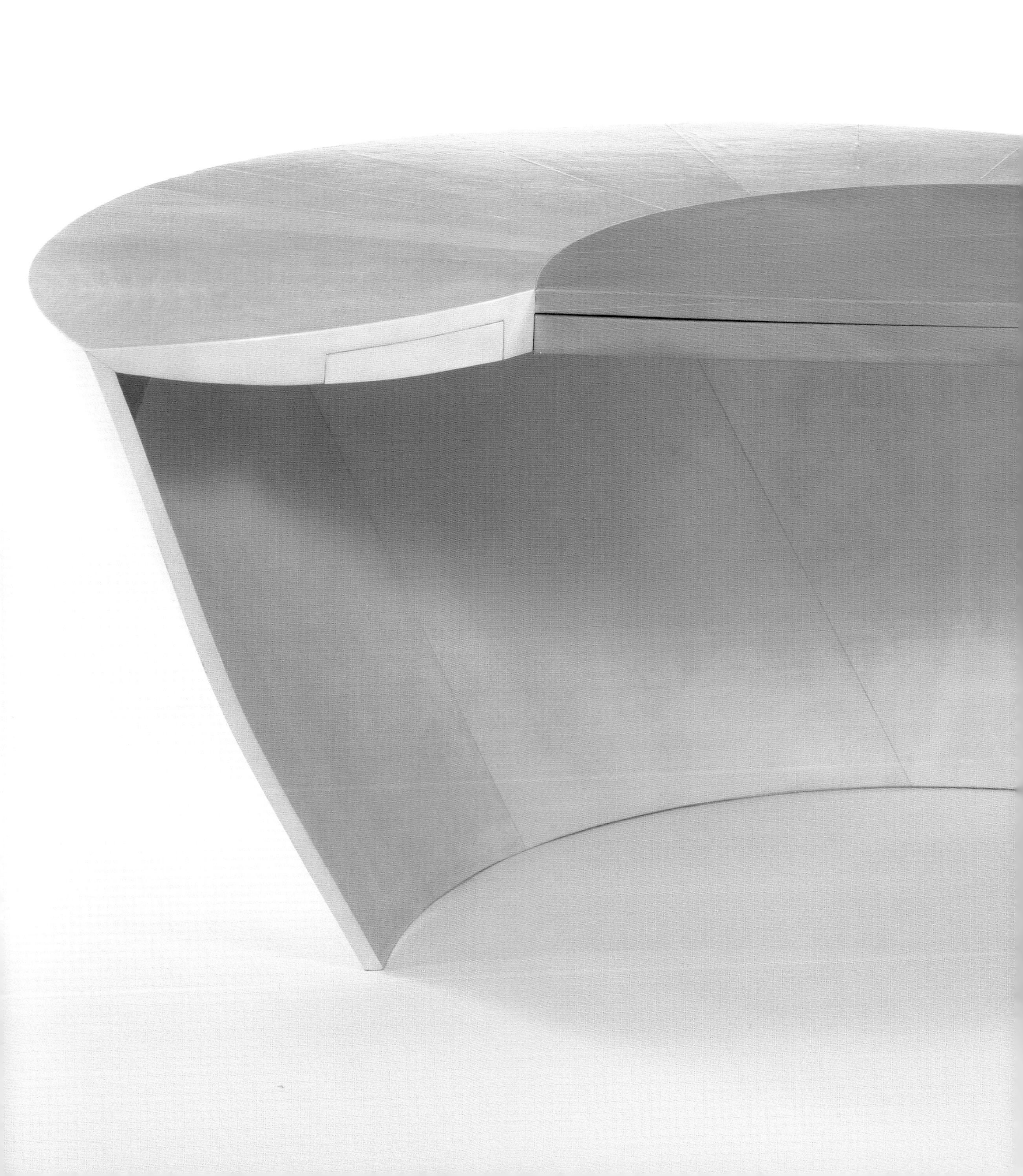

1989 Desk, Appartement Model

French, 1991
Sylvain Dubuisson (born 1946)
Wood veneered with sheets of parchment, blotter covered with gray leather. H. 28⅛ in. (71.5 cm), L. 63 in. (160 cm), D. 43¼ in. (110 cm)
Purchase, 1996

With all its allure of precious refinement, what is most striking about this desk is its simplicity of visual form. It appears to be a simple organic curve, like the shape of a shell but resulting from a mathematical progression. A far cry from the utilitarian vocabulary, it refers more to the gestures of calligraphy. With this piece, Sylvain Dubuisson broke with the tradition of men's desks—the free quality of its design contrasts with the convention of imposing rectilinear form.

The formal aspect of this curve is the outcome of sophisticated woodwork, and the preliminary drafts show the complexity of the calculations required to build it. Its surface is sheathed in parchment, emphasizing the sweeping roundness of the shape. The parchment sheets are cut so as to conform to the body of the piece, from the tight arc of the base to the broad curve of the top, in a radiating movement imposed by the conical form.

The manufacturer, Fourniture, created three molds for the model, allowing for different dimensions as well as finishes. Titled *1989*, the first model, Direction, was produced in that year for the Fourniture factory managers. A second was made in 1990 in conjunction with the Mobilier National for the office of then Minister of Culture Jack Lang. The third version, made in 1991, was called "Appartement," made so far in three examples, including one retained by Dubuisson himself, and this one, which previously belonged to the renowned French decorator Henri Samuel.

—C.R.

Jean-François Fouilhoux's keen interest in Chinese ceramics dates back to his days at the Ecole des Arts Appliqués in Paris. A visit in 1969 to the Guimet Museum of Asian Art inspired him to pursue a career as a ceramicist. In the Far East, the term "celadon" describes a porcelain or porcelaneous stoneware whose green surface, ranging from olive to pale green, imitates the natural hues of jade, the symbol of balance and softness. The green surfaces are obtained by reducing certain oxides, such as iron, barium, calcium, and titanium, at the end of firing. After years of experimenting piece by piece, Fouilhoux managed to reproduce the mythical green color achieved by his predecessors, the ceramicists of ancient China.

From 1986 on, when he had thoroughly mastered the techniques of the potter's wheel and the classic glazes, Fouilhoux devoted his attention to celadon, updating a formal tradition with the reliefs and crevices of his sculpted forms. Once modeled, his pieces might have up to ten coats of glaze, with several intermediate firings. The accidents of form give a vibrant modulation to the glaze: transparency where the coating is thin and translucency where it is thick.

The meeting of the unctuous surface of the glaze and the irregular edges of this bowl give it a decidedly contemporary character, but the modeling of the interior seems to be inspired by a Rococo baptismal font. The piece achieves a harmonic tension between the energized contemporary form and its coolly classical surface treatment.

In 1989 Fouilhoux was recognized for his success in celadon at the highly esteemed Mino International Competition in Japan, and in 1995 he was awarded the German Max-Laueger Prize. In 1998, in Auckland, New Zealand, he won one of the most prestigious international prizes for contemporary ceramics, the Fletcher Challenge Award. —F.B.

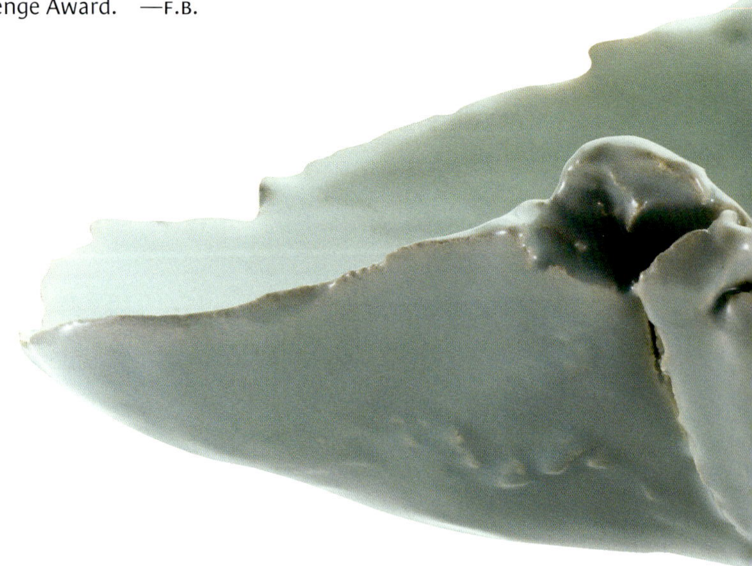

Bowl

French, 1996
Jean-François Fouilhoux (born 1947)
Celadon porcelaneous stoneware.
H. 7½ in. (19 cm), W. 25¼ in. (64 cm),
D. 11¾ in. (30 cm)
Fnac fund

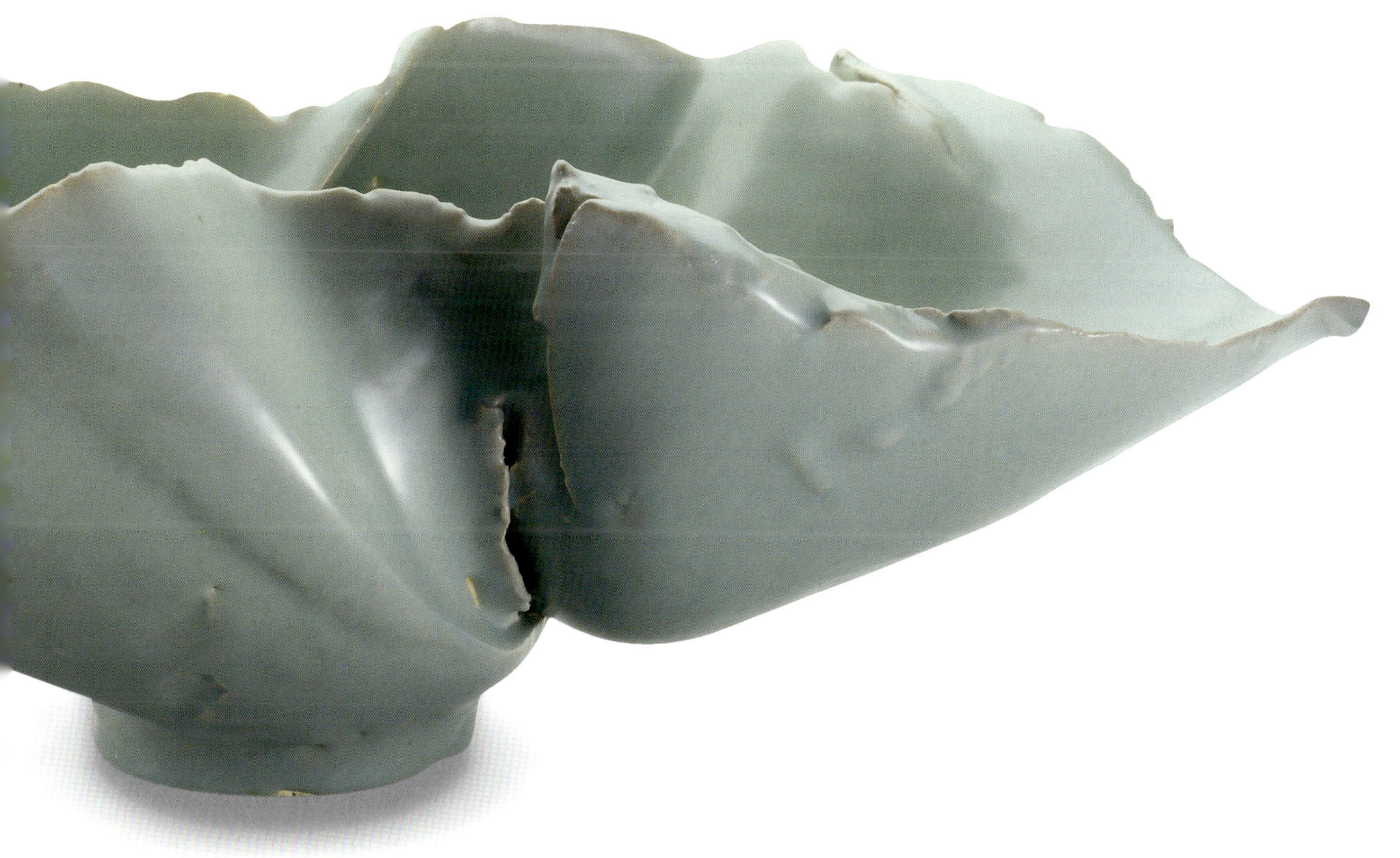

Copyright credits

Every effort has been made to locate and contact the copyright holders of the objects herein illustrated. If omissions are noted, please contact the publisher; corrections will be made in subsequent printings.

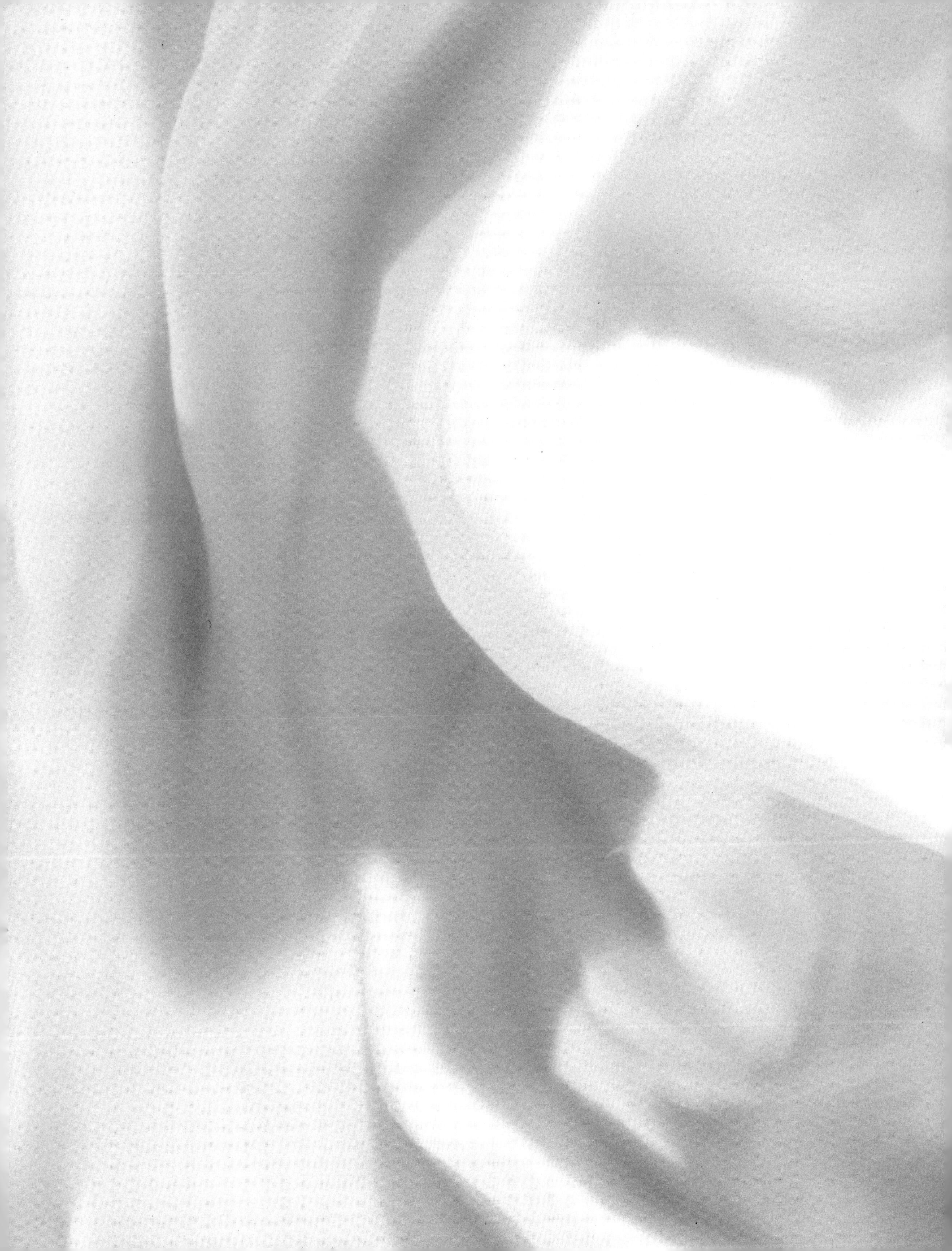